Redeploying the State

Redeploying the State

Corporatism, Neoliberalism, and Coalition Politics

Hishaam D. Aidi

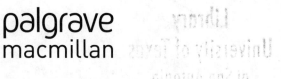

REDEPLOYING THE STATE
Copyright © Hishaam D. Aidi, 2009.

All rights reserved.

First published in 2009 by PALGRAVE MACMILLAN® in the United States—a division of St. Martin's Press LLC, 175 Fifth Avenue, New York, NY 10010.

Where this book is distributed in the UK, Europe and the rest of the world, this is by Palgrave Macmillan, a division of Macmillan Publishers Limited, registered in England, company number 785998, of Houndmills, Basingstoke, Hampshire RG21 6XS.

Palgrave Macmillan is the global academic imprint of the above companies and has companies and representatives throughout the world.

Palgrave® and Macmillan® are registered trademarks in the United States, the United Kingdom, Europe and other countries.

ISBN-13: 978-0-230-61159-7
ISBN-10: 0-230-61159-1

Library of Congress Cataloging-in-Publication Data

Aidi, Hishaam D.
    Redeploying the state : corporatism, neoliberalism, and coalition politics / Hishaam D. Aidi.
        p. cm.
    Includes bibliographical references and index.
    ISBN 0-230-61159-1
    1. Privatization—Egypt. 2. Privatization—Mexico. 3. Corporate state—Egypt. 4. Corporate state—Mexico. I. Title.
    HD4343.A79 2008
    338.962'05–dc22   2008021594

A catalogue record of the book is available from the British Library.

Design by Scribe Inc.

First edition: January 2009

10 9 8 7 6 5 4 3 2 1

Printed in the United States of America.

For Rachida, my mother

Contents

Acknowledgments

This book's genesis lies in a graduate seminar, "State Reform in Latin America," that I took with Robert Kaufman in the spring of 1996. A Ford Foundation–funded trip to Mexico that same year, with the country still reeling from the crisis of 1994, and ongoing discussions in the Arab media and academic circles about successful neoliberal reforms in Latin America led me to consider a comparative project. I am most grateful to Lisa Anderson, Robert Kaufman, and David Waldner for their support and guidance in pursuing this project. I am indebted to many colleagues and friends for their comments on various drafts of this study—Joel Beinin, Mona El-Ghobashy, Steve Heydemann, Mahmood Mamdani, Anthony Marx, and Charles Tilly. I am also thankful to the Ford Foundation for its support and to Linda Herrera, then of Ford's Cairo office. During my months in Cairo in the spring semesters of 1997 and 1999, I was based at the French research center Centre d'Etudes et de Documentation Economiques, Juridiques et Socials (CEDEJ). I am grateful to Patrick Haenni, Dina al-Khawagga, Françoise Clément, and the CEDEJ staff for their assistance and hospitality. All insights contained in this book are the result of exchanges with colleagues in New York, Mexico City, and Cairo; all errors are mine.

Acronyms and Glossary

ANTAD:	Mexican National Association of Self-Service and Department Stores
BUO:	Mexican Labor Unity Bloc
CANACINTRA:	National Chamber of Transformation Industries
CCE:	Coordinating Council of Mexican Entrepeneurs
CGT:	General Confederation of Workers
charro:	Mexican labor boss
CNOP:	Mexican National Federation of Popular Organizations
CNT:	National Chamber of Labor
COCM:	Confederation of Workers and Peasants of Mexico
CONCAMIN:	Confederation of Industrial Chambers
CONCANACO:	Confederation of National Chambers of Commerce
COPARMEX:	Employers' Confederation of the Mexican Republic
CPN:	Mexico's National Proletarian Confederation
CROM:	Mexican Regional Labor Confederation
CT:	Mexican Labor Congress
CTM:	Mexican Workers' Confederation
DMNL:	Democratic Movement for National Liberation, (Egyptian Communist organization)
feddan:	unit of land used in Egypt (1.038 acres)
fellahin:	a peasant in Egypt
FESEBES:	Federation of Unions of Goods and Services Companies
FICORCA:	Trust for Foreign Exchange Protection
Gobernacion:	Mexican Ministry of Government
Hacienda:	Mexican Ministry of Treasury
HPC:	Egyptian Higher Policy Committee
LFT:	Mexican Federal Labor Law
munadil:	freedom fighter

NAFINSA: Mexican State Development Bank
PAN: Mexico's National Action Party
PRI: Mexico's Institutionalized Revolutionary Party
PRD: Mexico's Party of Democratic Revolution
PROMAP: Program for the Modernization of Mexican Public
              Administration, 1995–2000
PSE: Mexico's Economic Stability Pact
RCC: Egyptian Revolutionary Command Council
RMC: Egyptian rural middle class
SPP: Mexican Ministry of Programming and Budget
SECOFI: Mexican Ministry of Commerce
SEMIP: Ministry of Energy, Mines, and Parastate Industry
SEPAFIN: Ministry of Natural Resources and Industrial
              Development
SOE: state-owned enterprise

I

The Politics of Privatization

In 1967 when the popular Egyptian folk singer Sheikh Imam sang his dirge "Ghifara Mat," mourning the death of Che Guevara and daring Nasser to be a true *munadil* (freedom fighter) like the slain Argentine revolutionary, he was promptly arrested and imprisoned for three years. Sheikh Imam's lyrics reflected the gloom that had settled over Egypt after the 1967 War, as heady dreams were dashed and grandiose promises shattered. After the 1952 Revolution, Egyptians—leaders and laymen—had looked toward Latin America for solutions and prescriptions for economic autonomy and freedom from the neocolonial yoke. Nasser sent delegations to South America and received Che Guevara and Raoul Castro and embarked on a project of state building and development inspired in part by Brazilian leader Vargas's state-labor alliance and corporatist legal code and Argentine leader Peron's antiparty political movement. By 1967, though, Egypt was in a deep economic and political crisis: the country lacked the hard currency to finance its import-substitution policy and welfare commitments to workers, bureaucrats, and the peasantry and was facing growing unrest from students, leftists, and Islamists calling for the return of Sinai.

Three decades later, Egyptian state elites were looking toward Latin America for a different kind of deliverance, casting an admiring eye at the market revolutions that swept across Chile, Mexico, and Argentina and the neoliberal guerrillas who defeated vested interests, eviscerated bloated bureaucracies, and steered their inward-looking economies toward the world. Egyptian eyes settled on Mexico, where economic restructuring was carried out swiftly, without the bloody repression that characterized economic reform in Chile under Pinochet. Since the mid-1990s in conferences, symposia, and articles, Egyptian policy makers, academics, and commentators have touted the "Mexican model," with analysts lauding Mexico's pacted transition to a market economy, technocrats' ability to reverse capital flight, and the Mexican ruling party's adaptability,[1] even as the Mexican model was coming under criticism in Latin America.

This book is a comparative study of Mexico's (1988–2000) and Egypt's (1996–2007) experiences with structural adjustment, particularly privatization, and Egypt's efforts to replicate the "Mexican model." Both Egypt and Mexico (prior to reform) were populist-distributive dominant-party authoritarian regimes that relied heavily on external revenues—oil, aid, and loans—and embarked on economic reform programs after external shocks led to fiscal crises and an inability to finance populist policies and debt repayment. However, while Mexico privatized much of its public sector with little agitation from labor, liberalized trade, and drew foreign investment (twenty-one billion dollars in 1993 alone), Egypt has managed to privatize less than half of the state-owned enterprises slated for sale. Due to labor protests and for fear of unrest, Egyptian reformers have not been able to overcome labor resistance and divest the larger state-owned enterprises (SOEs). Likewise, while Salinas reformed the upper echelons of the state bureaucracy, weakening statist ministries, and created a pro-reform coalition that included foreign and domestic capital, Mubarak, after promoting a mini-investment boom in 1998, has not been so successful.

The question I am addressing is the following: why has the Egyptian state, which is more repressive and authoritarian than its Mexican counterpart (which allows sexennial elections), been unable to overcome the opposition of a labor movement that is smaller, less organized, and more repressed (a military order passed by the Free Officers in 1953 banned all strikes) than the Mexican labor movement? Differently put, Mexican leaders were able to lay off 500 thousand workers, while Egyptian leaders have been unable to lay off the projected 650 thousand workers necessary for far-reaching divestiture.[2] Through agitation or the threat of agitation, Egyptian workers have been able to hinder the reform process, while the Mexican labor movement, which is larger, better organized, and less repressed, was unable to resist privatization. I contend that Mubarak's inability to overcome workers' resistance to reform and to direct different societal actors toward his developmental goals derives less from the organizational strength of the Egyptian labor movement or the labor elite's veto power than from the Egyptian state's low capacity. In Mexico, reformers could use the ruling party to mobilize support for reform, co-opt opposition, and maintain stability. Egypt's National Democratic Party, for historical reasons, lacks the Mexican ruling party's (PRI) channels of access and representation and the capacity to deliver public goods. Despite efforts by Sadat and Mubarak to build an Egyptian PRI and imitate Salinas's National Solidarity Program, the Egyptian state remains a "lame Leviathan," a fierce but weak and isolated state with limited control over society.

Reform and Resistance

The process of privatization in Egypt has been repeatedly halted by labor agitation or the anticipation of such agitation. Between 1982 and 1993, Mexico sold or liquidated 891 of its 1,155 SOEs;[3] Egypt in 1991 put 314 SOEs—40 percent of the public sector—for sale; and, according to the Egyptian Public Enterprise Office, 142 SOEs have been partially or totally privatized, and 172 SOEs are still owned by the state, which also holds stakes in 695 joint venture companies. In total, less than half of the SOEs slated for sale have been liquidated, and less than 20 percent of the entire public sector has been sold.[4] Most scholars have attributed Egypt's inability to privatize to a lack of will, which purportedly stems from a reluctance to relinquish control of the public sector as a source of patronage and the fear that any sizable state sell-off would unleash popular discontent.[5] This at first blush seems like a plausible argument. Market reform obviously cuts against the interests of groups that were benefiting from the preexisting development strategy of import substitution industrialization and could lead to social unrest.

But it is not evident that Egyptian elites lack the will to reform. The controversial Law 203 of 1991, which provided the legal basis for widespread privatization, was passed, restructuring the public sector and creating holding companies. Between 1991 and 1993, scores of small SOEs at the local level were sold. In 1996, a new cabinet pushed the privatization process forward, and by 1998 twenty companies of the 314 slated for divestiture were partially divested. By 1998, twenty thousand workers had been dismissed, and, although economic liberalization led to a rise in unemployment and a fall in living standards, Egypt's privatization drew in $3.3 billion.[6] In November 1998, a World Bank official lauded Egypt's privatization effort for not having created social unrest, and an International Monetary Fund (IMF) report praised Egypt's "remarkable" privatization program, ranking it fourth in the world (after Hungary, Malaysia, and the Czech Republic).[7] Egyptian reformers also appeared willing to subcontract SOEs to private interests that could peacefully shed "excess labor." But frequent strikes and serious labor disturbances in 1998 and 1999 forced reformers to hedge in privatizing and delayed the passing of the new labor law first proposed in 1993, until it was finally adopted in 2003. In the 1990s, economic liberalization measures went forward in other areas: trade barriers and tariffs were reduced considerably, portfolio investment lured, and the exchange rate unified, but adjustment has been slow in areas that triggered resistance from labor. Mubarak's team seems to be committed to neoliberal reform on all fronts, but privatization schemes stalled or were abandoned because of labor protests and the threat of such protests.

The problem is how to deal with labor during privatization. In 1996, the Egyptian state employed 4.2 million people out of an active Egyptian population of 12 million, and the public sector employed 1.3 million people; 11 percent of total employment was in the public sector, 21 percent in the public administration and 68 percent in the private sector.[8] One study by a British consulting group found that 30 percent of the labor force in SOEs was redundant, 40 percent of the workers had a second job, and 40 to 45 percent were under- or unqualified. Yet shedding the excess labor through divestiture was and remains to be a daunting and politically explosive task. As Amin Ugumar, director of employment creation at the Social Fund for Development (SFD), put it, "If we dismiss 500,000 people the rate of unemployment will reach 20 percent and the social situation will become explosive. This means revolution. Besides, the state would have to pay $1.8 billion in compensation which it cannot finance."[9] Concurring with Ugumar, some observers argued that international financial support was crucial to the progress of the privatization process. The Social Fund for Development was established to alleviate the pain associated with privatization and received $672.5 million from international donors, of which $117 million was allocated to fund the early retirement compensation to fifty thousand laborers in thirty companies slated for sell-off.[10] But despite the international aid and expressed interest of regime cronies and foreign investors in buying failing SOEs, the Egyptian state lacks the capacity to restructure labor-intensive enterprises because of its inability to control and contain labor discontent.

The Argument

I present three interrelated arguments: First, I argue that the capabilities of the Egyptian and Mexican regimes can be understood through a historical analysis of the state-building and incorporation periods following the populist revolutions that brought Nasser and Calles to power. The postrevolutionary regime in Mexico would have more success in integrating society. The Nasserist revolution was not as transformative of Egyptian society as its Mexican counterpart; the Egyptian revolution did not decimate the power of the landed elites and never successfully incorporated urban political groups. While Mexican state builders used the PRI to incorporate and mobilize the popular classes into the regime, Nasser, inspired by Peronism and the Brazilian Estado Novo (New State), banned political parties, attached labor and the peasantry to the state, and channeled participation into the state bureaucracy. While Mexican corporatism relied on the active inclusion and participation of the lower classes, regularly reaching out to workers and peasants for electoral support, Nasser opted for the passive inclusion of labor and the peasantry, granting them numerous welfare guarantees in exchange for political quiescence and absolute docility. Finally, while party corporatism granted workers voice and sanctioning power making unionists more representative and responsive to the rank and file, state corporatism extended benefits to workers and in effect divorced upper-level unionists from the base, making their careers hinge more on state approval than on the workers' votes, which increased chances for dissent and defection among the rank and file.

Thus while state-society relations in Mexico were mediated by the ruling party, and state elites could control the lower classes through thousands of unionists and local political bosses (*caciques*) who were party members, the state-society configuration in Egypt would remain fundamentally different even after Nasser created a single party (the Arab Socialist Union, later the National Democratic Party), lacking the PRI's numerous middlemen through which to mobilize the support of urban voters. Both the Egyptian and Mexican regimes have historically employed strategies of indirect rule, using labor unionists and rural notables to control the lower classes. But after the 1986 and 1988 electoral debacles, when labor and rural elites failed to deliver the vote, Mexican leaders decided to sideline these traditional power brokers, many of whom were resistant to reform and, through the PRI and Pronasol, cultivated new pro-reform intermediaries in the labor, peasantry, and private sector. Mexican reformers reconstituted the regime's base and revitalized the state's capabilities by developing new intermediaries in the private sector and lower classes who could help administer the public good and mobilize support for the new economic-political project. In Egypt, while the rural middle class is still a reliable ally, the labor elite—the state's intermediaries in urban areas—have consistently failed to deliver rank and file; workers, indeed the popular classes in general, are increasingly finding that allegiance to Islamist power brokers (who have resisted the state's attempts at incorporation) is materially more beneficial than loyalty to the state or ruling party.

My argument thus disagrees with the standard view that the Egyptian regime has not restructured its public sector because of a lack of political will and access to external revenue, which is used to placate vested interests. My argument is also at variance with the "moral economy" thesis, which may account for the "symbolic protests" of the 1970s, 1980s, and early 1990s but cannot explain the waves of full-blown strikes of the past decade and the growing demands for a new workers' confederation and a labor party.[11] I also differ with the more recent thesis that Egyptian labor has been able to block privatization because of the labor leadership's influence on the policy-making process.[12] While I concur that corporatist institutions in Egypt are weak and the party-state has been unable to subordinate labor to its political will, I do not think this institutional weakness has afforded the union elite "substantial influence" and veto power over the decision-making process. While some high-level unionists did oppose privatization in the early 1990s, the Egyptian Trade Union Federation (ETUF) leadership did not resist Law 203 of 1991, which passed to facilitate public sector reform, and in 1996 the confederation issued a statement in support of privatization; in 1999 the ETUF executive council declared its support for the controversial new labor law.[13] Unlike in Mexico, where strong party and corporatist institutions could contain and isolate labor dissent at different levels of the union hierarchy, the privatization process in Egypt has been repeatedly halted by the political agitation of rank-and-file workers and shop-floor leaders over whom the trade union confederation and National Democratic Party (NDP) have little control. Because of weak party institutions and the trade union federation's structure—where, since 1959, the ETUF remains the single official union organization, with a hierarchical structure allowing only one federation to represent workers in any given industry and where top-level unionists are selected and protected from being voted out by lower level unionists—the Egyptian state simply lacks the capacity to control the political behavior of low-level unionists and rank-and-file workers.

The Egyptian state's isolation, along with dwindling resources, has limited reformers' ability to co-opt opponents and mobilize urban constituencies for reform. Mubarak's inability to finance welfare commitments to the lower classes has meant that the regime's populist coalition is fraying as workers and peasants are flocking toward the Islamist and leftist opposition. With widespread poverty and the urban poor's mobilization by Islamist groups, Egyptian reformers fear that an attempt at political liberalization and inclusion could flood the political arena with the "logic of distribution" rather than the "logic of accumulation." Bereft of intermediaries, unable to incorporate the Islamists' social capital, and incapable of reaching directly to the popular classes, Egyptian leaders are increasingly opting for exclusion and coercion. Despite attempts to strengthen the ruling party, increase participation, and shore up support in urban areas, Egyptian leaders' failure to establish some type of pro-reform bargain with labor is leading to an exclusionary corporatism. And the more access to the state is closed off, the more political agitation occurs outside the party and corporatist framework, further isolating and weakening the regime.

My second argument also challenges the conventional wisdom that Egypt—and, more broadly, Middle Eastern states—has not reformed its economy because of its access to external revenue and foreign aid. The poor record of economic reform in the Arab world is often attributed to low state capacity, specifically the regimes' inability to contain "popular backlash" against adjustment, which is in turn chalked up to the reliance on external rents.[14] One version of this rentier state argument holds that, while Latin American states also rely on external rents and loans, the loans come from international financial institutions and with stringent economic conditionalities, whereas Arab states avail themselves of rents from Western governments that require little more than support for U.S. foreign policy and stability in the Middle East. Incumbent leaders, the argument runs, enjoy significant financial autonomy and have neither the interest nor will to reform their economies.[15] This line of argument is problematic. To begin with, rentier state theory tells us little about the institutional origins or evolution of the modern Egyptian state whose corporatist bargains were put in place before the flow of Soviet or American aid, nor can it explain the institutional building that has taken place since 1979 when Egypt became heavily dependent on American rents. The Egyptian state was born in a context of military conflict different from that of Mexico's, which grew out of a civil war and revolution. The size and complexity of the Egyptian state apparatus would be shaped not only by the nationalist struggle against the British but also by the Palestinian-Israeli conflict. The wars of 1948, 1956, and 1967 would affect the process of state building and incorporation in ways neglected by most rentier analyses: by strengthening the military, narrowing alternatives available to regime elites, and paving the way for nationalization.

I demonstrate that the claim that aid to Latin America comes exclusively from private sources and with strict economic conditionalities is also overdrawn; the case of Mexico shows how economic reformers relied heavily on aid from international financial institutions (IFIs) but also benefited from generous politically motivated funding and bail-out packages from the United States. Some political economists observe that structural adjustment in Mexico was bankrolled and sponsored by the United States more than any other reform process in the developing world.[16] The political nature of Egypt's and Mexico's relationships to the world economy and the United States is critical to understanding their reform experiences. Egypt's geostrategic location as a "front-line state" would shape that country's institutional development and engender a relationship with the United States that was political and "special" like the Mexican-American relationship, albeit underpinned by a different security and balance of power calculus. Mexico, like Egypt, has benefited from "soft money" and also evinces a budget with "soft constraints"—and, in fact, has lower rates of direct taxation than the Egyptian and Middle East and North Africa (MENA) average. I argue that the reason Mexico was able to reform, while Egypt is stalling, is because it could: Mexico's institutional capabilities, greased by oil rents, aid, and loans from the United States, IFIs, and commercial banks, could contain opposition and mobilize support for painful reforms. In comparing the two countries' institutional capacity, I do not simply focus on extraction and allocation capacity, as most scholars of the Middle East do, but I look at the state's capacity to deliver public goods, channel participation, respond to societal demands, and reverse policy course.

I also argue that the link between access to external rents and reform is neither simple nor direct. External revenue may lower the costs of repression allowing rentier states to forestall democratization,[17] but the cases of Egypt and Mexico show that while subsidizing authoritarian rule, external revenue can also promote economic liberalization and institution building. When asked about the lack of democracy in Egypt, in a now famous speech in January 2002, David Welch, the American ambassador, replied that "the United States considers Egypt to be a friend and we don't put pressure on our friends."[18] But the United States did press for economic reform. In June 2004, the United States granted Egypt three hundred million dollars in "cash transfer assistance" as a "reward" for reform steps taken, and Welch stated that the United States was prepared to offer two billion dollars in loans if privatization—particularly, of state banks—went forward.[19] Similarly, in the 1990s, the privatization process in Egypt often went forward when external resources were flowing, funding welfare and retraining programs for workers laid off by divestiture; and the process frequently would stop when these funds ran out or in face of domestic resistance. In other words, external rents can preserve authoritarian rule but do not necessarily impede market reform. The rentier effect in Latin America and the Middle East, while significant, is refracted by differing institutional contexts.

The third argument of this book involves policy diffusion and learning between states. Scholars have recently observed that as the United States establishes a presence in the Middle East, American-style models of capitalism, previously prescribed to Latin American allies, will be recommended to American client-states in the Middle East.[20] This observation is certainly true of Egypt and Mexico, two states dependent on American support, but it ignores the extent to which Egyptian policy makers and scholars were drawn to the "Mexican Miracle." If Egyptian state builders after 1952 were inspired by southern European and Latin American corporatism, since the mid-1990s Egyptian reformers have attempted in a number of ways to imitate the "Mexican model." Egyptian technocrats and bureaucrats have also lauded Salinas's antipoverty program, Pronasol, which used funds from privatization sell-offs to deliver welfare to targeted areas. With World Bank approval and financing, the Egyptian regime created the Social Fund for Development, which was modeled on Pronasol.

In praising the "Mexican Miracle," IFIs and Western policy makers often pointed to the opening of the economy to international competition; the drastic privatization and "deregulation" process; and the pacted agreement among business, labor, and the state, whose annual renewal became a major political event and which became a crucial institution underpinning the reform process and which distinguished adjustment in Mexico from that in Argentina and Chile.

Yet many experts who advocate the Mexican model misunderstand the degree of state intervention involved in that country's "neoliberal" revolution and the institutional legacies upon which Salinas built.[21] Increasingly, economists are noting that neoliberal reforms in Latin America were underpinned by extensive institutional interventions by the state. These scholars argue that what typifies the Mexican model is not its purported laissez-faire character but the economic transformation managed by a political party and underpinned by institutional interventions and "restricted democracy." Mexican technocrats used the preexisting institutions of the party and electoral systems to transform state-society relations and build a pro-reform coalition. The Mexican experience would be held up as exemplary and appeal to policy makers in other developing countries even after the peso collapse of 1995 and the subsequent austerity measures, which triggered the largest plunge in Mexico's GDP since the Great Depression of the 1930s and led to a widespread repudiation of Salinas's economic project as the economy shrank by 6.2 percent in 1996.[22] But the "Mexican Miracle" was represented differently by different interests.[23]

While Mexican officials, IFIs, the United States, and policy makers in different parts of the world were hailing the country as an "IMF success story," scholars (and even some Mexican policy makers) were pointing to Mexico as a case of effective and targeted state intervention similar to that of the East Asian newly industrialized countries (NICS) and noting that it was insufficient state intervention on the part of Salinas that led to the 1994–95 crises.[24] I examine this debate over Mexico as an exemplar of successful neoliberalism. A closer look at Salinas's reform policies illustrates the contradictions that often exist in state behavior between "image" and "practice," rhetoric (in this case, neoliberal) and policy.[25] The Mexican state intervened in allocating capital and market opportunities to business cronies, protecting banks from competition, overvaluing the peso, guiding investment, and disciplining small and medium-sized businesses who opposed trade liberalization. The state aggressively intervened in the polity to build a coalition for reform, rewarding supportive unionists, co-opting more pliant opponents, and extirpating union bosses (*charros*) opposed to the sell-offs.

Reforms in Mexico did not lead to state withdrawal as much as to new kinds of intervention; through market reforms, the Mexican state was able to expand its social bases and enhance its capabilities by allocating the provision of public goods to compliant private intermediaries. "Deregulation" gave way to "re-regulation"; rather than "shedding" (or in the words of Latin American economists, "disincorporating") state-owned enterprises, privatization often resulted in public-private ventures where the state would outsource functions, like port management and customs administration, to big business. Even in Egypt, I show how the limited growth and investment boom, which occurred in 1998 and 1999, prompting the *Economist* to call Egypt an "IMF Success Story," was achieved through dirigisme: the state intervened to allocate credit, protect the local currency, shield local manufacturers from foreign competition, bail out public banks, and invest in profitable businesses such as real estate. I question some Egyptian analysts' understanding of Mexico as a neoliberal success. One reason the Egyptian Social Fund has yet to develop the institutional reach of Pronasol or yield the political returns is because it is being created from scratch, while Pronasol was built upon successive antipoverty programs introduced by Mexican presidents since the 1950s.[26]

This study thus offers a critique of neoliberal theory, of the claim that privatization would lead to the retreat of the state, free the private sector, and spark economic growth and higher living standards. Aside from the now indubitable fact that market reforms have not raised living standards in Latin America, I argue that privatization has also not led to state withdrawal but rather to a redeployment of the state and new types of intervention. Divestiture has not unleashed an independent, dynamic private sector but rather produced a new relationship between state and capital and engendered public-private ("straddling") arrangements where the regime grants big-business market opportunities in exchange for the private sector's providing public goods and fulfilling some of the state's social control functions (such as monitoring smaller businesses and providing services formerly provided by the state). In Egypt, while the public sector is being restructured, the state is not shrinking; the civil service is actually expanding, and more joint ventures are appearing.

Analysts have evaluated the success of privatization by looking at a variety of indicators: the efficiency and productivity of enterprises transferred to private ownership and the role of divestiture in increasing government revenue, in reducing the fiscal burden, and in improving consumer welfare. While I consider the number of SOEs sold and the size of the public sector after privatization, since I am concerned with the state's capacity for social control and labor opposition to reform, I pay close attention to the public-private arrangements that have emerged from divestiture and how that "recombinant" property regime has enhanced state capacity and helped leaders achieve economic and political objectives. It is important to recall, as David Stark has argued apropos Eastern Europe, that there are "new forms of state ownership" and that counting the number of SOEs sold to the private sector tells us little about how the state retains control of these firms through public-private ventures.[27] Thus, rather than ask how many SOEs are sold or divested, I prefer to examine how the state intervenes and through which institutions and societal power centers it manages economic activity; such an approach can better illuminate the nature of the state-society and state-market configuration.

Privatization in Mexico, and to a lesser extent in Egypt, appears to be another phase in the continuing formation of these postcolonial states, where in bringing the private sector into the governing coalitions, the regimes expand their foundations and enhance their capacity for social control. By contracting state enterprises and state functions to trusted allies in the private sector, Mexican and Egyptian reformers create a new set of intermediaries in the propertied classes through which the state can govern and manage the economy. Privatization is thus a way for cash-strapped regimes to gain allies, draw capital, and enhance capabilities, but the recurring irony is that to privatize the state must have high capacity.

Plan of the Book

This book fits into the growing literature that attempts to deparochialize the study of the Middle East, a region long excluded from comparative research because of its purported cultural, political, and economic exceptionalism.[28] I try to explain Egypt's "political blockage" through a comparison with Latin American cases and their experiences with state and market reform; the ensuing analysis compares the historical trajectories of state formation in Latin America and the Arab world, assessing the impact of domestic institutional legacies and external rents in two countries heavily reliant on American largesse. By demonstrating how privatization in Egypt is stalling because of the nature of the state's institutional linkages to labor and the regime's isolation from society, which can be traced to its founding moment, I am offering a critique of the rentier state theory, which is influential in the study of Arab, African, and Latin American states.[29] And in showing how, rather than withdrawing the state, reformers in Egypt, Mexico, and Algeria (discussed in the concluding chapter) redeployed state institutions, this study contributes to ongoing attempts to reassess the political science and economics literature of the past decade on the politics of privatization and state retrenchment.

The next chapter provides a brief literature review and shows how this book's thesis fits into ongoing theoretical debates over state formation, corporatist legacies, and market reform and presents a causal model to illustrate how Egypt's and Mexico's differing experiences with privatization can be understood by looking at the periods of state building and incorporation. The path-dependent argument presented in this study rests on the assumption that state capacity is shaped historically by the state's internal structure, the relationship between the state and society, and the structure of society, which can facilitate or constrain state intervention. Chapter 3 thus offers a comparative historical analysis of the state-building periods in Egypt and Mexico, contrasting the political contexts (civil war in Mexico versus intrastate war in Egypt) and the revolutions' disparate accomplishments. Chapter 4 lays out the sociohistorical status quo ante detailing the institutional legacies of incorporation—particularly the nature of state-labor and party-labor relations in the two countries—on the eve of economic reform.

Chapters 5 and 6 examine party-labor and state-business relations in Mexico, explaining how de la Madrid, Salinas, and Zedillo were able to transform the social base of the state. Chapter 5 shows how Mexican officials manipulated corporatist mechanisms of control—party institutions and the Federal Labor Law (particularly the strike and exclusion clauses)—to overcome labor opposition and (re)incorporate workers and other groups alienated by structural adjustment. Chapter 6 looks at how Mexican reformers were able to restructure key bureaucratic institutions and draw the support of an estranged private sector and overcome the resistance of small and medium businessmen; the chapter concludes with a discussion of the "Mexican model" and its appeal to Egyptian scholars and policy makers.

Chapters 7 and 8 examine how in response to worker opposition, which has repeatedly derailed privatization, Egyptian state officials have begun redesigning and restricting boundaries of participation in legislative and trade union elections to build support for pro-reform policies. But unlike Mexico, where state officials reshaped the political arena to absorb opposition from the left and the right, Egyptian leaders are using the ruling party (NDP) to mobilize the support of the "winners" of adjustment; they are recasting the Egyptian electoral landscape to include the middle and upper classes but exclude the populist sectors most opposed to adjustment. Chapter 8 details how as a state-business alliance is cemented and business is brought into the NDP, Egypt is moving toward a soft bureaucratic authoritarianism with organized labor economically excluded and politically demoted from its already subordinate position as a junior coalition. In the final chapter, I ponder how Egypt's turn toward neoliberalism is

being accompanied by an institutional shift to an exclusionary party corporatism and provide further evidence for the thesis that an inclusionary
party corporatism affords states a greater capacity for reform by looking at
additional cases—particularly Algeria, which shows the perils of an exclusionary approach to reform.

Novelist Octavio Paz has likened Mexico's dense institutional setting to
a pre-Columbian stepped pyramid, saying that Mexicans over the centuries built a multitiered set of institutions that became one of the "seven
political-science wonders of the world," and scholars of Mexico used to
argue that this burdensome institutional heritage would not be favorable
to economic restructuring and democratization.[30] In a similar spirit, scholars have noted that the behemoth Egyptian state dates back five thousand
years to when Pharoah Menas unified the Delta and Upper Egypt under
one central authority and created a "total bureaucracy"[31] later expanded
by Muhammad Ali and Nasser and that today poses the most significant
obstacle to the country's development. Commentators regularly speak of
Egypt's "political blockage," "regime inaction," and the Egyptian "government's strategy of immobilism" without exploring or explaining the historical roots of this institutional incapacity and inflexibility. By focusing
on the period since regime formation, I hope to show how Mexico's dense
institutional context has proven conducive to economic transformation,
while Egypt's has not. The aim is to explain how political outcomes in both
Egypt and Mexico can be understood as resulting from the same processes
of state formation, coalition building, and dependency on external rents
and American largesse. The comparison is particularly pertinent given the
influence that Latin American political ideas and models of development
have had on Egypt.

2

State Formation, Incorporation, Political Parties

Concepts and Theoretical Considerations

Since the early 1980s, students of the Egyptian political economy have called for a comparison between Egypt and Mexico and the two regimes' attempts at reform. John Waterbury noted how under Sadat the Egyptian regime was becoming structurally similar to the dominant-party system in Mexico; Egypt and Mexico, in fact, figure prominently in his four-case study of public sector reform. Nazih Ayubi's textbook on the Arab state speaks frequently of the "Mexicanization" of the Egyptian state. Historian Roger Owen uses the dominant-party system of Mexico to illuminate attempts at simultaneous economic and political liberalization in Egypt. A conference organized by Egyptian and Mexican scholars in 1996 produced an edited volume that dealt explicitly with Egyptian and Mexican efforts at economic liberalization. Analysts have also traced Egypt's Islamist violence and Mexico's Zapatista insurrection in Chiapas to neoliberal policies.[1] In the last decade, Egyptian policymakers and academics, critical of their country's economic reform process, have extolled the virtues of the "Mexican model" and issued studies on how Egypt could expedite its privatization process by replicating the Mexican example.[2]

Despite variations in regime type and developmental levels, Egypt and Mexico are strikingly similar cases. Both Mexico and Egypt are corporatist, dominant-party regimes that rest (in Mexico until 1994) on leftist populist-distributive coalitions. Mexico is unique in Latin America in that it is a single-party corporatist regime resting on a coalition of urban and rural sectors. Like Mexico, Egyptian elites who came to power after the 1952 Revolution carried out land reform and established a populist authoritarian regime based on a coalition of workers and peasants. Mexico also resembles Egypt in its special relationship with the United States and its dependence on external revenues. Before Salinas's tax reforms, Mexico had the lowest taxation rate in Latin America and to this day a rate of direct taxation lower than Egypt's, and Mexico's strong dependence on American largesse, analysts have suggested, partly explains why it was one of the last states in Latin America to transition to democracy.[3] The Mexican state's rentier character makes the comparison with Egypt particularly appropriate, given the standard wisdom that what typifies the state in the Middle East (and some would say precludes cross-regional comparison) is the region's exceptional reliance on external rents.

A key difference between Egypt and Mexico, which I argue can explain their differing experiences with privatization and state reform, is the method of incorporation and state-building. In their survey of the corporatist regimes in Latin America, Collier and Collier note the different forms of control and support mobilization used during the incorporation period, and identify two broad types of incorporation experiences: state incorporation and party incorporation. I contend that, while in Egypt regime and coalition formation occurred according to the state corporatist paradigm, in Mexico the regime was founded following the model of party corporatism.[4] In the case of state incorporation, incorporation was undertaken through the legal and bureaucratic apparatus of the state, and the aim was to create a legalized and institutionalized labor movement that was depoliticized, controlled, and penetrated by the state. In the case of party incorporation, the main mechanism of incorporation was a political party, or political movement that later became a party; and a fundamental goal of political leaders, in addition to control, was the mobilization of working class support through this party. This mobilization contrasted sharply with the depoliticization characteristic of state incorporation.

Put differently, the argument of this study is that to understand the differing experiences with privatization in Egypt and Mexico today, it is crucial to look at the founding moment—or incorporation period of each regime—to identify not only the vested interests and opponents to reform but also the institutional links that the state formed with different social sectors—labor, peasantry, and capital. Scholars of Western Europe, from E. P. Thompson to Gøsta Esping-Anderson, have underlined the powerful and character-shaping effects of the incorporation of the masses into the political arena. Esping-Anderson's seminal study of the European welfare states showed that the terms under which the working class was incorporated gave rise to different kinds of welfare states and has illustrated how different working class mobilization patterns and cross-class coalitions led to different bargains between classes and the state and, consequently, different capacities for managing accumulation and distribution.[5]

In Egypt, the labor movement was depoliticized and attached to the state bureaucracy; the Free Officers' goal was the control and "preemptive demobilization" of labor. In contrast, in Mexico, though, labor was mobilized and tied to a political party and became a coalition partner on which the state greatly relied for electoral and political support. Although in both cases, the state played a dominant role in labor affairs, in Mexico, the state's links to labor were mediated by the PRI. This difference would prove crucial during the reform process because social control exercised through the Mexican ruling party turned out to be more effective in mobilizing social actors than the control carried out by the Egyptian state bureaucracy. Egypt's National Democratic Party simply did not grant reformers the capacity to co-opt opposition and to mobilize workers' support: patronage in the cities is not as adequately distributed as in rural areas, channels of representation are limited, and there are few reliable intermediaries (in the unions) who can deliver the rank and file.

An important factor explaining the Mexican regime's ability to retain the loyalty of workers while privatizing was not the presence of more inducements as opposed to constraints—Egyptian corporatism offers ample inducements and constraints—but rather the type of inducements. Inducements in the form of welfare benefits and subsidies, as exist in Egypt, are less likely to induce loyalty (particularly in the context of reform when benefits are being cut) than inducements that offer career incentives and formal channels for representation, expression of grievances, negotiation, and bargaining. The inducements and institutions of control I focus on are, first and foremost, the right to strike and the reconciliation and negotiation boards generated by this right; second, the electoral mechanism, which most effectively allows state leaders to gauge public opinion, mobilize certain groups, and exclude others; and, third, the labor confederation exclusion clauses and bylaws used to isolate recalcitrant unionists. During privatization, de la Madrid and Salinas made use of these linkages—tightening the administrative review of proposed strikes, awarding many candidacies to select unionists, altering the procedures covering wage negotiations and corporate bargains. In Egypt, the lack of institutionalized channels for bargaining and diminishing state resources has undercut the state's attempts to gain the support of the lower classes making repression and exclusion the most likely alternative for reformers.

Overcoming labor opposition is a necessary condition for economic reform, but it is not a sufficient one. The process also involves the undertaking of institutional reforms that will draw the support of previously alienated social actors, as the private sector was in Egypt and Mexico. Mexican state elites were more effective at drawing the private sector (which had never been fully incorporated into the PRI) because of their institutional interventions, namely their negotiated pacts and the creation of pro-reform agencies within the state bureaucracy. The processes of capacity building and coalition building are related. Coalitional support for economic reform could only be built if bureaucratic reform was undertaken and new institutions were created, a difficult process that paradoxically could only succeed if reformers had the adequate coalitional support. The process of state-capacity building is a political struggle, and it is useful to illuminate the conflicts that occur among different political forces over the state's organizational form. In the following chapters, I examine both the state-building period, when the elites' ideologies, political goals, and survival strategies dictated the size and political purpose of the state bureaucracy, and the current structural adjustment period, when reformers are engaged in a battle with etatists over the economic borders of the state.

To recap, the centerpiece of this argument is a comparison of the incorporation periods. The historical circumstances and nature of intra-elite conflict during the periods of incorporation in Egypt and Mexico bred different coalitional arrangements and different strategies of controlled mobilization and, consequently, populist-distributive coalitions that, despite apparent similarities, are undergirded by different bargains, links, and institutional configurations. The Mexican regime that emerged relied on the electoral support of labor and rural interest; the regime created by Nasser depoliticized the popular sectors and drew support primarily from the military and the rural middle class. These differing institutional profiles can help explain the record of privatization and state-business rapprochement in Mexico and the limited success of these projects in Egypt. The extensive electoral, organizational, and clientelistic ties existing between the Mexican state and labor (and, after 1987, state and capital) and mediated by a sprawling, institutionally robust political party granted reformers a degree of control and sanctioning power unavailable to Egyptian state elites.

Capacity and Control

Migdal has defined state capacity as "the ability of state leaders to use the agencies of the state to get people in the society to do what they want them to do," and, although not concerned specifically with economic restructuring, he emphasized how participation could enhance the state's social control and its ability to impose itself on social actors. This concept of social control is valuable to understanding how state elites can deal with "tenacious elements blocking state aspirations"—like labor resisting privatization.[6] The capacity to control labor is an aspect of power in that it implies forcing unionists and workers to comply and accept policies that they would not otherwise accept. Knight and Sened contend that bargaining power derives from the possession of "power resources," which they define as "the attributes (capacities or means) of actors (individuals or collectivities) which enable them to reward or punish other actors."[7] By this logic, the power of a social group like labor is manifest not only when it blocks a policy but also when government officials anticipate a reaction from that social group and do not pursue a policy that would adversely affect them.

Burgess has developed a compelling framework for analyzing the bargaining game that is triggered when a labor-backed party adopts market reforms, noting that in some cases there is a party-weighted distribution of "sanctioning power," whereas in other cases, where labor has threatened to withdraw from the ruling coalition or effectively done so, the distribution of sanctioning power is weighted more toward workers.[8] The extensive co-optation that occurs in state corporatist cases (such as Brazil and Chile) creates a union leadership insulated from the base and looking more toward the state and Labor Ministry than the grassroots level, with sanctioning power weighted more toward the state, while in cases of party corporatism, from the founding moment, sanctioning power is weighted toward the rank and file, and unionists are more representative and accountable to the base and better able to enforce the corporatist bargain. Thus, sanctioning power in Egypt seems to be weighted toward workers rather than toward the state, while the reverse seems to exist in Mexico.

How does one study state sanctioning power and capacity in the policy area of privatization? Ikenberry contends that a state may exhibit strength in some domains and weakness in others, so that as far as privatization is concerned, the ability to intervene does not imply the ability to withdraw; in fact, "flexibility—the capacity to break with past patterns of behavior—is the key component of state strength."[9] Both the Mexican regime in the mid-1980s and the Egyptian regime in the early 1990s were losing votes and facing popular grassroots opposition that had in effect created "parallel governments" replacing state institutions in providing services in local communities. In both countries, leaders tried to shore up support for the state, while facing dwindling state resources. Yet while the PRI was able to rebound and regain support neutralizing the challenges from the left, the Egypt ruling party is still in a crisis, losing votes and struggling to gain the support of urban constituencies.

One poignant example of the Mexican state's flexibility and the Egyptian state's rigidity was the states' reactions to the earthquakes of 1985 and 1992. Both regimes were paralyzed in face of the disasters. In the wake of the September 17, 1985, the Mexican military was seen as incapable and the government uncaring, and grassroots organizations mushroomed challenging the traditional PRI patronage machines in poor neighborhoods. Likewise, in Egypt, as the state fumbled for a response, the Islamists were out in the affected neighborhoods offering everything from blankets and shelter to counseling and loans. Yet while the Mexican state under Salinas responded to the loss of support and legitimacy by thoroughly purging the Ministries of Agriculture and Urban Development and then establishing Pronasol, Egypt is still unable to regain turf lost to Islamists, and since 1992 its main response has been repression.

It is important to disaggregate the different dimensions of "stateness" to identify which capabilities are most useful for shifting the state's social bases. Scholars of the Middle East tend to focus largely on one aspect of state capacity, and that is extraction. But there are multiple arenas for state-society interaction, not just extraction. As one author observes, "The idea of a generalized state capacity is meaningless. The capacity 'to get one's way in spite of opposition,' for instance, shares little with the capacity to 'mobilize consent' or 'to institutionalize cooperation.'"[10] Grindle has identified different types of capacity needed in responding to an economic crisis, among them technical capacity defined as "the ability to set and manage effective macroeconomic policies," administrative capacity defined as "the ability to perform basic administrative functions essential to economic development and social welfare," and political capacity which refers to "effective and legitimate channels for societal demand-making, representation, and conflict resolution." Although I discuss how technical capacity in Egypt and Mexico has been strengthened, I believe that what has facilitated reform in Mexico and hampered it in Egypt is not technical capacity but the latter two capabilities: the capacity to administer the public good, that is, to provide services, and the capacity to channel participation and respond to societal demands.[11]

To understand a state's ability to control social actors, it is useful to view people as rational actors who will shift their loyalty to the state, as opposed to another social organization, only if the state can offer incentives in the form of material rewards and systems of meaning. Mobilization can bind the populace or a social group to the state by getting individuals to comply with the state's demands, to participate in state-run or state-authorized institutions, and to view the state as legitimate.[12] The Mexican state enjoys more power of social control because during the incorporation period leaders mobilized both labor and peasantry and established through the PRI institutions of compliance, participation, and legitimation. In Egypt, only the rural middle class was mobilized into a mass organization and used as intermediaries to rule the hinterland; with regards to labor, the goal was "demobilization," "depoliticization," or what Thomas Callaghy has termed "departicipation," for fear that mobilized workers would join the Communist Party or Muslim Brotherhood. To borrow Luhman's concepts of "passive" and "active" inclusion, while Mexican labor was actively incorporated in the governing coalition, Egyptian labor was passively included—with the concomitant absence of essential links of bargaining and cooperation between the state and the Egyptian labor movement.[13]

How can reformers persuade unionists and workers to accept and cooperate with a divestiture program? Political economists have lauded countries such as Mexico where reformers have managed to induce the cooperation of labor through *concertación*, that is, consultation with affected groups.[14] David Stark and Laslo Bruszt have defended the merits of an inclusive, bargain-driven strategy and of participation:

> Instead of ignoring the enfranchisement of the non-propertied classes (without shares but with stakes) or instead of viewing these as an obstacle to economic development, [our] perspective endorses a broader expansion of political rights, from participation at the ballot box to participation in negotiations about the disposition of assets and the distribution of liabilities. Bringing actors informed by competitive evaluative principles to the negotiating table can contribute to economic development not simply by securing broader support for economic reform (through a reduction of uncertainty about the future) but also by reducing opportunities for rent-seeking by opening up these negotiations to public accountability.[15]

Organized labor was very much a junior partner in the economic pacts established by de la Madrid and Salinas, and reformers often overrode labor representatives, but the fact that Mexican corporatism was founded on an electoral bargain afforded regime elites the institutions by which to negotiate the implementation of a reform program, to marginalize resistant unionists, and to build alliances with a crop of pro-reform unionists who could control the base. In Egypt, the corporatist pact was an "imposition," and the Egyptian state never developed the requisite bargaining links with social actors so that at present, although Mubarak has been trying to integrate the populist and Islamist opposition into the parliamentary system and find new intermediaries in civil society, the only institutionally possible alternative seems to be another imposition—this time of a neoliberal project. Despite attempts to forge new links to labor and capital, Mubarak's strategy of reform thus far seeks to gain the electoral support of the upper classes, while excluding populist Islamist groups, and to ram through painful measures rather than risk derailing the reform agenda with free elections. Salinas reformed the economy while retaining labor's

Table 2.1 Hypothesis

State capacity (IV) ➡ Successful public-sector reform (DV)
(Effective social control) ➡ (Ability to overcome opposition to reform)

	Founding moment	Aftermath	Institutional legacy	Structural adjustment
Egypt	Intra-elite conflict revolves mainly around political issues (i.e., return to parliamentary democracy); transport workers are the only segment of labor mobilized; only quiescence and control, not electoral support, of labor sought; rural middle class electorally mobilized into coalition; controlled mobilization takes a different strategy than in Mexico.	Populist distributive coalition created; labor attached to bureaucracy; workers depoliticized and controlled; workers and peasants granted myriad benefits. (The resultant regime is based on state incorporation and passive inclusion)	Ineffective social control; few institutional links between union movement and the state. Despite several attempts to link unions to a political party, labor remains tied to state bureaucracy.	Inability to privatize labor-intensive SOEs; unionists and workers are opposed to reform; state cannot overcome opposition; labor protests increase; workers and unionists defect to opposition parties; regime is loosing support; repression and exclusion is are increasing.
Mexico	Intraelite conflict centers around political and economic issues (i.e., the role of the state in the economy); worker and peasant support sought by warring elites; workers and peasants armed and mobilized politically.	Populist distributive coalition created; labor tied to ruling party; workers mobilized electorally and granted benefits. (The resultant regime is based on party incorporation and active inclusion)	Effective social control; extensive linkages between party and union movement. State can effectively co-opt opposition and undertake unpopular policies.	Ability to privatize; militant unions co-opted or marginalized by the PRI; extensive privatization. Reforms by Salinas draw support of disgruntled workers and private capital.

support, whereas Mubarak has not been able to maintain popular support. The Egyptian leader simply lacks the social control needed to redeploy the state apparatus and build a new support coalition. One caveat: I am aware of the Mexican state's limitations—its difficulties in providing public security, quelling rural uprisings, and controlling capital flight—but in examining its capacity in the area of privatization, one can see that the regime has effectively enlisted private sector support and contained labor opposition. The causation of the hypothesis I am presenting is that state capacity is a necessary variable for public sector reform.

Incorporation and State Building: States and Intermediaries

The process of incorporation and the building of ties between the state and popular classes is an aspect of state formation. Tilly has understood the process of state building as involving principally the transformation from indirect rule to direct rule—a transition from mediated states who rule through local elites to unmediated states that have direct institutional links to social groups and could directly distribute public goods.[16] In mediated states, local elites would carry out functions for the state from taxation and conscription to settling disputes and turning out the vote. This, as discussed below, was the role played by the rural middle class after Nasser's land reform. Weber's discussion about the patrimonial ruler, the landowning elites (*honoratiores*), and the "mediatized" subjects can elucidate Nasser's coalitional strategy and "limited revolution" and, more broadly, the logic of the mediated state:

> The patrimonial ruler cannot always dare to destroy these autonomous local patrimonial powers . . . if the ruler intends to eliminate the autonomous *honoratiores*, he must have an administrative organization of his own which can replace them with approximately the same authority over the local population . . . [A]s a rule the prince found himself compelled to compromise with the local patrimonial authorities or other *honoratiores*; he was restrained by the possibility of an often dangerous resistance, by the lack of a military and bureaucratic apparatus capable of taking over the administration, and, above all, by the power position of the local *honoratiores*.[17]

Tilly argues that the power of these middlemen is weakened as the state delivers more public goods and creates institutions to directly deliver goods and services, and the intermediaries are "integrated . . . directly into national administrative hierarchies."[18]

But several scholars, mostly Europeans, have expressed skepticism about this view, arguing that the state reform that occurs during structural adjustment does not involve a transition to direct rule but rather entails the state's resort to new private intermediaries. Thus privatization does not so much result in a withdrawal of the state and a "shedding" of public enterprises as much as it results in cash-strapped states subcontracting ("discharging") SOEs and administrative functions (e.g., management of labor relations, customs administration, social security) to allies in the private sector through which the state can still indirectly exert control over the economy and polity.[19] Privatization, in this view, involves a redeployment of the state and is but another phase in the ongoing formation and consolidation of the postcolonial state; this phase entails a "passage from one modality of government to another," which involves "not so much a loss of control as an option for indirect government, using private intermediaries."[20] Insofar as it grants private actors market and accumulation opportunities in exchange for state control, privatization in this sense is part of the incorporation process, as regimes in crisis decide to co-opt the social and economic capital of different social groups.

Different explanations have been advanced for the emergence of this type of "recombinant" property regime, including economic uncertainty and institutional weakness. One analyst attributes the trend toward joint ventures in Latin American reformers to the weakness of property rights: "When property rights are weak, there is a greater need and potential for discretionary alliances between public elites and the state, leading to the effective privatization of what should a public good."[21] Both the Egyptian and Mexican postrevolutionary regimes relied on indirect rule and on intermediaries, yet what occurred in Mexico during the adjustment period was a transition not so much to direct rule but to the emergence of a new kind of indirect rule based on a new bargain with a new set of private intermediaries; the statist intermediaries were in effect replaced with pro-reform "interlocuters" who could provide public goods. The differing success that the two regimes have had in finding new intermediaries can be explained by examining the different corporatist contexts.

Intra-Elite Conflict and Coalition Building

Why does incorporation sometimes involve the mobilization of popular classes and sometimes demobilization? Why do state elites sometimes seek to incorporate and gain the active political support of only urban groups, sometimes urban and rural groups? Why do state builders sometimes incorporate but depoliticize both groups? Nelson and Huntington's classic study of political participation linked elite politics to mobilization by arguing that every political leader, "even in completely non-democratic systems," has to have some "group or groups that are his source of strength and support."[22] The Colliers contend that "progressive" elites will often mobilize labor to gain support for a statist development strategy. Waldner has also put forth a compelling framework showing how elite conflict, coalitional formations, and state-building patterns shape development strategies.[23] These approaches, though, neglect the important role played by mobilization in coalitional strategies and in state building. Mobilization (or demobilization) is a potent strategy of political entrepreneurship and determines the configuration of the resulting coalition.

An analysis of intra-elite politics and choices made by actors within the state can explain why the incorporation period took the specific form it did in Egypt and Mexico. The instability of prerevolutionary Mexico dictated a coalitional strategy that made mobilization a rational option. Since elites wanted to increase labor's weight as a popular resource, radical populism in Mexico involved more concessions and a degree of power sharing with labor, which led to the development of numerous electoral and bargaining links between the state and labor. Between 1952 and 1959, Egypt experienced an antiparty, depoliticizing incorporation period similar to that which unfolded in Brazil. Nasser's Free Officers came to power via a coup in 1952 and were not reliant on the support of labor or the peasantry. Unlike Mexico, where elite conflict centered around the economic role of the state making labor's active political and military support vital, Nasser did not need labor's backing to pursue his development plan. As Chapter 2 shows, the support of transport unions was important for Nasser in his power struggle with Naguib in March 1954, but the mere quiescence of most workers was sufficient.

Nasser's political objective of depoliticization and control of labor is evident in the institutional structure of the Egyptian Trade Union Federation (ETUF), which as Bianchi notes is strikingly similar to the Brazilian labor code and union confederation, the General Confederation of Workers (CGT).[24] The organizational structure is hierarchical or "pyramid shaped." In exchange for pledges of loyalty and renouncing the right to strike, union leaders were given unprecedented legal guarantees concerning job security, promotions, and retirement benefits. The singular, hierarchical structure of the Egyptian union movement and the state's co-optation of top leadership have had a profound influence on the state's ability to control the working class. Nasser's desire to prevent collective action by unions led to an extensive use of inducements and constraints. But the ETUF's institutional structure simply lacked the co-optive resources to allow mid- and lower-level leaders to express the voices of their constituencies or to rise upward in the union hierarchy. Turnover was minimal, and extensive intervention by the Labor Ministry insured that only clients would advance. Conflicts and divisions in the ETUF structure simmered beneath the official calm as long as the state was benevolent to the popular sectors; but efforts at state reform, starting with Nasser in 1965, then Sadat in 1974, and revived by Mubarak in the 1990s, brought the schisms within the labor confederation to the fore.

In Mexico, where the goal of incorporation was to mobilize and politicize the working class, the labor code promulgated placed fewer constraints on unions and labor activities than in Egypt. The Mexican regime favored credible, accountable labor leaders who could deliver the workers' vote; unions were after all a vehicle for support mobilization, and labor could in theory withdraw from the PRI and ruling coalition (as it threatened to do in 1954), so representation was preferred to coercion. Mexican leaders relied heavily on institutions of representation and bargaining. The new constitution granted labor the right to form unions and to strike. And unlike Egypt, there was not a single central confederation. Within the PRI, there were several confederations in addition to the Mexican Workers Federation (CTM), which enhanced the state's ability to control labor. With regards to representation, the party structure granted Mexican unionists of all levels more access than their Egyptian counterparts.

"Bringing Parties Back In"

Political scientists have recently shown a renewed interest in the role of political parties in regime transitions. Yet despite Joan Nelson's hypothesis put forth over a decade ago, noting that whether labor unions would adopt a cooperative or oppositional stance to reform is often determined by "political institutions," particularly "party systems and union ties," the role of political parties in capitalist transformation and state reform has not been sufficiently studied.[25] One of the more cogent critiques leveled at Peter Evans's "embeddedness" thesis involves his "neglect of politics and political parties" and how the latter can enhance state autonomy.[26] The Mexican state's ability to control and co-opt labor and proceed with privatization rested on the linkages and resources provided by the PRI. The most significant party union institutional links utilized during the reform process were (1) electoral incentives that drew aspiring unionists, (2) the Exclusion Clause used to isolate dissident unionists and workers, and (3) the "tripartite conciliation and negotiation boards," historically a forum for workers to press their demands on wages and workplace conditions but used by reformers to gain the cooperation of unionists. Moreover, by voting for the PRI, workers and unionists participated in a system and could be represented at all levels of government; state officials benefited from this system of "representation qua control."

In Egypt, for historical reasons, a different scenario obtains. The launching, abolition, and reincarnation of successive ruling party organizations meant that the existing National Democratic Party (NDP) lacks the rootedness, support, or legitimacy that decades of political influence have given mass parties elsewhere. Regarding the control of labor, successive political parties from the National Union, Liberation Rally, Arab Socialist Union, and most recently the NDP interfered in union elections at national and federation levels but not at the local level both for lack of capacity and apparently to bestow a semblance of legitimacy. Except for the brief period when the Arab Socialist Union was functional (1964–66), labor lacked any effective instrument of pressure or bargaining. In lieu of a party, Nasser preferred using the state and public sector to control labor and large sections of the populace.

The challenge posed to the NDP by informal leftist groups and to a lesser extent by the leftist Tagammu Party (NPUP) can also be understood as a product of the state incorporation period. The absence of a ruling party that mobilized workers and responded to labor's interests left the opportunity for leftist parties and grassroots groups to perform that function. An important difference between party and state incorporation was that in the former "organizational space" was largely filled with cooperating mass organizations and an encompassing party so that the challenges of new opposition movements posed different problems.[27] The ASU's short-lived career and the NDP with its slogan of "stability, democracy, and capitalist development" never drew labor's allegiance, and space for a leftist alternative always present was quickly occupied by the Tagammu and other groups when Sadat allowed limited pluralism in 1976. In Mexico, on the other hand, the government had in place mass organizations that could act as interlocutors between the regime and the mass base; dissident movements were quickly isolated.

It is during the process of privatization that the abilities of ruling parties and states to control labor are put to the test, and it is during this context that Egypt and Mexico's differences rose to the fore. Privatization in Mexico hurt the interests of labor, undermining contracts and weakening the bargaining power of unions, but, given the range of benefits, CTM leaders preferred staying within the parameters of the alliance. The NDP lacks the multiple levers of control over the union movement available to the PRI. To implement privatization, Egyptian reformers have opted to restrict participation in the labor hierarchy and the party system even further. The institutional structure of the ETUF simply does not allow for much turnover of personnel or upward mobility from the base, and so it does not give mid- and upper-level unionists incentives to take up positions and issues favored by the rank and file. While upper-level unionists generally support privatization, lower-level unionists are increasingly preferring to join the disgruntled rank and file rather than support state policy. In 1998 after a wave of strikes, textile workers in Kafr al-Duwwar withdrew their support for labor representatives elected to the board of directors; one unionist noted how it was getting increasingly difficult to take the labor confederation's side against rank-and-file interests: "We could stand by the workers and be adamant but we are still trying to do our job. It is getting rather difficult, though."[28] Since 2004, Egypt has seen an unprecedented wave of workers' strikes that repeatedly delayed, if not halted, the privatization process in Egypt; the state cannot provide incentives to maintain the workers' quiescence.

State Reform and Political Parties

Scholars of economic reform, particularly students of the East Asian NICs, have long stressed the importance of center-right coalitions. But as Robert Wade has observed, most analyses of coalition building suffer from "thin politics"; the process of coalition building in the context of adjustment is insufficiently explained, and coalitional strategies are undertheorized.[29] While Mexican reformers have found partners in civil society to back the development effort, the Egyptians are still searching for allies, and as the reform process moves forward the NDP is losing electoral support. Why have the Egyptians not been able to enlist the support of societal actors?

David Mares' analysis of trade policy in Colombia can help conceptualize the politics of coalition building. In his framework, state elites can influence the policy preferences of societal actors and undertake major policy changes by exploiting the problems of collective action facing key groups in society. State actors can use rents to raise barriers to collective action by opponents of policies preferred by the state. David Mares argues that institutions and rents can be used to either impede or allow the collective action of social groups.[30] The institutional structure of the Egyptian trade union confederation, for instance, served to impede collective action on the part of labor unions and to check the upward mobility of lower-level unionists. Chaudhry has similarly observed that Middle Eastern leaders often allocate rents strategically to preempt collective action by businessmen.[31] Leaders can also threaten to eliminate existing institutions to influence the policy preferences of social actors. This strategy was used repeatedly by Mexican reformers: labor's acquiescence was secured partly with the threat of eliminating the PRI's corporatist sectors. Likewise, the Mexican state used the Economic Stability Pact as an instrument to distribute or withhold important rents (e.g., government contracts) to change capital's behavior. Mubarak has similarly introduced institutional innovations to draw the support of the private sector, such as the NDP's Economic Committee.

Administrative reform was crucial for changing the preferences of social actors in Mexico. Mexican business's cooperative response to liberalization would not have been possible were it not for the reform of the upper echelons of the state bureaucracy (and the rise of the Ministry of Planning and Budget) and the centralization of power within the presidency. A question I address is, why were Mexican reformers able to implement these reforms while Mubarak, who since 1991 has brought numerous market-oriented technocrats into the upper echelons of the bureaucracy, has not yet been able to impose a reformist vision on the state apparatus?

Political leaders face the dilemma of insuring their own political survival by using the bureaucracy as a reservoir of favors for supporters or of undertaking administrative reform and using the bureaucracy for economic goals and risking the alienation of supporters. The bureaucracies of Egypt and Mexico have not been immune to these survival tactics. In Mexico, the incoming president historically rewards thousands of loyalists and potential supporters with bureaucratic positions. Nasser's policy of guaranteeing every university graduate a position in the bureaucracy was a textbook case of a leader using the bureaucracy for control and support. Yet, if far-reaching civil service reform is politically very difficult (and has been carried out in neither Egypt nor Mexico), it is not clear why limited piecemeal reform creating "pockets of efficiency" cannot be achieved.[32] In other words, elite macroeconomic agencies, such as the Mexican Ministry of Programming and Budget (SPP) in Mexico, can be created or reformed, insulated from intrastate politicking, while preserving patronage opportunities in other parts of the state apparatus. Mubarak has attempted to create such "pockets" as seen in the establishment of the Public Enterprise Office (PEO) and the Higher Policy Committee (HPC), but these agencies lack the capacity and societal support and are still vulnerable to outside depredation. This, too, can be explained by examining the differing corporatist contexts.

The mobilization and incorporation of various social groups into the PRI relieved the Mexican state of many of the clientelist pressures that have captured the Egyptian state. Reformist leaders in Mexico could divert societal pressures into the PRI and use the party as a reservoir of patronage, thus maintaining their support while reforming the state itself. In Egypt, where the state was used for control and participation, reformers lack this luxury. The absence of a strong rooted party politicized the Egyptian state even further, and bureaucratic politics gained a special significance. This is not peculiar to Egypt; in other states in the region, attempts to "demobilize" populations and limit participation, particularly in the absence of a strong party, often diverted "participatory impulses" into the state bureaucracy.[33] In Mexico, leaders used incorporation into the PRI as a strategy to restrain the independent bases of peasants, labor, and a variety of other groups. In Egypt, Nasser's distrust of parties led him to use the state bureaucracy as an instrument of control and to incorporate threatening power centers into the state apparatus.

The Egyptian state today can now no longer serve as the linchpin of a populist coalition, which is slowly unraveling. The historical beneficiaries of state largesse are experiencing material losses as public expenditure is cut. With the structural adjustment process underway, the bureaucracy—historically the main institution for containing the populace—is not proving such a useful tool. The NDP's electoral mechanism and patronage machine is being administered and manipulated from above to reconstitute the state's social bases, but the country's weak party system and the participation deficit are proving to be serious obstacles. In the early 1990s, Amir Salem, the director of Cairo's Legal Center for Human Rights, observed that only 7 percent of Egyptians were members in a party, union, or syndicate.[34] In 1999, only 4.1 percent of Egyptians between the ages of eighteen and twenty-five were reported to be members of political parties, compared to a national average of 8.4 percent.[35] A study released on the eve of the March 2007 referendum on constitutional amendments noted that "less than 5 percent of Egyptian citizens are organized in political parties,"[36] so that even counting the four million working in the bureaucracy, the overwhelming majority of the population is not in any of the regime's participatory institutions. With limited control over the population, the regime is unable to incorporate different social groups—Islamists, urban poor—and is instead opting for exclusion and political closure. The polarized political situation, with the ideological and political stand-off between the state and the Islamist opposition, seems to have made an inclusionary coalitional strategy next to impossible and led regime elites to opt for exclusion.[37]

Rents and State Capacity

Before analyzing the state-building periods and the specific corporatist bargains, it is worth considering the canonical account on domestic coalitions and Middle Eastern states. I contend that despite the demobilization and departicipation of the popular sectors, Egyptian state elites rely on coalitional support. The conventional wisdom on the Egyptian regime's coalitional underpinnings is that labor's "passive loyalty" is very important for the stability of the country and legitimacy of the ruler; but, given the state's financial autonomy, the state is in no way beholden to any constituency. Labor, in this view, cannot block any attempts to reform, because workers are bought off with ample benefits and lack any organizational strength to resist. If market reforms are not being implemented, it is because regime elites lack the will. John Waterbury, an influential proponent of this view, underlines the lack of political will to reform, stressing labor's lack of organizational strength and inability to resist measures that have violated labor's entitlements: "When organized labor has chosen to confront the state . . . it has invariably been smashed." Speaking of labor's purported inability to resist reforms, he opines, "Entitlements were originally bestowed and not won. Hence the emerging interests did not develop the organizational sinews and history of struggle and cooperation that would have afforded them a coherent defense of their interests . . . I posit that those who have not won their acquired rights through organizational trials of strength will probably not be effective in defending what they had been granted."[38]

My argument is directly at variance with the above conclusion: I believe that the fact that benefits were paternalistically extended to labor without mobilization implies that crucial organizational ties with which the state (or party) can control labor were not formed. Because of Leviathan's gratuitous benevolence, institutions of negotiation, and cooperation, which benefit workers but in a reform period are an asset to the state's control capacity, were never effectively established in Egypt. In the 1990s, lower-level unionists and rank-and file workers opposed to privatization began to agitate and protest beyond the state's control; unable to appease all protestors and dissenters with cash payments or early retirement plans, the regime would resort to a mix of repression and exclusion. The laws and institutions that Mexican labor fought for during the 1930s and 1940s to empower unions against unfavorable policies turned out to be the very same institutions used by Mexican reformers to atomize and control labor dissent today. While analysts have argued that state corporatism, by strangling the union hierarchy to the state bureaucracy and forbidding strikes, has emasculated the union movement and weakened labor's ability to mount protest and block policy,[39] I argue the converse: that state corporatism's stymieing of autonomous union activity and credible representation, combined with the criminalization of strikes, deprived state elites of various institutional mechanisms for bargaining that would allow reformers to contain dissent and mobilize support.

The argument that Egypt's access to external revenue in the form of aid, labor remittances, and earnings (from tourism, the Suez Canal, and oil sales) allows it to postpone needed reforms, buying off any societal resistance to reform is ultimately unpersuasive. This argument explains little about Egypt's and Mexico's differing experiences with market reform or the institutional development of these states. Both Egypt and Mexico historically have had low taxation rates and relied heavily on externally generated revenue. Miguel Centeno's study of war and state formation in South America argues that one reason military conflict has not led to administrative development or enhanced the fiscal capacity of the Latin American state is because of the flow of external rents: "The easy availability of external financing allowed the [Latin American] state the luxury of not coming into conflict with those social sectors that possessed the required resources."[40]

According to numerous sources, the Middle East, compared to Latin America and other regions in the developing world, is not undertaxed.[41] A World Bank study showed that in 1985, total taxes—that is, direct and indirect taxes combined—as a percentage of GDP and the ratio of direct to indirect taxes (56:46) in the Middle East were on average higher than in all other regions of the developing world including Latin America. In 1985, the percentage of direct taxes of income and wealth was 56 percent in the Middle East and North Africa, while in Latin America it was 46 percent.[42] Several studies have shown how throughout the 1960s and part of the 1970s Mexico was one of the countries with the lowest income tax rates as a percentage of GDP in the world. Roger Hansen's classic study of the Mexican political system ranks Mexico seventieth among seventy-two countries in terms of extractive capacity. And by most accounts, Egypt has a higher rate of direct taxation than Mexico. From the late 1970s onward, until de la Madrid's tenure and Salinas's tax reforms, Mexico relied heavily on oil earnings and loans from private banks. In comparing recent taxation levels in Egypt and Mexico, we find that Egypt's tax revenue as a percentage of GDP in 1997 was 16.56 percent, while for Mexico it was 13.04 percent.[43]

Political economists have noted the rentier character of the Mexican state. Mexico became a rentier state in the late 1970s at about the same time Egypt became dependent on American aid. In 1978, Mexico gained access to oil rents, which would be used to finance the PRI's populist coalition and serve as a "lubricant" for the spoils system for the remainder of that decade and through the 1980s.[44] The rentier state paradigm posits that the distributive Middle East state's lack of need to tax its populace not only vitiates political representation but generally severs the links between the state and domestic constituency, leading to extreme autonomy. But to argue that the Egyptian state's autonomy from society and various coalition partners grants it the freedom to act at will would be erroneous and ahistorical. The Egyptian state's institutional detachment from the popular sectors is more a product of Nasser's coalitional strategy of demobilization than of an inherently rentier economy. In both Egypt and Mexico, corporatist bargains and coalitional arrangements were in place before both countries became heavily dependent on foreign aid: in Mexico, this massive dependence began toward the end of Echeverria's presidency in 1978 when bank loans began flowing, and oil prices rose; and in Egypt, it was after the 1978 Camp David Accords. In both countries, reforms were attempted and abandoned long before rents began flowing in the late 1970s. Egypt did have access to rents prior to 1979 from the United States and the Soviet bloc, but as I demonstrate in the next chapter, external revenue began streaming into Egypt following the decisive, initial stages of state building and after the populist bargains and institutions were in put in place.

Moreover, in terms of a state's capacity to reverse course and transform society, extractive capacity is not a reliable indicator. As Weiss has emphasized, "there is no clear correlation between extractive and transformative capacity. States with very high extractive capacities, for instance Sweden, exhibit little of the transformative capacity of the low-taxing state like Japan."[45] Egypt has long had higher taxation rates than Mexico but does not have Mexico's capacity to channel participation and respond to societal demands. With regards to state reform and coalition building, the institutions of concern should be institutions of participation, not just of extraction. Mexico's connectedness to the popular sectors and Egypt's detachment are the result of the political calculus that drove the countries' respective incorporation projects and not the product of the rent dependency that developed in the 1970s. As powerful as external flows and international pressures may be, they are mediated by domestic institutional arrangements and circumstances. State-society configurations and the distribution of power within the Mexican and Egyptian states refracted and channeled external pressures and ultimately shaped policy choices.

Rents and Market Reform

Analysts have increasingly been noting that access to external rents can actually facilitate economic reform and not necessarily lead to its postponement. Chile is often highlighted as a case where successful economic restructuring was aided by the state's "unusual" access to foreign exchange from the sale of copper and World Bank loans.[46] Comparativists who underline the role of rents concede that Egypt and Mexico are heavily dependent on external revenue and funded state expansion through rents and only began considering reform after the price of oil fell. According to this argument, reform occurred in Mexico because the country almost defaulted in 1981 and did not benefit from an international bailout. Since most of Mexico's borrowing was from private banks, capital dried up as oil prices fell, and leaders had little choice but to restructure its economy. So Mexico received funds guided by market efficiency considerations, whereas Egypt got money from public creditors, IFIs, and donor countries for political reasons and could use its political/geostrategic value to postpone reform; that is to say, Mexico had access to "economic rents," while Egypt availed itself of "security rents."

But Mexico's access to rent was also based on a political calculus. Mexico may not receive an annual two billion dollars from the United States like Egypt, but it received substantial American aid, and its reform process was supported by Washington more than any other country in Latin America. For economic and geopolitical reasons, Mexican leaders could always count on receiving an American bailout in crisis situations. Finally, the fact that in Latin America external revenue came from commercial banks, while in the Middle East the lending was from states, does not make the domestic institutional context any different; reformers were still faced with domestic contexts and coalitional arrangements shaped by differing incorporation patterns.

American largesse may indeed, as Eva Bellin has argued, subsidize Arab states' repressive capabilities, allowing leaders to defer democratization, but significant institution building has still taken place. External revenue can help forestall political liberalization, but it can still bankroll and advance economic liberalization. Both the United States and IFIs have an expressed interest in the economic restructuring of Egypt, though they may differ on the pace of reform. Mubarak often used the country's strategic importance for American interests to stave off pressure from the IMF (which he calls the "International Misery Fund"), but that did not always work. (Despite his appeals to the United States, the IMF in 1994 still refused to approve the third installment of the 20 percent debt relief by the Paris Club scheduled for July 1994.)

The relationship between rents and reform is also linked to the variable of economic crisis. The variable "crisis" is often brought in by scholars as a deus ex machina to explain structural change. How exactly do you measure the severity or depth of a crisis? The severity of a crisis obviously involves an element of subjectivity, since state elites perceive crises differently. Moreover, the crisis in Egypt was and remains deep: as Luciani has wryly noted, Egypt can be said "to have faced a fiscal crisis throughout its modern existence."[47] The "crisis" argument is also tautological: a crisis is deemed severe and change inducing after reform has happened; if change did not occur, then the crisis was not deep enough. The crisis argument, like the will argument, assumes that reformers have the capacity to restructure but do not want to because it is not in their interest as long as rents are flowing and there is no money crisis. The crisis explanation does not elucidate the Egyptian experience. Neoliberal reform is in the interest of the cash-strapped Egyptian regime. Privatization can draw investment, enhance the state's legitimacy with the upper classes, and strengthen the state's capacity as the regime finds new allies in the private sector. Mubarak has not privatized most of the SOEs slated for sale because he risks losing control of labor and creating unrest in an already deeply polarized society.

3

The Founding Moment

Elite Conflict, Coalition Formation, and Regime Consolidation

I don't believe the 1952 revolution had any positive features, since democracy is still missing. Even its social reforms led to the failure of our economy. The greatest failure of the revolution is the lack of democracy, which I believe led to our defeat in 1967. Egypt has never experienced a democratic government from 1952 until now . . . The revolution embraced the slogan "raise your head, my brother, for the age of oppression is over," but it replaced it with the heavy foot of Abdel Nasser that kept people's heads down.

—*Awad El-Morr*[1]

To assert the primacy of politics in the incorporation periods of Egypt and Mexico would be to state the obvious. The political struggles of the pre- and postrevolutionary periods are critical to understanding the origins, profile, and support bases of the Mexican and Egyptian states. Different political rationales drove the processes of regime formation and coalition building in the two countries. Establishing control over the lower classes involves political mobilization, which can be violent and destabilizing, but the successful institutionalization of mass support increases state builders' capacity to consolidate their rule and policy agenda. Regime elites in Mexico and Egypt sought to limit the duration of mass mobilization, direct it through approved organizational channels, and guide social groups toward different elite-defined objectives. How state elites directed mass participation would have a powerful effect on the institutional profiles of the postrevolutionary authoritarian regimes.

The historical context in which the regimes were born shaped the leaders' strategies of coalition formation. In Mexico, intra-elite conflict before incorporation necessitated the electoral mobilization of the popular sectors, and subsequent conflict during the period of regime consolidation led to the creation of a dominant-party system. If the Mexican state was born in an environment of civil war and revolution, the modern Egyptian state would appear in a context of intrastate war, specifically in the wake of the 1948 war, and develop in the shadow of the Palestinian-Israeli conflict; the wars of 1948, 1956, and 1967 would have decisive effects on state and party formation in Egypt. The Free Officers came to power in 1952 with the aid of the military only, and, despite the critical support provided by trade unions during the intra-elite power struggle in March 1954, Nasser did not attempt to cultivate the electoral support of labor. Instead, after destroying the power base of large landowners, Nasser sought to control labor and the peasantry using the state bureaucracy. Nasser forged electoral links with the smaller landed elites who, along with the military and the state bureaucracy, formed the base of his support.

The process of coalition building involves the expansion of state structures. Postrevolutionary elites will expand the state apparatus in order to centralize power and achieve the revolution's goals; the size and shape of the state is the product of struggles between the postcolonial regime and societal actors, on the one hand, and the regime and international actors, on the other. The coalitions that emerged in Egypt and Mexico were populist-distributive, but the specific bargains tying the state/party to the popular sectors differed in both countries and would produce disparate state structures. The differences in bargains can be explained through an analysis of the incorporation process and that period's coalitional struggles. Gaining the cooperation of the labor movement is often crucial for prevailing in the intra-elite conflict that occurs during the process of state building. Embattled political elites, particularly leaders who want to pursue statist and protectionist economic policies, often try to increase their power by mobilizing labor. Although elite conflict in Egypt did not center around the degree of state intervention, in both countries the dynamics of the power struggle determined the subsequent coalitional strategies that led to electoral mobilization in Mexico and "departicipation" in Egypt.

Revolution and Labor Mobilization (Mexico 1910–34)

There is ample historical evidence showing how and why the conflict among elites in Mexico led to the mobilization of workers and peasantry. The instability of postrevolutionary Mexico dictated a coalitional strategy that made mobilization a rational option. The Mexican Revolution of 1910 triggered the collapse of Porfirio Diaz's long-standing oligarchic state, and the assassination of Francisco Madero in 1913 set off a civil war that raged until the victory of the Constitutionalist forces in 1916. In this setting, with the oligarchic elite weak and lacking any substantial control over the population, peasant and labor unrest was rife, and different political factions appeared to court the support of the popular groups. Soon after the 1910 revolution, a split began to appear within the "revolutionary family" between the accommodationist faction (with ties to the oligarchic forces), represented by the supporters of Francisco Madero and Venustiano Carranza, and the populists, who sought to mobilize labor and peasant. The first major episode of labor mobilization occurred in 1914 when Victoriano Huerta assumed the presidency, and the Constitutionalists (the group opposing Huerta for being a counterrevolutionary linked to the oligarchic state) formed six Red Battalions of fifteen thousand workers to fight for the Constitutionalist cause; workers, in turn, fought in exchange for labor's right to organize the working class throughout the country.[2] Historians point to several factors that made labor's support crucial for elite factions: workers' new organizational strength; the military importance of railroad, port, and petroleum workers; labor's political significance in urban areas; and the continuing threat of working class violence.[3]

Although Adolfo de la Huerta began the state-building process in 1920, Ruth Collier has shown that the Mexican incorporation project occurred in two phases: an early phase in the 1920s and a later one in the 1930s under Cardenas; in both phases labor support proved crucial for regime consolidation. Both Presidents Alvaro Obregon (1920–24) and Plutarco Elias Calles (1924–28) sought to build a stronger state and to gain control over regional caciques who had gained power in the previous decade of armed conflict. But rivalries among the Sonoran leaders—Obregon, Calles, and De la Huerta—narrowed the support base of the presidency, as Obregon became identified with the agrarians, de la Huerta with the cooperativists, and Calles with labor.[4] The splintering of the coalition meant that Calles came to the presidency reliant on labor as his main source of support. In 1923, when de la Huerta staged a rebellion challenging Calles's succession to the presidency, the Regional Confederation of Mexican Workers (CROM) formed militias and took up arms in Calles's defense, playing a decisive role in the outcome of the conflict. A host of concessions was granted to maintain labor's support, including greater political influence at various levels of government. The federal labor law was revised, the role of the tripartite commissions increased, and the state supported the CROM's efforts to establish hegemony over the labor movement. To keep labor in the coalition, the government also granted unions an expanded social security program, a system of retail outlets selling subsidized goods to workers, and a number of agencies and banks to serve workers.

Calles's radical populism drew a conservative backlash from the private sector, the agrarians, and the church. During the Maximato (1924–28),

Calles would abandon his progressive policies toward labor, and, following president-elect Obregon's assassination for which the CROM was blamed, even previous pro-labor policies were reversed. A conservative labor code was passed, undoing the state-labor alliance that had existed during the 1920s. But even during this conservative hiatus, regime consolidation remained high on the agenda. Since the revolution, no presidential succession had occurred peacefully, and Obregon's assassination underlined the need for a mechanism to institutionalize presidential succession. Partly in response to this need, in 1928, Calles founded the National Revolutionary Party (PNR). Calles established the PNR to contain factional rivalries and as an institution that would support a strong state and unite both military and civilian elements of the "revolutionary family." Because of the hostility toward the Calles-CROM alliance, the labor confederation was not included in the PNR, and the party coalition was initially an alliance of regional caudillos and rebellious caciques and their factions.[5] Despite having little popular support, the PNR was an important instrument for Calles who used it to gain control over the presidency and to centralize political control.

Cardenas-Calles Conflict (1934–40)

Since the state-labor alliance had been broken, when Cardenas assumed power in 1934, he was again faced with the question of labor incorporation and coalition building. As a state builder, Cardenas sought to weld together a coalition that would allow him to strengthen the presidency and the party against civilian caudillos and against the army, which was still not subordinate to the state. In confronting Calles's conservative supporters, popular sector mobilization was necessary. Scholars have shown how few coalitional alternatives were available to Cardenas in battling the Calles group and how a populist coalition with radical labor and peasant groups was his only viable strategy.[6] When Cardenas armed peasants and formed workers' militias, his coalition also became a counterweight to the military. With that base of support he was also able to establish his autonomy from foreign and domestic capital and carry out the far-reaching reforms for which the Cardenas period is known.

To gain popular support, Cardenas offered benefits that were ideological, political, organizational, and material. He defended the cause of urban and rural workers and committed the state to intervene in the class struggle on behalf of the working class. He strengthened labor organizations, granted labor officials positions throughout the government, and encouraged workers to strike and demand wage increases; he also introduced socialist education into schools, distributed more lands to the peasantry, promoted the collective ownership of land, and even armed groups of peasants and workers.[7] The Cardenas-labor alliance was taking shape in 1935 as the Calles-Cardenas power struggle intensified. Since Calles's establishment of the PNR, Cardenas had become increasingly dependent on labor support; and labor, alienated by Calles's pro-business tilt, broke with Calles and threw its support behind Cardenas who emerged triumphant in 1936 as Calles was exiled. During this period of regime consolidation, unions were drawn to Cardenas's nationalist economic program, which emphasized state ownership and regulation and which workers saw as an important means through which to realize their socioeconomic demands. Unions would subsequently begin to loosen their ties to the PNR, now known as the Partido de la Revolucion Mexicana (PRM).[8]

As with Calles's alliance with labor in the 1920s, Cardenas's state-labor coalition provoked opposition from capital, the middle class, the church, and factions in the military threatened by the formation of worker-peasant militias. Nora Hamilton observes that Cardenas's populist coalition precipitated a political showdown because it "suggested that while the state continued to perform the functions of accumulation in the interests of the dominant class, it had abdicated its social control function and was in fact participating on behalf of the subordinate class."[9] Right-wing factions joined forces and formed the National Action Party (PAN). Labor policy was at the heart of this conflict. The initiative to form worker militias had rankled military leaders. Labor discontent was also at the root of the tensions between foreign capital and the Cardenista state and the expropriation of the foreign oil companies in 1938. The political alliance with labor and state intervention in the labor market polarized relations between the state and capital. As conservative sectors within the state and society mobilized, Cardenas's alliance began to splinter. The beginning of the retreat from populism was evident in the dramatic decline in 1938 of land distribution in rural areas and of strikes in urban areas, as well as in the choice of the conservative Avila Camacho as presidential successor.

After 1938, with the rise of a conservative opposition to Cardenas and his reform program, Lombardo Toledano, head of the CTM, pledged support to the Cardenas government. Calles had failed to institutionalize his populist coalition in a party. Cardenas sought to cement his alliance with the populist sector organizations through their formal incorporation into the party. The centerpiece of this effort was the reorganization of the PNR into the PRM in 1938. To broaden and strengthen working class and peasant organizations, the PRM was organized on a sectoral basis with four sectors (labor, peasantry, popular, and military), and party membership was not individual but collective, based on membership in labor unions or organizations affiliated with one of the other sectors. Each sector was to retain autonomy and to serve as a channel of political recruitment and candidate selection.

Cardenas's concessions to labor provoked an anti-populist backlash and calls by the private sector and the middle classes for inclusion in the ruling coalition. To regain the loyalty of these alienated groups and insure the survival of the regime, Cardenas's successors swiftly made several pro-capital concessions and institutional changes. During the presidencies of both Camacho and Aleman, policies encouraging foreign investment were introduced, and while the state-labor alliance was maintained various pro-labor measures were reversed. Lombardo Toledano, the CTM's Marxist ideologue, was forced out of the position of secretary general in 1941, and the state no longer promoted unionization, strikes, or wage gains for workers.[10] To prevent future polarization and contain elite conflict, the one-party system was reorganized. The PRM's popular sector was strengthened to serve as a counterweight to the labor and peasant sectors. Membership in the popular sector was expanded to include public employees, professionals, and small businesses, and the National Confederation of Popular Organizations (CNOP) was created as a new confederation for the popular sector to counter the CTM, which had served as the party's main mobilizing agent. By 1946, the PRM had been reorganized into the PRI.

Another regime-consolidating conflict-preventing mechanism was the 1946 electoral reform, which created legal measures to insure the dominance of the transformed PRI. The new law narrowed the political arena by introducing new requirements for the registration of political parties; the aim was to enhance the state's ability to control the electoral process and the opposition by limiting the existence of small parties, especially local and regional parties, religious parties, and parties of the far right or left.[11] By the mid-1950s, Mexico had a well-institutionalized dominant-party regime supported by a broad centrist coalition. Labor, without its left wing, continued to play an important legitimating role in the state's coalition. Not only did labor's support help state elites consolidate political control after the 1910–20 revolution, but the mass support of disciplined labor organizations was particularly significant during the moment of presidential succession, which was vulnerable to disruption. Also, although the private sector was never fully incorporated into the PRI, since the conservative backlash of 1946, there were links between the state and the private sector. Mexican state builders never decimated the private sector as Nasser did in Egypt, and it was not until Lopez Portillo's nationalizations that the private sector would be alienated again.

Expanding the State

In the period of institution building from the 1920s to the early 1940s, Mexican leaders developed the coercive, administrative, and extractive capabilities of the state apparatus. In Mexico, as elsewhere in Latin America, political elites expanded the state's administrative role in the labor sector to address the crisis of participation that accompanied the mobilization of different social groups between 1910 and 1920, particularly the entrance of industrial workers into the political arena. The leadership's strategy was to achieve social control by increasing state capacity. In building the Mexican bureaucracy, Calles and Cardenas relied on the populist sectors and elite bureaucrats. Capital and the middle classes were excluded until the mid-1940s when, along with the military, they were brought into the ruling coalition. The expansion of the Mexican state bureaucracy was driven by the needs of state builders like Cardenas and his allies—the populist sectors and elite bureaucrats.[12] Cornelius similarly describes how Cardenas forged the coalition out of peasant and worker militias, not only to counter the army, but also to create a social base of support from which to establish bureaucratic autonomy from foreign and domestic capital and carry out his reforms and distributive policies. Mexico's leaders established specific administrative structures to mediate labor's participation. Agencies such as the Ministry of Labor and Social Welfare and tripartite conciliation and arbitration boards offered workers new channels through which to press their demands about economic issues and workplace conditions.

Mobilization proved advantageous to labor as well. In order to mobilize support successfully, an exchange was necessary in which real concessions and a degree of power sharing were offered in exchange for the support. After deciding to mobilize labor, it was in the interest of state elites to increase the power of organized labor and its weight as a coalitional partner. Radical populism and party incorporation in Mexico thus involved more concessions and a more favorable political position for labor (than the cases of state incorporation). In this vein, the PRM structure was used to increase the state's capacity. Direct linkages between an expanded state administrative apparatus and mass organizations were mediated by the party and were crucial to creating a reliable base of support for the regime. The PRM played an active role in promoting Cardenas's agrarian reform and the nationalization of the petroleum industry, which cemented ties between groups such as organized labor and the official party. After 1940, the party's principal responsibility would become the mobilization of popular support during elections.[13]

In summation, radical populism and party corporatism in Mexico entailed popular mobilization, the formation of a state-labor alliance mediated by the PRI, concessions to labor, and substantive progressive reforms. The state's populist agenda provoked a conservative opposition and polarization along class lines. State elites would respond by making a policy turn toward the right, forming a multiclass party to channel and institutionalize the political participation of both the popular sectors *and* capitalist classes. The party would incorporate some of the conservative sectors—middle classes who had opposed radical populism. Mexican corporatism tried to ease this polarized situation, to reestablish the support of the dominant economic sectors that were alienated by populism, and at the same to retain popular support for the regime and newly created political structures. Egypt would follow a different path of incorporation and controlled mobilization. Nasser and the Free Officers came to power without the aid of labor, and the coalitional arrangements that would emerge in Egypt were different than in Mexico. Workers were granted a multitude of benefits, but labor unions were not strengthened or politically empowered, and labor policy was not so progressive as to elicit a conservative backlash.

Labor and the Wafd Coalition (1919–52)

The oligarchic alliance that existed in Egypt between the large landowners, the British, and the monarchy before 1952 was similar to the oligarchic system in prerevolutionary Mexico, which saw an alliance between the *hacendados* (landowners), foreign capital (especially land companies), and the Porfiriato, as Porfirio Diaz's thirty-one year regime was known. But unlike Mexico, in Egypt there was still a (British) colonial presence and the Wafd Party, which began as an anti-British movement and had developed into a strong electoral machine with a predominantly rural coalition, representing the interests of the oligarchy, the landed elite that had links to international capital. The large landowners who dominated the Wafd were against any reform in the areas of land tenure, rent, and the taxation of agricultural property. The Egyptian industrial bourgeoisie, often identified with the Sadist Party, acknowledged the need for agrarian reform, but they were also linked to large landowning interests by family and social ties and derived much of their capital from agrarian interests; the business class shared the pashas' social conservatism and fear of unleashing the anger of the impoverished rural and urban areas. During the 1930s and 1940s, foreign and indigenous industrialists promoted considerable industrial development, although most national capital came from large landowners linked to the European-dominated cotton market and went into agriculture.

Since the 1920s, the Wafd and its rivals had competed for the leadership of the trade union movement. As Beinin and Lockman observe, the Egyptian labor movement's entry into the political scene had occurred with the nationalist revolution of 1919 with the demands of the nascent working class merging with the political movement for national independence.[14] The persistence of low wages and poverty among workers and rising militancy in the context of economic crisis and nationalist struggle led the Ministry of Social Affairs to speak of the "labor question" (*mas'alat al-umal*). Competing political forces realized that a controlled workers' movement could provide a mobilizable source of support in urban areas and fought to control the labor movement. In the wake of the 1919 revolution, the bourgeois nationalism of the Wafd emerged as the dominant ideological and organizational force within the labor movement. The Wafd's support base was in rural areas because of its appeal to rich, middle-level peasants and rural notables who delivered the poorer villagers. But no political party had a mass base among the poor peasantry and workers.

By the end of World War II, an economic and political crisis had developed in Egypt. The Wafdist regime was coming under attack, and labor was becoming more militant. Deeb has shown how, through the 1920s, Egyptian workers were largely passive in face of Wafdist domination, and trade unions were simply instruments of the Wafd and other parties.[15] By the 1930s, calls for an independent workers' movement grew louder as it became more evident that neither the Wafd nor Prince Abbas Halim were responding to labor's economic and political demands. The so-called Liberal Age (1932–52) of parliamentary politics had failed to create political stability. The Wafd came under criticism in the postwar period for its reluctance to mobilize the masses to fight for the full evacuation of British troops from Egypt. The Wafd began to lose control over the labor movement. The newly formed Egyptian communist organization (Democratic Movement for National Liberation [DMNL]) gradually became the leading force within the workers' movement and achieved its greatest popularity during the postwar nationalist mobilizations that took place from January to June 1946 and from October 1951 to January 1952. In the postwar period, the MB also emerged as a rival to both the Wafd's bourgeois nationalism and the DMNL's communism, vying for influence within the labor movement as well as in Egyptian society at large. The parliamentary system's bankruptcy and the protracted economic crisis following World War II offered these forces the opportunity to challenge the regime. The working class was used by different political contenders as "a social battering ram" to destabilize the old regime, and many nationalists, including socially conservative Wafdist leaders, encouraged labor agitation.[16]

The strikes of 1946 and 1947 at Shubra al-Khayma and Mahalla al-Kubra placed the "labor question" squarely on the nationalist agenda as an urgent issue that, along with land reform, the Free Officers would have to consider upon assuming power.

In describing the coup of 1952, one historian makes an important point: "The Free Officers did not accede to power by the consent of any large section of the Egyptian public, prior or even concurrent. They were not chosen. They took power forcibly. The public simply acquiesced."[17] The Arab-Israeli war of 1948 had turned Nasser against the Egyptian monarchy and parliamentary system and led him to form his underground Free Officers movement to topple the regime; when he assumed power, Nasser was suspicious of preexisting political actors and institutions. Unlike Mexico, the Free Officers were not indebted to labor or any other social group, and they had considerably more leeway in forging a coalition and consolidating their regime. The Free Officers relied on the military and the bureaucracy to consolidate their power base and abolished the institutions that had permitted the ancien régime to exercise power—parties, parliament, the monarchy, and the courts—before proceeding to depoliticize the public altogether. Parties were dissolved; former party leaders were either imprisoned or forbidden from engaging in political activities. The brief flirtation with "popular participation" of the Liberal Age was abandoned, and an approach of departicipation, or political isolation (al-azl al-siyasi), was adopted. These decisions made in the aftermath of the 1952 takeover would have a far-reaching impact on the Egyptian state's capacity to control and galvanize support. This context was different from the participation crisis that faced leaders in Mexico. In Egypt, we have a "reverse type participation crisis," where the challenge facing the Free Officers was not how to mobilize and admit lower classes but how to restrict the participation of political actors who had been active under the ancien régime.

The incorporation and coalition-building projects in Egypt were carried out in roughly three phases: (1) the military coup and its aftermath, 1952–54; (2) the March Crisis and its aftermath, 1954–56; and (3) the Suez Crisis and its aftermath, 1956–62. The Free Officers passed the land reform law of September 9, 1952, to build support for their rule. Agrarian reform was intended not simply to gain rural support but to break the power of the large landowners, redirect their capital into industrial development, and expand the market for Egyptian industrial goods. The economic rationale was that the bonds that the state issued in exchange for confiscated lands would be invested in industry, since those holding the bonds were ineligible to purchase additional agricultural land. The land reform would also expand the market for Egyptian industrial products because peasants who received lands would have more to spend on consumer goods.[18] Land reform was the only structural economic reform adopted by the Revolutionary Command Council (RCC) before the Suez War of 1956. The RCC's early economic policy was to encourage private capital to develop the nation's industrial base, though the government did take the lead in planning new heavy industrial projects, such as railways and Helwan Iron and Steel, and in arranging the necessary capital to finance them.

The political rationale behind the land reform was to stabilize the countryside and neutralize extremism in urban areas. Land distribution, it was believed, would reverse the processes of absenteeism and rural migration into the cities. But as I elaborate below, this much-touted land reform did not radically transform the traditional social structure in the countryside. According to several studies, land reform led to the limited redistribution of wealth in the countryside because the policy placed a ceiling on individual landholdings of two hundred feddans (a feddan, an Egyptian unit of land, is equal to 1.038 acres). The larger landowners, absentee and provincial, did indeed disappear, and their influence in the local affairs of the provinces did increase. But those who owned under one hundred feddans, particularly from ten to fifty feddans, emerged not only as the newly privileged group but also as the favored clients of the state with connections (through kin and economic relationships) with members of the military and the bureaucracy in the city.[19]

Land Reform and Coalition Building

Nasser sought the active political support of one social group—the rural middle class (RMC), the rural notables who had received the confiscated land and supplanted the rural oligarchy. For their political cooperation and resources, Nasser gave the RMC subsidies, favorable prices, and rent and wage laws and attempted to gain their electoral support for the National Union first and then in successive party organizations the Arab Socialist Union and National Democratic Party. In this sense, in Egypt, as in Brazil under Vargas, there was no mobilization but a "politics of accommodation" between the landowners (read RMC) and the state builders. Nasser would come to rely on the RMC to man the rural bureaucracy, control the peasantry, and insure the flow of capital from rural areas to urban industrial projects. The RMC's political role grew with the establishment of agricultural cooperatives and with the expansion of provincial and local government services. As state structures extended into the provinces, new state and local bureaucracies needed to be manned by members of the new small landowners. The larger farmers took advantage of these cooperatives particularly in the area of credit and dominated other local institutions, including village councils, credit banks, and "combined centers" (*wahdat mujamma'a*).[20]

The rural middle class also insured the functioning of the urban bias in Egypt's development strategy. Demand for export crops forced all smallholders, dwarfholders (whose land holdings were less than half a feddan), and tenant farmers into a single crop system; and terms of trade (input costs versus producer prices) were weighted against the tenant farmers. When the government bought crops from the peasants (*fellahin*) at low prices and resold them in the domestic or foreign markets, vast profits were extracted out of the countryside. One analyst describes the indirect tax that all cooperative members had to pay: "Agricultural income is actually taxed implicitly through the price differential policy applied on the main agricultural crops . . . taxing agricultural income implicitly this way may turn out to be regressive, thus worsening the relative position of the small farmers as compared to the rich farmers."[21] In the late 1960s and early 1970s, it became evident that this system presented few incentives to increase production and led to a severe agricultural crisis.

"Demobilizing" Labor

The Free Officers dealt with urban-based political rivals using co-optation and repression. As demonstrated by the Kafr al-Dawwar crackdown, the RCC labor strategy was to repress the left of the workers' movement so as to maintain an attractive climate for private capital. The RCC wanted to control labor within a corporatist system. But the creation of a successful corporatist system required that the RCC eliminate the communists from positions of influence in the union movement and build a significant base of support for the regime within the labor movement. The RCC's first initiative was to undertake a thorough revision of existing labor legislation. New labor policies were implemented to prevent labor unrest, increase the purchasing power of workers, and encourage greater productivity. Laws 317, 318, and 319 of December 1952 and subsequent decrees granted many of labor's long-standing demands, including the improvement of employment security by sharply limiting employers' freedom to arbitrarily dismiss workers, that is, not for misbehavior on the job but solely because of production cutbacks or other market considerations. In enacting this measure, Decree 165 of April 1953, the regime granted the single most important economic demand of the postwar workers' movement—job security—and in so doing, the Free Officers won the support of many workers and trade union leaders who saw this measure as a demonstration of the military's commitment to social justice.[22] The new Law of Individual Contracts also granted workers significantly improved material benefits: increased severance compensation, longer annual vacations, free transportation to factories in remote areas, and free medical care. But labor paid a steep price for these concessions: a military order issued concurrently with the new legislation banned all strikes.

With the enactment of land reform legislation on September 9 and the labor law of December 8, the new regime gained substantial support from peasants and workers, and the Free Officers felt confident to move against potential sources of political opposition. On January 17, 1953, all political parties were dissolved. These improvements in labor legislation and the special attention the RCC paid to cultivating good relations with trade union leaders explain why most labor leaders supported Nasser in his confrontation with Naguib. The crisis of March 1954 was of critical importance in shaping Nasser's coalitional strategy and power base.

Nasser-Naguib Power Struggle

Even after the dissolution of political parties in early 1953, the new regime was challenged by antiestablishment movements such as the Muslim Brotherhood (MB) and the DMNL and the Communist movement, both of whom shared the Free Officers' disdain for old-regime politics, and constituted alternative bases of power in the country. The Free Officers feared the political machines of the MB and the DMNL. The MB could rally mass support second only to the Wafd and, with its paramilitary secret organization and cells in the army, appeared to be, as the RCC described it, "a state within a state." Likewise, although splintered, the Communist movement was well organized on campuses and factories and had allegedly infiltrated the Free Officer corps. The MB and the DMNL had supported the Free Officers' coup and were expecting a role in influencing the revolutionary agenda. The Communists wanted progressive social reforms and called for a coalition of opposition movements including the Wafd to press for a return to civilian life. Moreover, the MB, more suspicious of the party system, pressed the Free Officers to refrain from a hasty return to parliamentary life.

The RCC banned all political parties, except for the MB, which was not considered a party but a political movement, and shared the regime's opposition to party politics. To fill the void and galvanize support, the regime created the Liberation Rally. Despite the progressive measures of land reform and pro-labor legislation, as a grassroots political organization, the Liberation Rally never succeeded in surpassing its rivals, the Wafd and the MB. As one historian put it, "overt Wafdist hostility to the regime and the Muslim Brotherhood's unease with the formation of a rival political front effectively blocked efforts by the Rally's organizers to create a civilian power base for the RCC."[23] As long as the MB, the largest mass membership organization in Egypt, remained allied to the regime, as they did uneasily until 1953, a stand-off prevailed. The RCC had in effect outlawed the parties but had not yet replaced the old system with a viable political alternative.

As the crisis between the RCC and MB intensified, a broad-based popular challenge to the legitimacy of military rule and the suspension of parliamentary democracy emerged. A pro-civilian rule coalition was developing and exploited the conflict simmering within the RCC. In late 1953 and early 1954, Supreme Guide Hudaybi of the MB and General Naguib were considering the possibility of overthrowing Nasser and placing real power in Naguib's hands.[24] The MB's cooperation with the Free Officers ended when Hudaybi realized the RCC would not pass his proposed Islamic laws. When Nasser signed an agreement with Britain over Sudan in February 1953, the MB saw the deal as a betrayal because it undermined the unity of the Nile Valley. On January 12, 1954, the MB led a rally at Cairo University denouncing Nasser as a pro-American dictator, and the demonstrators clashed violently with supporters of the Liberation Rally. Aware of the Naguib-Hudaybi contacts, the RCC responded by declaring the Islamist group a political organization and dissolved it in accordance with the decrees of January 1953. By early 1953, the RCC was opposed by every organized civilian political force from the pre-coup period.

Naguib saw the RCC's attack on the MB as a blow against his own base of support and a strengthening of military rule in the face of popular demands for the restoration of civilian rule. The clash between the RCC and the MB thus pitted Nasser against Naguib. Because Naguib had never been a member of the Free Officers, he served as a focal point for all of the political forces opposed to military rule. Naguib subsequently demanded more powers in line with his formal offices of chairman of the RCC, prime minister, and president of the republic. On February 24, he resigned from all his posts, bringing the crisis within the RCC to the public's attention. When Nasser assumed both the premiership and presidency, mass demonstrations erupted in support of Naguib and called for a return to parliamentary democracy with the participation of the Muslim Brothers, Communists, and Wafdists; even a section of the army (the cavalry officers led by Khaled Muhieddin) threatened to rebel. Considering the split in the army and the broad support he had from the Musim Brotherhood-Communist-Wafdist alliance, Naguib became the greatest threat to Nasser' faction in the RCC. On March 9, the RCC was obliged to reinstate Naguib as president of the republic, while Nasser stayed on as prime minister. Upon news of Naguib's return, supporters took to the streets of Cairo calling for Nasser's resignation. Nasser proceeded to organize his supporters among the junior army officers, while Naguib, still enjoying his victory, failed to mobilize his own supporters in the army, particularly, the cavalry forces. Nasser, intent on winning the power struggle, worked with a small circle of Free Officers (Zakariya Muhieddin, Salah Salim, and Anwar Sadat) to foster a crisis atmosphere and to create a situation analogous to that which existed prior to July 1952, in which the army would be the only alternative to corruption and disorder—and this is where labor's support proved crucial to Nasser's consolidation of power.[25]

After staging bombings in different parts of Cairo on March 26, the RCC passed resolutions permitting the establishment of parties to further exacerbate the chaotic atmosphere. With the announcement that the ban on political parties would be lifted, the MB, who had supported Naguib against Nasser, withdrew its support for the domestic coalition because it opposed the formation of parties and because it then seemed likely that the Wafd could return to power on July 24, 1954, when the RCC would dissolve itself as promised. On March 26, massive pro-Naguib demonstrations supporting a return to parliamentary democracy took place all over Cairo, but then pro-Nasser forces began to counter, and the Liberation Rally, with its connections to trade unions, proved vital in enabling the Free Officers to mobilize their own mass support. With Nasser's approval, Liberation Rally's chief officers, Ibrahim al-Tahawi and Abdallah Tuaymah, called their forces into the streets. By March 28, with their superior organization and with the aid of mob and police violence, pro-Nasser forces succeeded in cowing the opposition and compelling the RCC to stay in power.

The centerpiece of the mob activity was a general strike declared by pro-regime trade unions on March 27. Nasser approved of the action as long as the RCC did not officially have to recognize the strikers.[26] The leader of the transport union workers, Ahmed al-Sawi, organized the strike in conjunction with the heads of major oil and tobacco unions. On the evening of March 26, leaders of the transport union began a hunger strike and called for a general strike to force "the RCC to answer the people's call." The vanguard of RCC support came from the unions that could most effectively disrupt the daily operations of Cairo: transport workers, gas station attendants, and bank and cinema employees. If matters had not been resolved by March 29, electricity, gas, and waterworks were scheduled to shut down, which would have paralyzed the country. Nasser's strategy of mobilizing a segment of the working class in his favor thus succeeded: strikes and mob activity by workers intimidated and eventually neutralized Naguib's followers. By the end of March 1954, Nasser's coalition had begun to take shape. A pact with the MB neutralized the regime's most troublesome and potentially dangerous foe. Nasser had promised Hudaybi to restore the movement's legal status and, during the March crisis, released three hundred detained Muslim Brothers. In return, Hudaybi adopted an ambivalent public stance toward legalization of political parties and kept the MB out of the events of March 26–28.[27]

Labor emerged as a staunch supporter of the military regime, although many unions, particularly in Communist-dominated areas, stood against Nasser and the RCC. The conventional wisdom is that labor unanimously supported Nasser because of his welfare policies. In reality, labor was divided, and it was Nasser's superior resources and control over the means of coercion that got dissident unions to join the strikes. The response to the transport union leaders' call for a general strike was mixed. While the Cairo bus, tax, and metro workers participated, the Cairo tramway workers did not until their leader was assaulted by workers and police who then forced some of the trams to stop running. The strongest trade union resistance to the call for a general strike was in Alexandria where many union leaders called for an end to martial law, the dissolution of the RCC, and the establishment of a general federation of trade unions. As Beinin and Lockman show, on March 27 and March 28, the ranks of the trade unions were clearly divided for and against Najib and the restoration of parliamentary democracy, but by March 29 a large number of trade unions had either been persuaded or coerced to join the general strike.[28]

To maintain the loyalty of the pro-RCC unionists and neutralize the influence of the dissidents and communists, Nasser began to grant some further concessions to the loyal unionists. But despite the alliance between a section of the trade union leadership and the RCC, labor's calls for the right to strike or a greater role in economic policymaking were not granted. Instead of a greater political role, further benefits were paternalistically extended over the following decade. After March 1954, Nasser quickly implemented legislation improving wages, job security, and social benefits, thereby solidifying the state-labor alliance. But he still refused to mobilize or institutionalize the labor movement. Nasser initially refused to allow the formation of a union confederation for fear that it would be infiltrated by members of the Wafd, MB, or Communist Party. He moved to institutionalize the labor movement by establishing the General Federation of Egyptian Trade Unions in 1957 and a Ministry of Labor in 1959. In the 1960s, legislation was enacted requiring that workers constitute at least 50 percent of the management committees and that workers and peasants comprise 50 percent of membership in the National Assembly. Despite the show of repression at Kafr al-Duwwar, the continued stability of the new regime was heavily dependent on making real concessions to workers. The benefits served their purpose of tying labor to the state: throughout the Nasserist era, the working class did not violate the terms of the bargain struck in March 1954. Despite occasional strikes and collective expressions of discontent, there was nothing comparable to the labor unrest of 1946 and 1951.

In sum, the Egyptian scenario differs from the Mexican one where workers were mobilized electorally and given a role in policy making—in exchange for their role in the leadership's rise and consolidation of power. Cardenas relied on labor's support to overcome the conservative opponents to his nationalist development strategy. Nasser did not rely on labor to the same degree. The Free Officers' rise to power was not due to labor or any other group's support. Labor provided the foot soldiers during the March crisis, helping Nasser stay in power. But the power struggle between Nasser and Naguib did not involve a conflict over the economic borders of the state, so the former did not require labor's sustained, mobilized support to initiate his development strategy; the mere control and acquiescence of the working class would suffice. Also, as of March 1954, there was no plan for nationalization or for a quasi-socialist development strategy; the RCC was actually leaning toward a pro-capitalist strategy and was pondering ways to enlist the support of the Egyptian private sector.

"The Politics of Resentment"

As mentioned, the internecine conflict and left-right division within the RCC did not involve the degree of state intervention or industrial strategy but centered around the return to parliamentary democracy versus continued military rule. While it was Khaled Muhieddin, a left-leaning officer backed by the cavalry officers, who backed Naguib's call for a return to democracy, the remaining twelve officers who supported Nasser were not all pro-American or economically conservative. The disagreement did not revolve around the state's economic strategy, essentially because the Free Officers did not have an economic plan yet; there was as yet no import substitution strategy or quasi-socialist plan that would require labor's support against conservative elite opposition. In 1953, the Free Officers had proclaimed their commitment to six principles that were to influence their conduct of government: an end to imperialism, feudalism, monopoly, and capitalist control of Egypt; social justice and democracy; and the establishment of a powerful national army. These objectives outlined no particular strategy of development or desired mix between public and private sectors. As O'Brien observes, the Free Officers were "without an economic ideology and apart from land reform not even the most general ideas relating to economic organization had formed part of their pre-revolutionary discussions on the future of Egypt."[29]

Judging by the Free Officers' policies between 1952 and 1956, it appears that Nasser made an effort to work with the private sector that was defeated by unforeseen political and international circumstances. The initial years of military rule were marked by a strong conservatism in economic affairs, and Egypt's political revolution of 1952 only began to have its counterpart in the economic sphere after 1956. Robert Tignor has argued that one reason for the economic crisis of 1951–52 was that the initial stage of ISI had run its course, and "to develop further, Egypt needed to expand the industrial sector and make its manufactures competitive in export markets," a strategy that would have necessitated the cooperation of the private sector.[30] One of the earliest steps in favor of private capital was the military's crackdown on labor during the riots at Kafr al-Duwwar, a large private textile company. Despite the pro-labor legislation of 1953, the state continued to give preference to the interests of capital.

Unlike Mexico, then, where Calles and then Cardenas pursued a statist strategy that aimed to subordinate the private sector and benefit labor, in Egypt welfare benefits were granted to appease labor, but the regime was leaning toward a strategy that relied on private capital. The military regime's early courtship of business groups is reflected in a series of legislations—measures long advocated by the Egyptian Federation of Industries that were speedily implemented. The regime raised tariffs and lowered customs duties on raw materials and capital goods, as the federation had frequently urged. Generous tax exemptions and benefits were granted to businesses when the government increased its financial support of the industrial bank. New privileges were also accorded to foreign investors. Law 156 of 1953 on the investment of foreign capital allowed profits to be remitted abroad up to the value of 10 percent of the initial investment. Despite speeches on the merits of socialism, when asked for more detail on the socialist society that he envisioned, Nasser acknowledged that Egypt was not ready for socialism because its industrial sector was too small to be worthy of nationalization.[31] At this juncture, rhetoric notwithstanding, Nasser's ambition was to create a mixed economy in which the private and public sectors worked in close harmony. Pro-business policy statements were often made to reassure the private sector, such as when the Minister of National Guidance declared, "We are not socialist. I think our economy can only prosper under free enterprise."[32] Such statements were backed by actions such as the purging from the leadership of left-wing elements, as well as by the imprisoning of communists following the Kafr al-Duwwar riots of 1952.

The military turned against foreign capital after the Suez War of 1956. The French-British-Israeli invasion led directly to the sequestration of British, French, and Jewish assets. Until that moment, the RCC was still committed to fostering the private sector and foreign capital, but the invasion and Nasser's belief that certain foreign banks and insurance companies were sympathizing with the invaders infuriated the Egyptian leader and led to an order of full-scale nationalizations. After the war, it was possible to return sequestered companies to their previous owners, but the state was unwilling to renounce a new source of patronage, and the alienated private sector was understandably reluctant to invest and preferred compensation. In 1956 and 1957 the military called upon the Egyptian bourgeoisie to lead the drive for industrialization and diversification, but following the tumult of that year, Egyptian businessmen were in no mood to cooperate. When they failed to do so, their assets were nationalized as well.[33] Political factors were again important in these decisions. Some scholars have linked the nationalizations to tensions within the Syrian-Egyptian union. Others point to the state's incapacity to fully control capital and Nasser's fears of independent bases of power from which social actors could challenge his rule; private capital, he believed, was one such center of power that had to be absorbed into the state. But it's important to recall that before the 1956 invasion, Egypt's military rulers had sought to preserve the private sector. They underscored the importance of foreign investment and by early 1956 had resolved most of the major issues that had plagued the relationship between foreign capital and the state. The invasion, however, provoked such a xenophobic backlash that these plans were swept aside, private property expropriated, and foreign and "Egyptianized" businessmen expelled—actions that would have far-reaching and devastating effects on the Egyptian economy.

Regarding the role of organized labor, it is worth noting that even when Nasser embarked on a "socialist" public sector–driven strategy of development he did not rely on or attempt to gain labor's support, despite workers' attempts to use the 1956 war to extract further concessions and gain a more prominent role in ruling coalition. During the Suez crisis, trade unions mobilized support for the nationalization of the canal and wanted to participate in the national defense. Unions collected financial contributions for their members to assist the war effort. Over fifty local (military) committees, some with hundreds of workers, were established with the participation of trade union leaders and rank-and-file workers. The government, though, would not accept the prospect of armed workers led by communists, even if their aim was to defend the nation.[34]

The economic borders of the Egyptian state were shaped by intra-elite conflict and struggles between the state and various social groups but also by conflict between the Egyptian regime and external actors—foreign capital and other states. This occurred in Mexico as well, where state builders had to deal with external pressure from the United States and international markets in conjunction with domestic demands, which together would coalesce to push the regime to adopt nationalistic policies. After trying unsuccessfully to shape the outcome of the Mexican revolution (by sending American troops to topple General Victoriano Huerta in 1914), in 1923 the United States said that it would recognize neither Mexican sovereignty nor the Alvaro Obregon government, unless the Mexican regime agreed not to apply Article 27 to American assets. (Article 27 of the new constitution declared national resources the inalienable property of the nation and allowed the state to expropriate private property for the "national interest.")[35] The Mexican government gave the United States the requested assurances, but in 1925 Plutarco Calles passed the Alien Land Law—prohibiting foreign capitalists from owning land within fifty kilometers of the Mexican border and from having majority ownership in land-development companies—and the Petroleum Law, which made non-Mexican businessmen, who had owned their property before the revolution, request "confirmatory concessions."[36] President Cardenas would also clash with foreign petroleum companies. When Cardenas nationalized the petroleum sector, the United States demanded "prompt, effective and adequate indemnization," and for some years preceding World War II the U.S. State Department forbade U.S. government money from funding the Mexican oil sector unless U.S. companies were allowed back in. But as the United States also wanted to secure its southern border, coveted raw materials from Mexico, and needed diplomatic support in the war, the U.S.-Mexican relationship gradually improved.

Egypt's position as a frontline state in the Palestinian-Israeli conflict and its tortured relations with various Western states (Great Britain, United States, France) and Israel would have a sharper effect on the country's economic and political development. The Egyptian state was born in a context of interstate war, unlike Mexico, which emerged out of a civil war. From Calles and Cardenas's bargaining with American interests, one could see that, since the Roosevelt era, Mexico's relationship with the United States—like Egypt's—was governed by political and security considerations and not driven simply by market logic. Both relationships were driven by political rationales, but the calculus underpinning the United States' relationship with Egypt—a frontline state in the Palestinian-Israeli conflict whose stability was critical to the regional balance of power—would differ from the rationale underlying Mexico's "special relationship" with the United States.

Bureaucracy and Coalitional Politics

Bureaucratic expansion was an integral part of the state-building process in Egypt, and the state apparatus was expanded and structured with the aim of preempting activity by banned political forces in the country. After dismantling the monarchy and shutting down parties, the military regime relied on the bureaucracy to consolidate power and control societal actors. Nasser was able to assert control over the inherited bureaucracy by segmenting it into fiefdoms, which were then assigned to trusted lieutenants. Zakariya Muhieddin, for instance, gained control of the Ministry of Interior, which gave him access to the state security apparatus. By December 1954, Nasser had appointed trusted army officers to supervise the work of civilian departments. Nasser exerted control over the state apparatus by using his military appointees. By 1961, more than 3,400 of the 4,100 employees in the Ministry of Interior were either active or retired military officers.[37] The creation of committees and commissions directly responsible to him for the coordination of policy allowed Nasser to gain control over the activities of the state.

The nationalizations of 1956 fueled the expansion of the bureaucracy. The establishment of the Economic Organization, a parastatal body to manage the nationalized foreign assets, provided new job opportunities for educated Egyptians and leadership positions to the military men and their cronies. Between 1960 and 1963, the regime staffed nationalized private enterprises with members of its administrative and military constituency. As a pillar of the regime, the civil bureaucracy came to employ over one million in 1970. The military establishment grew to over three hundred thousand by 1973.[38] These two institutions were vital in building a support base, achieving control, and implementing state policy. High school and university graduates who depended on the military and bureaucracy for employment gradually became key regime constituencies.

The Free Officers were forced by political circumstances to turn to the bureaucracy. Since previously active political institutions had been dismantled or demobilized, the bureaucracy was the only civilian institution of control remaining. The Free Officers, who were fully cognizant of the inefficiency and corruption of the civil service, had wooed bureaucrats upon assuming power, because of the new regime's need for support and the lack of alternative allies. Bureaucrats, in turn, welcomed the Free Officers' reliance on the administration and supported the RCC's plan to expand. Historian Tareq al-Bishri attributes the bureaucracy's favorable response to the Free Officers to the common social origins of mid-level civil servants (who moved to administrative posts following the purges of upper echelons of the state immediately after the revolution) and to the Free Officers;

and, moreover, the Free Officers' agenda fulfilled many of the aspirations of Egyptian civil servants in terms of employment security, a low cost of living, and free education for their children.[39] It was ultimately a coalition of military officers, bureaucrats, and populist sectors that drove the expansion of the bureaucracy.

Immediately after the coup, the Free Officers appointed Ali Maher as prime minister, who outlined a major overhaul of the government bureaucracy. His plan for bureaucratic autonomy included purging the ranks and ending the patronage system by taking the power of civil service appointments out of the hands of individual ministries.[40] But because of his opposition to land reform and other RCC policies, Maher was replaced by Naguib; Nasser also scuttled Maher's plan for bureaucratic reform, which would have alienated bureaucrats, a sought-after constituency. The RCC needed the bureaucracy as an instrument of control. One of Nasser's first moves was to purge the state apparatus of individuals deemed disloyal rather than any fundamental restructuring, which would have alienated important constituents. Instead Nasser proceeded on an ad hoc basis, establishing state bodies to manage expanding functions, such as the Suez Canal Authority created quickly to bypass the old bureaucracy.

In the absence of effective parties, the bureaucracy and the new public sector became the Egyptian state's instrument of control, the sole target of societal demands and the main channel for participation. The competition for rents and patronage was intense both within and outside the state administration. The result was the formation of clientelistic networks that crisscrossed the state and that would render the bureaucracy incoherent and inefficient. The same clientelism existed in the public sector where control was valued more than efficiency. Fearing that managers could translate their important functional roles and high status into an independent base within the industrial system, Nasser created an intricate control system. The manager was placed at the bottom of a four-tiered hierarchy that included the enterprise head, corporate head, minister, and president and was constrained by a number of control agencies, including the Central Audit Agency, the Central Agency for Administration and Organization, and the Legal Department. In addition, Committees of the ASU were formed and used as watchdogs within the individual enterprises. To monitor the ASU watchdog committees, Nasser created several popular organizations within each industrial organization and assigned to them monitoring functions. Subsequently, in each large factory there existed a labor union, a joint labor-management consultative committee, worker members of the board of directors, and the ASU committee. All four groups acted as "popular" restraints on the managers, while their mutual rivalry, which forestalled the emergence of a power base, also prevented the efficient functioning of the enterprise.[41]

"Populism without Participation"

The pre-1952 coalition binding the pashas, the monarchy, and the British had never strongly pushed for bureaucratic capacity and autonomy. Despite their liberal view of parliamentary politics, the landed elites were never able to forge a stable progressive coalition for state autonomy. Given their common economic interests with the British-dominated export market, the pashas were more willing to compromise with the foreign power and the monarchy than to mobilize a middle- and lower-class constituency. The urban bourgeoisie did oppose foreign economic domination and did favor state autonomy, but without allies they were powerless.[42] The Free Officers did attempt to weld together a new coalition for state autonomy that would include the military, the urban and rural populist sectors, the rural middle class, and the bureaucrats to counter the oligarchy and foreign and domestic capital. But the partnership with the private sector failed due to international factors that eventually led to nationalization and the alienation of private capital. The strategy of state capitalism that Nasser would adopt after 1956 may have been the only alternative, the most feasible strategy of state building and coalition formation. Jobs, benefits, and patronage were doled out to bureaucrats, populist sectors, and the rural middle class in exchange for their support; and plans for administrative reform were abandoned.

In Mexico a similar populist distributive coalition emerged, but Mexican leaders had a different understanding of bureaucratic autonomy than their Egyptian counterparts. Mexican state elites did use local strongmen to maintain stability and to turn out the vote in rural areas, but the same kind of "politics of accommodation" as in Egypt, where a segment of the landed elite was spared and protected to become a rural comprador class, did not emerge. Land reform under Cardenas was thorough, distributing nearly eighteen million hectares of land to more than eight hundred thousand peasants and governors aiming to gain rural support; Cardenas allowed peasant leaders to hold major political and administrative posts, often even arming peasants so they could defend their land.[43] Mexican leaders were ultimately more reliant on the ruling and its links to the peasantry than their Egyptian counterparts.

Nasser, in contrast, sought no political engagement with his coalitional supporters, except arms-length electoral support from the rural middle class; state autonomy did not mean administrative reform and bureaucratic autonomy, but it meant the RCC's independence from coalitional constraints; this type of autonomy deprived the regime of organized, mobilizable support. In his comparative study of regime formation in Egypt and Turkey, Ilkay Sunar observes that the Nasserist and Kemalist revolutions were supported by "etatist coalitions," but subsequently different mobilization strategies led to different uses of the state bureaucracy:

> The RCC wished to win the loyalty of the masses without engaging them politically . . . the populist state was the distributive state par excellence; its strategy was to couple distributive incorporation with political exclusion. While Nasser incorporated them [the popular classes] economically through redistributive policies, he excluded them politically by eschewing organizational engagement with the popular classes. The outcome was "populism without participation." The early Republican elite in Turkey used the rhetoric of populism but did not incorporate the masses either economically or politically. The result was "populism without incorporation."[44]

The Mexican case, however, was populism *with* participation, and mass participation was channeled through the PRI. In Egypt, the absence of dense participatory linkages with societal actors and classes granted the Nasserist state an incapacitating type of autonomy.

Analyses of Nasser's heavy reliance on the bureaucracy as the principal mechanism of social control have emphasized the leader's military background and distrust of party politics, while others have underlined the state's weak capacity. Nasser, in the latter argument, simply lacked the capacity to gain the private sector's cooperation, and that incapacity is what led to nationalization. Chaudhry, in this vein, argues that it was the postcolonial Egyptian state's inability to tax, regulate, and discipline the private sector that led Nasser to expand the public sector and nationalize private assets. State weakness would eventually also produce an inefficient public sector. Moreover, the type of autonomy that Nasser sought allowed the state to dominate society but did not enable the regime to elicit cooperative action. In attempting reform, it became evident that the Egyptian state is not autonomous from bureaucratic and labor constituencies; it lacks the capacity to extract itself from postrevolutionary commitments. State autonomy under Nasser was conceived as the absence of institutionalized engagement with society led, and this ultimately produced an incoherent and isolated state.

Egypt and Latin American Corporatism

Historians have noted the influence of Marxism-Leninism, particularly Tito's brand of Marxism, on Nasser, when he began constructing the Arab Socialist Union in the mid-1960s.[45] Others have highlighted the influence of Southern European corporatism,[46] but few have noted how Nasser was drawn to Latin American variants of corporatism. When Peron came to power in 1946, Argentina was internationally isolated. Because of its perceived pro-Axis position during the war, both the United States and the Soviet Union were reluctant to grant Argentina membership in the United Nations. To counter American and Soviet "opposition" to Argentina in international fora, Peron actively tried to forge what came to be called an "Arab-Latin American bloc."[47] The Argentine leader began to build political alliances with Arab states, in particular, Egypt, Iraq, Syria, Lebanon, and Saudi Arabia, who voted as a single unit and could influence the vote of Pakistan and Iran. Peron's "courtship" of Egypt's Free Officers began (to Britain's dismay) immediately after the latter came to power. Peron saw Egypt, the Arab League's most powerful member, as crucial to the success of his "Tercera Posición" ideology, an alternative to capitalism and communism, which some have seen as a precursor of Third Worldism and the Non-Alignment Movement.[48] Egypt would become Argentina's largest export market and also the most willing recipient of Peronist ideas. Nasser was intrigued by Peron's populism, military rule, and aversion to party politics. According to the memoirs of Abdal Latif al-Boghdadi, one of the Free Officers, the RCC regularly debated aspects of Peronism and whether to maintain military rule as the Argentine strongman suggested or to return to multiparty politics.[49] Various authors have noted the influence of Peronism on the development of the Egyptian regime. Robert Bianchi's describes Nasserism as "a fascinating and often intentional Egyptian counterpart to Peronism." Abdal Maghni Said highlights the Free Officers' interest in Peronism and the Argentine regime's corporatist reorganization of the labor movement, though in the end, he notes, the trade union confederation Nasser ended up creating was modeled on the labor hierarchy of the Brazilian Estado Novo under Vargas.[50] Beattie also highlights the parallels between the Brazilian state and the post-1952 Egypt, which he dubs "Nasser's Estado Novo."[51]

Latin American scholars in turn have described Nasserism as "Arab Peronism" and noted not only Peron's influence on Nasser but the latter's influence on Peron's military clique.[52] In 1962, a book titled *The Nasserist Revolution* was published in Buenos Aires and by some accounts, had wide circulation among Argentine military officers.[53] In the mid-1960s, American scholars and policy makers were pondering the possibility of

"Latin American Nasserism," that is, of military juntas in South America who would overthrow elected governments and assume "modernizing and reforming possibilities that the military have assumed in the Near East."[54] Some nationalist commentators have gone so far to say that Peron was in fact a "disciple of Nasser."[55] Given that the working class was incorporated in Argentina almost a decade before Egypt, it is more likely that Peron influenced the Nasserist incorporation experience than vice versa. The ruling styles and incorporation patterns of Nasserist Egypt and Peronist Argentina are similar. Nasser, like Peron, was a poor institution builder and distrusted political parties, dissolving all parties after the 1945 elections. Peron would create the Peronist Party but would not grant it much power or leeway. In 1954, he finally created the Peronist Movement, which was made up of the Peronist Party, the Women's Peronist Party, and the General Confederation of Labor (CGT). Nasser would also establish the Liberation Rally, which he preferred to call a movement, not to mobilize the populace but simply to take up space. The Egyptian leader's hostility to political parties would begin to mellow only after 1964.

But the parallels between Nasserism and Peronism notwithstanding, the corporatist structure Nasser established looked more like the system introduced by Vargas during the Estado Novo. Unlike Peron's corporatism, which valued worker mobilization, the system introduced by Nasser closely resembled Vargas's Estado Novo with the single labor confederation, the prohibition on strikes, the high degree of inducements, and the constraints aimed at producing a docile, controlled labor movement rather than cultivating labor support. Given Nasser's opposition to worker mobilization and communism, it is not surprising that he would be drawn to Vargas's Estado Novo, which has been described as the "most full-blown" and "purest form of corporatism in Latin America" that rejected liberal politics, claiming that would allow communists to take over the state.[56] The system instituted was, in Philippe Schmitter's words, a preemptive, co-optive, "artificial" corporatism.[57] Scholars have noted that the absence of mediating political parties in Brazil led to coups and "high military involvement" between 1945 and 1964 to control popular groups.[58]

As in Brazil, the corporatist structures put in place in Egypt did not seek to mobilize unions but saw them as organizations through which to deliver benefits to workers. According to the Nasserist plan, unions could not have direct links with others; any links were mediated by a federation; the federation included unions in the same industry. The federations were grouped by economic sector into seven nonagricultural confederations with no single confederation embracing them all together. The state had the right to intervene in union activity and union elections. By making unions essentially social welfare agencies, Egyptian state officials limited unions' abilities to participate in wage setting and collective bargaining and created a cadre of docile but unrepresentative unionists. Given rural elites' control of the countryside, Brazilian state elites would not find mobilization necessary; likewise, in Egypt, the control over the peasantry by rural elites traditionally allied with the state meant that Nasser need not mobilize the peasantry, and he would opt instead for the limited and controlled mobilization of workers.

After Nasser's death, Sadat tried to reconstruct a single-party organization, and he too would look toward Latin America, but he would be more interested in Mexico where the PRI was seen as a paragon of stability and continuity. Sadat probably saw that post-Nasserist Egypt shared with Mexico the rural-urban support coalition, a single party, and the continuity of the postrevolutionary regime. John Waterbury argues that Sadat before his death was pushing Egypt "toward a political and economic system similar to Mexico's. It would be civilian, and his National Democratic Party would occupy the same preponderant position as the PRI."[59] The constitution that Sadat introduced in 1971 after purging the state included stipulations for sexennial presidential elections and the *dedazo*, whereby the incumbent president can select a successor; although it is not clear if these two features were directly copied from Mexico, the two institutions are unique to that Latin American country. In short, while Nasser's "political formula" blended elements of Peronism with Vargas's corporatism, Sadat and Mubarak seemed more drawn to Mexico's "perfect dictatorship," which experienced decades of stability unknown to other Latin American regimes.

"Egypt's Incomplete Revolution"

Several historians have argued that Egypt's revolution was not as transformative as has long been believed—certainly not as far reaching as Mexico's. This point is central to understanding the two regimes' institutional evolutions and differing state capabilities. Recently scholars have traced the institutional continuity from pre-1952 Egypt to the revolutionary regime, noting that the Free Officers may have abolished the monarchy and party system, but most of the pre-coup legal and judicial structures continued to function, though the officers tried to bring them under Nasser's political control. Nathan Brown, for example, argues persuasively that some of the welfare policies of the Nasserist period—such as the free public education—can easily be traced back to the 1930s and 1940s.[60]

Economists have also argued that Nasser's land reform was not as extensive as the regime and its cheerleaders claimed and did not succeed in replacing the pre-1952 patterns of land ownership and social control in rural areas. The failure of complete land reform and the continued prominence of landowning elites would have dire economic repercussions, as policy makers deferred to the interests of landowners. Agrarian reform was intended to bring an end to the feudal ownership patterns and to encourage large landowners to invest in industry; investment capital would come from the forced sale of land over the two hundred acre limit. But this did not quite happen: there was no significant rise in investment in industry largely because reforms were not as distributive as claimed and because the laws were easily evaded by landed elites. Nasser expropriated the estates of the royal family, but for others he set the maximum holding at three hundred acres. The 1952 land reform stated that "no person may own more than two hundred acres of land" but allowed owners to keep another one hundred acres by giving up to fifty acres to each of two children. Land over three hundred acres was to be taken by the government over five years and sold to small farmers in two- to five-acre holdings. The five-year implementation period, however, allowed owners to sidestep the law through private sales or transfers to other relatives.[61]

Although the reforms did put in place rent controls and tenant rights that improved conditions in villages (until their reversal in October 1997), only a small proportion of the land was actually redistributed. By one account, between 1952 and 1961, only 14 percent of total cultivable land in Egypt was redistributed, with ownership rights transferred to only 10 percent of the population.[62] In 1965, the top 5 percent continued to control 43 percent of the cultivated area, while 95 percent of those owning or renting land held less than five acres; 45 percent of agricultural families were still landless.[63] Since land reform was fairly limited, the Egyptian state gained the support of the small landowners who had benefited from the redistribution, but many in rural areas (an estimated 4.3 million in 1985) remained landless. The limited nature of land reform in Egypt undermined the country's industrialization and did not generate the same growth rates as Mexico or East Asia but actually increased inequality, exacerbating tensions within and between rural and urban areas.

It's ironic that that President Park Chung Hee of Korea, as Alice Amsden notes, claims to have been influenced by Nasser in his implementation of land reform in South Korea, given that reform in Korea was more far reaching and effective than in Egypt. In Japan, Korea, and Taiwan, where extensive land reform was carried out, the limit was 2.65 acres (while in Egypt the limit was set at 50 to 100 acres). In the 1930s, 3 percent of all farm households in Korea owned two-thirds of the land; by the 1940s, land reforms had decimated the landed elite and left only less than 7 percent of the population landless. By 1975 in Korea, less than 20 percent of the land was held in farms of two hectares or more (around five acres), while in

Egypt 47.5 percent of the land was in holdings above this limit, and almost one-third of Egyptian landholders (32.3 percent) had holdings in one acre, amounting to only 6 percent of this agricultural area.[64] As Dani Rodrik has observed, given that income distribution was relatively egalitarian, Korean leaders were not under pressure to redistribute incomes and could focus on accumulation and investment.[65] Nasser never gained enough capital from land reform and domestic constituencies, and his distributive commitments would lead him to try to mobilize capital at the international level. The issue of external capital flows is related to the question of institutional continuity before and after 1952. The degree of institutional continuity between pre- and post-1952 Egypt can help elucidate the impact, if any, of external revenue on Nasser's state-building efforts. Did external flows "skew" the fledgling Egyptian state's structures, as some have argued, or did these structures predate both the flows and the revolution?

Rents and State Building

Rentier theorists claim that the Egyptian state's weakness and inability to reform today is the result of a decades-old dependence on external revenue, which not only deprived leaders of the incentive to reform but produced the isolated Nasserist state, detached from the population and "suspended from above." I argue that Egypt is indeed reliant on external rents, which began flowing long before Camp David, but, contrary to Terry Karl Lynn who says the character of rentier states was shaped by the infusion of external capital flows during the critical initial phases of state building, I demonstrate that the Nasserist regime's coalitional arrangements and welfare commitment had already been established before Soviet and American aid began flowing.[66] Moreover, Nasser's state-building strategy took the direction it took because of the dearth of capital, in particular foreign capital, which necessitated the policies of land reform and nationalization.

Several scholars have noted that many of Nasser's welfare policies were put in place in the 1930s and 1940s. Brown has argued that the notion of a Nasserist social contract is "exaggerated" and that what we think of as Nasserist welfare commitments actually preceded 1952 and "can easily be traced back" to the period during and immediately after World War II: "Rents and price controls were imposed during the war . . . [H]igher education began to expand and become accessible to the middle class under post-war governments . . . Nationalist economic policies were not an invention of the Free Officers; rather they were made possible by Egypt's legal independence," following the 1937 Montreux conference, which proclaimed "the abolition of the capitulations" that had theretofore prevented the Egyptian government from claiming jurisdiction over non-Egyptian citizens. Despite some innovations in the legal arena, Nasser, according to this argument, essentially used preexisting state organs and political structures to govern. "The image of Nasserism as a bargain of welfare gains in exchange for political silence is thus perhaps less accurate," writes Nathan Brown. "Pre-Revolutionary governments laid the groundwork for the new welfare policies and some of the authoritarian tools later developed much fully under Nasser."[67]

But even accepting that Nasser expanded a preexisting welfare state, it is not evident that this expansion or that his coalitional strategy of inclusion of the lower classes was prompted or funded by external revenue. The critical phases of state building—shaped by intra-elite conflict, state-society struggles, and international circumstances—had been completed by the time external revenue began flowing. In September 1952, the law on agrarian reform was passed. The nationalization of the Suez Canal on July 26, 1956, was carried out because of the lack of external revenue—specifically in response to the United States' refusal to finance the Aswan High Dam and John Foster Dulles's withdrawal of an aid package on July 19. (President Truman had granted Egypt a ten million dollar subsidy for the purchase of wheat surpluses but had adamantly refused to sanction any military aid, for fear of triggering an arms race in the region and to avoid a backlash from pro-Israeli groups at home.)[68] This was followed in 1957 by the nationalization of other foreign assets in Egypt, including banks, insurance companies, and foreign trade agencies. It was *after* these nationalizations, which provided income for the government and assets for the public sector, that Egypt began receiving significant amounts of non-food aid. In 1958, Egypt negotiated its first twelve-year loan for economic development with the Soviets, who agreed to provide financing for the Aswan High Dam project.[69] Between 1959 and 1966, Egypt received $1.124 billion ($949 million in food aid) from the United States, $842 million from the Soviet Union, and $273 million from the Eastern bloc countries.[70] But it is not clear how this money skewed the Egyptian state's regulatory, extractive, and distributive institutions, as some rentier state theorists would predict; welfare commitments were in place before 1959, and, as discussed in the next chapter, the ASU, established in 1962, actually encouraged participation and tried to mobilize various constituencies. Just as it is not clear that the early phases of Egypt's state building were shaped (or "skewed") by external rents, it is not clear that rents post-1958 forestalled institutional development or participation.

The size and complexity of the Egyptian state apparatus would be shaped not only by the nationalist struggle against the British but also by the Palestinian-Israeli conflict; the wars of 1948, 1956, and 1967 would affect the process of state building and incorporation—in ways neglected by most rentier analyses that focus on revenue flows—by strengthening the military, polarizing domestic constituencies, and paving the way for greater state intervention. The conflict in Palestine, from the war of 1948 to the invasion of 1956, combined with domestic instability made Nasser obsessive about his autonomy and independence from different social groups and interests. The "bellicist thesis," which claims that states make war and vice versa, is not belied by the Egyptian case; protracted military conflict in the Egyptian case did lead to an "administrative growth," but not the state apparatus Weberian "bellicist" theorists predicted. Rather, the combination of successive wars and (later) external rents produced an isolated, militarized state with an enormous bureaucracy and few links to society. This context would set the Egyptian state on a different institutional path than Mexico. Lacking the manpower and administrative means to directly rule their territories, postcolonial states have often ruled through middlemen. Nasser, though, was reluctant to grant power to mediating institutions or agencies for fear that they would become bases of opposition, in contrast to Mexico where corporatist organizations were granted some autonomy.

4

The Institutional Legacies of Incorporation

The Party-Labor Alliance on the Eve of Privatization

A regime without parties is of necessity a conservative regime.

—*Maurice Duverger, Les Parties Politiques (1954)*

Corporatism has been described as an exchange based on an interplay between inducements and constraints, both of which are mechanisms used to influence behavior and achieve control.[1] If inducements are offered to produce compliance by the granting of advantages, constraints produce compliance by the application or threat of "disadvantages" or negative sanctions. The particular combination of inducements and constraints determines the resulting type of corporatism and the mix of control, representation, and mobilization. A critical factor explaining the Mexican regime's ability to retain the loyalty of workers while restructuring in the 1990s is the type of inducements employed; inducements in the form of welfare benefits and subsidies are less likely to induce loyalty (particularly when austerity measures are retrenching these benefits) than inducements that offer career incentives, channels for representation and the expression of grievances, and input in policymaking.

Inducements are particularly important in understanding the degree of social control. The granting of official recognition, monopoly of representation, compulsory membership, or subsidies from the state can make union leadership dependent on the state rather than on workers for their legitimacy and career success. This dependency, as Michel's "law of oligarchy" postulates, may encourage the tendency for labor leadership to become an oligarchy more responsive to the concerns of state agencies or political leaders with which unionists interact than to the needs of workers.[2] In Egypt, the extensive use of inducements and constraints produced a "crisis of representation" and an inability of leaders to deliver the rank and file in the context of reform. In Mexico, by contrast, party leaders gained the support of labor unionists by offering them inducements such as union subsidies, access to public office, and participation in policy formulation. Labor leaders in turn used these resources to offer inducements to union members in the form of higher wages, welfare benefits, and job security. When the state could no longer provide benefits in the context of reform, the PRI began to target benefits to select unions and leaders and closed off alternative channels of participation. The institutional legacies of incorporation in Egypt and Mexico are critical to understanding these differing reform experiences.

"Nasser's Estado Novo"

In 1961, the Egyptian Trade Union Federation (ETUF) was created by statute and granted a formal monopoly of representation. Nasser wanted an organization to control workers and prevent their mobilization by an alternative group. The ETUF has since been the single official union organization with a hierarchical structure allowing only one federation to represent workers in any given industry. The organizational structure is hierarchical or, as the trade union statute put it, "pyramid shaped." Local units are tied to functional and regional branches, which are centralized under a national confederation with headquarters in Cairo. The confederation, in turn, is linked with a parent ministry that supervises its finances and activities and consults with its leaders on public policy. Membership is compulsory, providing the organization with a guaranteed income that is supplemented by government subsidies. Unionists tried to influence state policy mainly through membership in the ruling party and positions that senior unionists got in the government. While constraints were abundant, inducements were also aplenty. Article 52 of the Egyptian Constitution declared that work was a right of all Egyptians and pledged the government's commitment to ensuring adequate employment opportunities. Under this article, the government guaranteed all workers just treatment in jobs, hours of work, wages, vacations, and insurance against accidents. Top-level unionists were selected, co-opted, rewarded, and often insulated from being voted out by lower level unionists. This institutional setup insured labor quiescence for decades.[3]

The Egyptian corporatist framework came to look increasingly like its Brazilian inspiration. The Estado Novo had also passed a generous social welfare legislation and subjected legalized unions to substantial state control through the Labor Ministry, creating "an apolitical labor movement made up of unions that would function as consultative organs of government." Vargas also introduced highly constraining corporative laws limiting the right to strike and "placing more constraints on union organization and leadership than any other labor law in Latin America."[4] The key characteristic of Brazilian corporatism that was replicated in Egypt with significant implications for state capacity and social control was the hierarchical structure of the union movement. The Ministry of Labor exerted control over the leadership selection within the union movement and union election procedures; at the union level, the ministry was given the power to choose the union directorate, which in turn chose the union officers. Through all these means, plus the use of extensive cooptation through the offer of jobs and material benefits, the government created a leadership whose interests and outlook dovetailed with that of the Ministry of Labor and the state rather than with the rank and file; this type of unrepresentative, co-opted unionist would be called *pelego*. A similar *pelego* situation would appear within the Egyptian union movement.

Most studies of the ETUF have highlighted the conflict of representation between top union leaders and lower level unionists stemming from the pyramid structure of the confederation.[5] The law established separate unions in each individual enterprise and required workers to become members in unions if three-fifths of workers in an enterprise were already union members. This provision permitted an employer to establish a union under his tutelage and require recalcitrant employees to join once three-fifths had done so. This law also permitted the establishment of separate unions for blue-collar and white-collar workers in a single enterprise and thus divided the membership base of unions, making it more difficult to unite workers in a given enterprise.

The hierarchical structure of the confederation has been a point of contention among middle- and local-level unionists since its inception. Middle- and lower-level unionists protested that the way industries had been merged into federations was not conducive to collective action. Following the ETUF's 1961 convention, fifty-nine federations were formed. The structure established in the law, however, provided for only twenty-one individuals on the confederation's executive committee, meaning that the other forty-four federations would not be represented. Complaints abounded on the lack of representation for a number of federations and local-level unions and on the lack of opportunity for career advancement of lower level unionists.[6] The hierarchical structure of the ETUF made the locals strictly subordinate to the federations, which as Marsha Posusney notes, "served to stifle the initiative of local leaders and restrict[ed] their ability to address the day to day issues of workers."[7] Lower level unionists were also dissatisfied with the union electoral system. The ETUF laws stipulated that at each level of the union hierarchy boards would select a president. Legislation passed in 1964 established an indirect electoral system specified by the 1964 law that allowed rank-and-file workers to elect unionists to their local board, who then in turn appointed representatives to the federation convention. The bylaws of most locals and federations, as well as the ETUF, further specified that the boards at each level would select their own president and other officials. The voices of the rank and file were thus muzzled by layers of institutions.

The institutional structure created by Nasser simply lacked the co-optive resources and representative channels for mid-level and for low-level leaders to express the preferences of their constituencies or to rise upward in the union hierarchy. Unionists of different levels were often at odds and working at cross-purposes. Successive political parties from the National Union, Liberation Rally, Arab Socialist Union, and most recently the National Democratic Party would interfere in union elections at national and federation levels. Since Nasser was concerned with control and depoliticization and not mobilization and representation, the institutional framework he established placed workers within an elaborate corporatist straitjacket. Institutions for the negotiation of wages and collective bargaining were never developed—channels vital for negotiating change and reform were absent. Nasser engaged in what one scholar calls the "politics of simulation,"[8] whereby the state establishes certain intermediary organizations and associations from above, with the intent of creating an organizational and political vacuum that others may not fill. This political calculus produced grave structural contradictions. Senior unionists were handsomely rewarded and insulated from electoral pressures, while often simultaneously holding top positions in the ETUF, in the Labor Ministry, and in the ruling party. The institutional reforms carried out by Sadat exacerbated this conflict of representation: he reduced the number of federations to only sixteen and, between 1976 and 1981, passed laws strengthening the administrative and financial controls of the confederation over the federations and of the federations over their local affiliates. These tensions remained manageable as long as the Egyptian state was benevolent to popular sectors. But efforts at state retrenchment, starting with Nasser in 1965, Sadat in 1974, and then Mubarak in the 1990s, brought to the fore the conflicts and schisms existing within the labor confederation.

"Representation Qua Control"

Although organized labor in Mexico had to support the government and, in receiving benefits from it, became dependent on the state, the Mexican union movement was not penetrated to the same degree as Egypt (or Brazil.) The new constitution granted labor the right to form unions and to strike. A corporative labor code was promulgated, but it put fewer constraints on union activities than in Egypt. Unlike Egypt, there was not a single central confederation. Within the PRI, there were several confederations in addition to the Mexican Workers Confederation (CTM): the Mexican Regional Labor Confederation (CROM), and the General Confederation of Workers (CGT), and the newer Mexico's National Proletarian Confederation (CPN), Confederation of Workers and Peasants of Mexico (COCM), National Chamber of Labor (CNT), and Mexican Labor Unity Bloc (BUO). The multiplicity of confederations enhanced the state's ability to control labor and increase impediments to collective action; state elites could play one confederation off against another. By channeling participation into different sectors, the party organizationally separated the blue-collar workers from white-collar government employees and the peasantry. In this way, different groups were atomized, allowing the PRI to be the sole adjudicator of intersector relations and preventing a united front from emerging.[9] In 1966, the Labor Congress was created to embrace groups that fell outside of the PRI's perview, like the BUO and CNT. The Labor Congress also helped the union bureaucracy to consolidate its control over the labor movement. But the CTM, under the leadership of the powerful Fidel Velazquez, remained the dominant force within the Labor Congress.

The Mexican regime had more co-optive capacity than the Egyptian state and maintained the populist coalition mainly through negotiation and accommodation within the framework of the PRI. The Mexican state employed coercion to dampen labor-capital conflict and used labor bosses to control the rank and file's demands in exchange for personal rewards. But although *charrismo* (labor bossism) certainly exists, as Thompson and Roxborough showed in a survey of Mexican unions, it is not an accurate description of state-labor relations, because Mexican unions display great diversity in terms of how internally democratic they were, as indicated by the frequency of competitive elections, the closeness of elections, and the rate of turnover of leaders.[10] The Colliers similarly note that the charro model fails to capture the Mexican regime's preference for the use of "hegemonic" rather than "coercive" mechanisms of control: "A key aspect of the functioning of the regime was not only state capacity to buy off union leaders or otherwise to ensure their compliance as puppets of the regime that would do the bidding of the state, but the capacity of union leaders to represent their constituencies as well as to discipline them. In the Mexican regime, unions were a vehicle for support mobilization as well as control."[11]

Unlike Egypt, where charrismo was the rule, in Mexico, the state needed to maintain labor's active support; a minimal use of coercion and a degree of representativeness insured a mutually beneficial relationship. The state's reliance on labor's electoral vote turned out to be an effective way of insuring labor's participation in the political process. And the distribution of political rewards to progovernment leaders through the PRI was crucial in getting labor leaders to support the government's policy preferences. The regime thus wanted credible working class representatives as union leaders; that way the state could minimize its resort to coercive measures. Elective posts at the federal, state, and local levels were distributed as incentives and rewards to regime supporters; the positions also allowed labor to demand concessions from government officials and private employers. At the state and local level, control over elective offices even reinforced labor leaders' control within worker organization. Trejo Delarbe argues that the union bureaucracy in alliance with the state maintained its "hegemony" over the labor movement during a period of about four decades, an accomplishment that would have been inconceivable without the capacity to perform a representative function.[12] Newell and Rubio identify three stages by which the state achieves compliance from labor: first, a process of conciliation and accommodation of opposing interests; second, a political and material cooptation; and, finally, if all else failed, resort to repression.[13] This is not to say that inducements were equally distributed. Financial assistance and unionists' access to political mobility opportunities in the PRI were granted to selective pro-government labor organizations.

Mexican corporatism was thus based on a balance of constraints and inducements, control and representation, but there was more of the latter than the former. Central to the regime's political controls was the structure of the PRI. In terms of providing "survival strategies" and meaning, the PRI's ideological hegemony was unparalleled in Mexico. The PRI monopolized and manipulated symbols of the revolution and embodied a set of values that had widespread acceptance throughout Mexican society and served to legitimate the actions of the state.[14] Because of its linkages to different social groups, the Mexican ruling party could mobilize support for government policies and allow the state to manage sweeping economic and political changes. But the PRI is not a fixed entity; it has evolved considerably. The PRI's very large coalition included a variety of groups and constituencies whose interests had to be reconciled and, to the degree possible, accommodated in order to contain dissent. Scholars have long debated the extent to which the party actually represented the disparate interests within it. Roger Hansen has argued that the PRI was always meant to control interests and did not represent the peasant and labor sectors that made up two-thirds of its coalition. Miguel Angel Centeno in turn holds that the PRI was representative in the 1960s but grew less so in the 1980s, and it was this exclusionary turn that led Cauhtemoc Cardenas's PRD to break away.[15]

The PRI may have grown less representative since the 1960s, but up to 1988 when reforms began chipping away at labor's privileges popular sectors were controlled and enjoyed a degree of representation. The organizational links between the PRI and the mass organizations, like the CTM, for example, provided a vehicle for dispensing concessions, which maintained the support of constituency groups and kept them from defecting to more militant organizations. This vast system of limited participation and leadership cooptation, coupled with the distribution of other material benefits, helped control the leadership, of course, but through those leaders, the mass organizations and their grassroots base. This hegemony would be challenged in the 1980s by Cardenas's leftist PDR, which maintained that the PRI's espousal of neoliberal reforms violated the revolution's goals. To understand why the PRI proved more resilient and far reaching than its Egyptian counterparts, it is necessary to examine the institutional development of the dominant parties in Mexico and Egypt.

Party Formation in Egypt

Upon ascending to power, Nasser abolished political parties and severed all preexisting ties between labor and parties to prevent the politicization of the working class. But he would quickly realize the importance of structuring political life and that to embark on his path of development he needed at the very least the "symbolic participation of the masses." He subsequently established successive political organizations: the Liberation Rally (1954), the National Union (1956), and the Arab Socialist Union (1961). As is evident from their names, these organizations were not referred to as "political parties"; the discourse of the 1952 Revolution had expressed an animosity to party politics, given the corruption and disunity associated with the liberal politics of the interwar era.

The Liberation Rally was established after the March 1954 crisis to fill the political vacuum, to impede the participation of the prerevolutionary elite, and to prevent the Communists and Muslim Brotherhood from mobilizing the masses. Branches of the Liberation Rally were established in all the major cities, and the rural middle class emerged as a crucial constituency that would control the countryside and deliver the rural vote. The only organizational link between the ruling junta and labor was the Workers' Bureau of the Liberation Rally. Under the 1956 constitution, the rally was abolished, and the National Union was created. If the Liberation Rally was founded shortly after the 1952 coup to fill a political vacuum, the National Union was created in 1956 to reinforce national unity in face of the invasion. Rural notables formed the core of the National Union as well. The National Union elections of 1959 revealed the importance of the regime's rural base, which had more representation than urban constituencies. Binder explains this rural focus, noting that "the National Union was not really an instrument of political mobilization. It was rather an instrument to preclude political mobilization by rival groups. . . . the regime wished to avoid the risk of mobilizing urban political elements into a new and untried structure."[16] The dominance of the rural middle class was also reflected in the composition of the assembly elected in 1956. As Anouar Abdelmalek wrote, the assembly was made up of a "large number of prosperous men, and most of the provincial delegates favored the old system of agrarian dominance."[17]

When the ETUF was established in 1957, the National Union made no attempt to attract workers' support; industrial workers, in fact, were hardly represented in the party. Both the Liberation Rally and the National Union lacked the capacity and resources to penetrate the labor movement, to engage unionists of all levels, and to gain the support of the rank and file. The Liberation Rally lacked the capacity to reach into hundreds of union locals. The National Union had greater institutional capacity than its predecessor, with branches in various localities, but these offices did not get involved in local union affairs. State elites never granted these two parties the resources necessary to penetrate and control the labor movement, and they never developed the grassroots support, nationwide appeal, or legitimacy the Wafd had enjoyed.

Nasser did briefly consider using the ASU to mobilize the popular classes. Founded in 1961 when the regime explicitly adopted a socialist ideology and passed the July Laws expanding the state's role in the economy, the ASU sought to gain the active support of labor and the peasantry. The National Charter of July 1962 stipulated 50 percent at least of all elected seats to be reserved for workers and peasants. Nasser realized that to implement his development goals he would need more than the populace's passive support; he granted the RMC a prominent position in the ASU and began to address conditions in the Egyptian village in order to expand his social base. In January 1965, he contemplated not standing for "reelection" and devoting himself to mobilizing people and building an effective ASU to undertake a socialist industrial transformation. The creation of the

ASU reflected a shift in Nasser's coalitional strategy. While the RMC delivered the rural vote and the resources necessary to finance state-led industrialization, the popular classes would support the socialist project and counter the resistance of the middle classes. Nasser also had an interest in using the ASU as a civilian counterweight to the military, then under the powerful Field Marshal Amir. Nasser established a vanguard organization within the ASU, headed by Ali Sabri, the party's preeminent leftist ideologue who wanted to expand the regime's base beyond the rural middle class.[18] Sabri also wanted to bypass the state bureaucracy and attach the public sector, civil service, and corporatist sectors (labor and professional syndicates) to the ASU's Alliance of Working Forces.

The ASU had some success in incorporating labor. By the early 1960s, the ETUF had been consolidated, and elections were being held throughout the union structure supervised by the ASU. In July 1963, on the eve of the 1963–64 trade union elections, a law was passed requiring that all candidates for union office be members of the ASU. Unlike its predecessors, the ASU's larger membership base and branches in various localities provided the capacity to monitor and intervene in union affairs. Reports from that period describe workers as exhibiting a high level of ideological and group consciousness, as evidenced by the greater campaigning activity and responsive leadership. The ASU rivaled the ETUF in providing channels of communication between unionists and the state. The ASU's Workers Bureau established workers' committees to defend workers' grievances, but these often competed with and had more influence than unions. Ali Sabri's camp successfully used these committees to counter the power of the bureaucracy and SOE managers. In numerous cases, workers' candidates, by allying themselves with the ASU Youth Organization, defeated candidates proposed by the management of state-owned enterprises (SOEs)[19]

The ASU's success with labor, however, was short-lived. Nasser tried to build a mass party with cadres and apparatchiks but withdrew his support for the organization after the 1967 war. Despite the presence of peasant and worker candidates in many party and administrative bodies, there were no new elections at any level of the union hierarchy between 1967 and 1970. Migdal sees this as another instance of Nasser "undermining his own agency," fearing that it was becoming a threatening power center. Cammack disagrees, saying that the ASU had fulfilled its goals and was no longer needed. The party, in his view, was intended to help Nasser counter the military, maintain stability in the countryside, and prevent the emergence of new strata of rich peasants outside state control and incorporate the RMC and peasantry so as to insure a flow of resources to boost urban development and industrialization.[20] By late 1967, with the defeat of the military and the ensuing purge of the state, these goals had been achieved, and Nasser saw it fit to demobilize the ASU. Further mobilization and cultivating of labor's support was not on the Egyptian leadership's agenda and would not be again until the 1990s. Whatever the reason, Nasser demobilized the ASU following the 1967 war; the conflict in Palestine would again affect the institutional development of the Egyptian state.

Unlike the PRI, the ASU was created after the corporatist organizations were established and represented a bold attempt to build institutional links to control the popular sectors and introduce a new discourse and ideology to underpin the ETUF's existence. With its demobilization, labor lacked any effective instrument of pressure or bargaining. Nasser's fear of power centers meant labor was never allowed to develop institutions for bargaining and participation; to achieve the socialist agenda he wanted, Nasser would have required the mobilization at all levels of the ETUF, but he feared the consequences of mass participation. The only form of representation labor now enjoyed was through workers' representation on SOE management boards. The Law of 1963 gave workers four seats on a nine-member board that was required to meet monthly. Nasser reverted to the bureaucracy and public sector for control.

The launching, dismantling, and rebuilding of successive ruling party organizations meant that the existing NDP party lacked the organizational reach, support, or legitimacy that decades of political influence had given most mass single parties in the Third World. When Sadat introduced multiparty elections in 1976, he revived the ASU's moribund political apparatus and named the new organization the National Democratic Party. Sadat's rationale was similar to Nasser's: the single party was to be used as a vehicle for mobilizing rural support and to exclude the urban-based rival movements such as the Muslim Brotherhood and the Wafd. And again the representative system was heavily biased toward the rural areas, particularly since the New Wafd was also courting rural elites.[21] NDP leaders recruited unionists of all levels into the government party; high-level confederation leaders held top positions in the NDP. But by the mid-1980s, a number of high-level unionists had resigned from the NDP, and many mid-level unionists were running on the tickets of opposition parties; in the 1984 elections, the Socialist Party had on its membership roster presidents and vice-presidents of three major unions—from construction, defense, and printing federations. Opposition parties—the Tagammu (NPUP), the Wafd, and the Socialist Labor Party—proved more effective than the NDP in drawing the votes of workers. One study examining the relation between the strength of the union movement in each province and the degree of electoral support for the NDP found a persistently negative correlation in the parliamentary elections of 1976, 1984, and 1987.[22] The NDP's lack of support in urban areas eventually pushed Mubarak to adopt a number of reforms, including more party supervision of union elections in different regions and conferences at the regional level between NDP officials and unionists—all intended to gain labor's electoral support among them.

It is during the process of privatization that the ruling party's (and state's) ability to control labor is put to the test. In Mexico, CTM leaders complained bitterly about the economic reforms and threatened mobilization to improve their negotiating position within the PRI, but they neither organized serious protest against the reforms nor took steps to withdraw from the party-union alliance. In Egypt, on the other hand, since 1991, labor protests and violent strikes have become more frequent. Activists have publicly called for a new confederation or for the withdrawal of the ETUF from the NDP; defections of lower level unionists to opposition parties and movements are common.

Party-Labor Relations on the Eve of Privatization

Party union linkages in Mexico are extensive. The electoral mechanism is the most significant linkage: by voting for the PRI, workers and unionists participate in a system and could be represented at all levels of government; the state, in turn, benefited from this system of "representation qua control." Financially, the CTM owed its survival to the support of the PRI. Despite statutory requirements that workers and affiliates pay dues, the CTM never developed an effective system of self-financing and was forced to rely on financial subsidies from the state—channeled through the PRI. In addition to economic and legal subsidies (such as provisions in collective labor agreements), Middlebrooke notes that the PRI also provided the CTM with "political subsidies," such as the state's use of force against opposition political and labor organizations. By dominating all these branches of government, the PRI enjoyed multiple levers of control over CTM leaders, and the Federal Labor Law (LFT) gave the state extensive authority to intervene in labor affairs. The PRI provided political, ideological, and organizational resources that allowed the state to maintain legitimacy, mobilize support, and control the organizations of the popular sector. Control was exercised through a fundamentally cooperative alliance of state-labor and state-peasant relations, mediated largely by a hegemonic party. Given the benefits they received, CTM leaders preferred staying within the parameters of the alliance. From the beginning, the CTM was granted more relative autonomy than the Egyptian workers' confederation; in privatizing, reformers manipulated these party-union linkages and used the confederations as bargaining partners and institutional tools.

In Egypt, since the incorporation period, the main instrument for state intervention in labor affairs has been the Ministry of Labor. With the ban on strikes and unionists incapable or unwilling to promote rank-and-file concerns, workers increasingly took their grievances to the state rather than to the union leadership or political party. This interaction reinforced the compact of reciprocal rights and responsibilities between labor and the state that Nasserism had introduced. When the ASU was in power, the main linkage between party and labor was the Workers' Secretariat, a bureau that sought to bypass the state bureaucracy, penetrate the ETUF, and subordinate the unions to the ruling party. The Workers' Secretariat and the Vanguard, led by cadres and workers, tried to organize elections that would increase worker and peasant presence throughout the party hierarchy, but after the 1967 war, Nasser dismantled these institutions.

Sadat shared his predecessor's distrust of the left. He abolished the ASU and reformed the structure of the union movement, greatly increasing the powers and privileges of the Confederation of Labor, isolating it from its own constituency. In 1976, he passed a law that exacerbated the hierarchical structure of the union movement by dictating that it have a pyramid form where the lower bodies were subordinate to the higher ones. The law also formalized the system of having officers at all levels elected indirectly by the boards. Bianchi holds that this law was Sadat's attempt to tighten his control over labor by buttressing the authority of the ETUF hierarchy and increasing the (administrative and financial) controls of the senior unionists over the federation leaders and of the federation over the locals.[23] Sadat delinked labor from the party structure but still tried to co-opt top union leaders and insulate them from rank-and-file pressures; the confederation and federation leaders were expected to toe the NDP line and maintain industrial peace. This was the extent of the NDP's reach, however; aside from confederation and federation leaders who got top party positions, the NDP offered little career incentives to lower- and middle-level unionists. The NDP's limited reach and offerings coupled with the ETUF's inhibiting hierarchical structure restricted opportunities for upward mobility and voice by labor unionists and rank and file. In November 1976, the ETUF declared that it would not align itself with any of the newly established political platforms. Many began advocating the establishment of an independent workers' party.

During union elections, the state would intervene (often via the Labor Ministry) at the confederation and federation levels, insuring that state-sponsored NDP candidates would win defeating other locally elected NDP candidates. Consequently, a select few high-level state-backed NDP unionists would receive attractive positions in the NDP, but most others did not. During the 1984 elections, several union leaders—including the heads of two of the most important federations in the country (the engineering, metal, and electrical workers' federation), representing about 100 thousand public sector manufacturing workers, and the Construction Workers' Federation, Egypt's largest union, claiming nearly 550 thousand members)—resigned from the NDP in protest over second-rate positions they were offered and joined opposition parties.[24]

The NDP and the Labor Ministry do not intervene effectively in union elections at the local level to give some semblance of legitimacy but also for lack of capacity. Workers can more closely monitor the election results at that level, and lower level union leaders have little contact with regime elites. This creates a schism within the ETUF between pro- and anti-government supporters. Often candidates opposed to the government position on privatization, for example, can win office at the local level. But once elected to the local board, the unionists will rarely get appointed to the Federation Congress or elected to the Federation Board. The state thus shuts out the lower level unionists, the very leaders that could deliver rank-and-file cooperation. These unionists often vote as independents or join opposition parties or unofficial workers organizations such as the Voice of Workers. This split weakened the ETUF's capacity to control the rank and file and pushed workers toward alternative parties and movements.

Ruling Party and Economic Reform

When the reform process began in Egypt, the NDP's weakness became evident, as the ruling party lacked the institutional linkages and manpower to deliver benefits and disseminate the party's message. Since the late 1970s, NDP leaders have attempted to establish ties with business, agricultural interests, and organized labor. Business and agricultural interests are better represented within the NDP than labor and other urban constituencies, which have not been sought-after constituencies. Sadat, like Nasser, simply wanted labor controlled and demobilized, and so he reorganized the labor corporatist sector. The NDP's principal link to the ETUF is through senior confederation leaders who hold positions in the NDP (often simultaneously with posts in the state bureaucracy) and sit in the Egyptian parliament to fulfill the constitutional commitment of 50 percent representation of peasants and workers.

A central reason for the weakness of all Egyptian political parties is their narrow base of support. In the case of the NDP, the rural vote is mobilized with the support of the rich peasants, the regime's main coalitional ally since 1952, and the control they exert in rural areas through clientelistic circles makes it possible to distribute NDP patronage. A few local notables often decide how an entire village would vote. "Villagers tended to vote in blocks, with each individual casting his ballot for the party his entire clan had agreed to support," writes Sadowski. "Clans, in turn, tended to negotiate their votes with local notables; they would throw their ballots to the candidate who offered the most generous patronage."[25] The regime does not have such support in urban areas. The NDP's constituencies in urban areas are businessmen and bureaucrats, and businessmen do not have the same clientelist control as rural notables. The party's humiliating performance in urban areas in 1990 prompted Mubarak to call for the "structural reorganization" of the party with the objectives of "greater institutionalization and differentiation." More specific goals were the creation of "communication networks" between different levels of the party and greater interaction with the base—thus the establishment of the Bureau of Political Affairs and Security Office[26] and easier registration procedures intended to attract more workers.

The PRI's legitimacy, resources, and leverage vis-à-vis labor by far surpassed that of the NDP. Despite the economic downturn and hardship imposed by the reform measures, as the next chapter describes, the PRI during the adjustment period still enjoyed a reputation as a party that for sixty years "delivered the goods"; and for anyone aspiring for an elective post, the PRI was the best option. The structure of the PRI shows the extensive penetration of the three corporatist sectors into all levels of the party. The party employs tens of thousands of people in its offices and affiliates nationwide. The PRI can also be an effective way for achieving employment in the government sector; through its unions, the party controls many jobs in the private sector as well as state-owned industries. It was these structures that reformers would use to contain labor opposition to privatization.

5

Privatization and the Populist-Distributive Alliance

Privatization required that reformers transform the social base of the Mexican state. This chapter examines how state officials manipulated the corporatist mechanisms of control to overcome labor opposition and incorporate (in some cases, reincorporate) workers and other groups alienated by adjustment. Particularly during Salinas's *sexenio*, state elites reworked the PRI's corporatist framework and manipulated the clientelist links between the state and labor leadership, on the one hand, and the union leadership and the rank and file, on the other, to insure labor docility and neutralize the challenge of the leftist Party of Democratic Revolution (PRD). Unlike Egypt, the Mexican regime benefited from the presence of several mass organizations, and the PRI's cooptive capacity facilitated the control of these popular organizations.

Although de la Madrid initiated neoliberal reform measures in 1983, it was Salinas who, after the PRI's electoral defeat in 1988, realized that top-down reforms could not be sustained without popular support and reached out to workers and unincorporated middle class and popular groups. Salinas took advantage of institutions linking the PRI (and the state) to organized labor to enlist union support for privatization, manipulating mechanisms that controlled strike activity, union formation, and worker demand channels. These institutions of control would prove crucial to the reformers, who would shield them from the privatization process. As Middlebrooke and Zapeda put it, "In marked contrast to the 'state withdrawal' agenda that economic reformers pursued in other arenas, government officials in the 1980s and 1990s showed little interest in dismantling the complex array of legal and administrative controls regulating wage and contract negotiations, union formation and strikes,"[1] for it was these levers that helped neutralize labor opposition. The strike and exclusion clauses of the Federal Labor Law (LFT) were interpreted stringently against anti-reform unions. Salinas's control over strikes and the manipulation of the union registration process weakened the unions' bargaining position and split the labor movement, marginalizing resistant unionists and co-opting pro-reform ones as intermediaries. The PRI's social sector was revamped and expanded, with more patronage being delivered to the rank and file, sidestepping the more resistant *charros*. When traditional corporatist and clientelist mechanisms proved insufficient, Salinas used electoral reforms and the PRI-labor electoral linkage to reshape the electoral arena in favor of pro-reform candidates and unionists. Salinas's thinking after 1988 was simple: if the PRI was to have the capacity to win future elections without rampant fraud and violence, it had "go to the base" and could not rely on the sectoral organizations and the caciques who ran many of them.

Salinas's coalition-building strategy had a deliberate logic of timing, sequencing, and targeting. Through party reforms, Salinas's team wanted to promote just enough institutional change to facilitate economic reform and to recoup the PRI's electoral support, knowing that opening up the PRI to internal and external competition could jeopardize adjustment. Mexican reformers were trying to structurally revamp the PRI while maintaining power and to reform the economy while using the party structure as an instrument of governance and coalition building. In constructing a pro-reform coalition, Salinas did not totally exclude labor; organized labor was weakened but not totally marginalized, because reformers still needed labor for campaigning and vote gaining. In fact, after whittling away at the CTM's power and weakening charros to facilitate privatization, Salinas's labor policy began to change; as the 1994 election approached, he began to restore privileges and benefits. It is this flexibility and responsivity on the part of the Mexican state that stand in contrast to Egypt's low capacity. The Mexican regime stands out in Latin America for its ability to use the state-labor alliance to contain opposition to economic polices that inflicted tremendous hardship on workers and still maintain organized labor's support on macroeconomic policy and in elections. The financial crisis of 1994–95 did trigger a backlash against the PRI and Salinas's economic project, with scores of peasants and workers leaving the ruling party, but the economic and institutional reforms put in place in the previous years were not be threatened.

Pronasol, the antipoverty program, which has been called Salinas's "greatest institutional innovation," was central to the reformers' new coalition-building strategy. Pronasol helped Salinas reverse the PRI's declining electoral strength. The program helped mobilize and incorporate new social groups by getting them to participate in the state's new economic and political project. Pronasol, however, was not the "innovation" it has been touted to be, but it reflected Salinas's retooling of preexisting institutional mechanisms to construct a massive bureaucracy that was crucial in reconstituting the regime's faltering base. Pronasol's strength was its establishment, through welfare distribution, of new linkages between the government and the urban and rural poor who had voted for Cardenas in 1988. Given the success of this "institutional innovation" in building support, scholars have wondered how Salinas was able to establish such a massive bureaucracy (seemingly) overnight. The question is important because state elites in other countries—including Egypt—have tried to build a similar welfare program, a patronage machine designed to galvanize support for neoliberal reform, but are not having Salinas's success. An analysis of the institutional origins of Pronasol reveals that this successful program was the result of administrative reforms initiated by Lopez Portillo and continued by de la Madrid, which made use of the PRI's corporatist sectors and the Mexican state's local and municipal branches. Moreover, as with privatization, Pronasol was successful in reconstituting the state's support base, but it is not clear that the program reduced poverty.

The 1988 Debacle

The economic expansion of the ISI era financed the distribution of material benefits to labor and peasant organizations within the PRI coalition. But the crisis of 1976 and the subsequent devaluation severely strained the state's social pact with the popular sectors. The onset of the debt crisis in 1982 and the collapse of oil exports left the country with a negative growth rate in GDP. When de la Madrid took office later that year, inflation was at 100 percent; the public deficit was 16.9 percent of the GDP; and the country's foreign exchange reserves were depleted. The austerity argument signed with the IMF committed Mexico to stabilization and structural adjustment programs and made it clear that the state's new economic strategy was directly at odds with the old populist distributive commitments.[2] The stabilization program imposed severe hardship on workers, sharply limiting wage increases, cutting government spending, relaxing price controls, and retrenching subsidies for union transportation, electricity, natural gas, and gasoline. Income inequality grew, and the proportion of the population living in extreme poverty rose.

Reformers were faced with a dilemma. Since privatization and neoliberal reform violated the regime's commitments to labor, it seemed necessary to either weaken labor as a coalitional partner or otherwise reform the state-labor alliance. Rising inflation and the emergence of the PRD as a challenger made it necessary to maintain the cooperation of labor confederations, which could restrain wage demands and try to regain working class votes. In the mid-1980s, the ruling party was failing electorally. By one account, a trend of "loosening party attachments" had appeared. Between 1983 and 1987, over 20 percent of the population previously aligned with the PRI or other parties had moved into the "nonaligned camp," so that nearly half of Mexican voters were no longer sympathetic to a particular party.[3] The main reason for the PRI's loss of support was declining resources and patronage. As living standards declined, corporatist organizations were increasingly seen as ineffective representatives of workers and the poor, and new local organizations (*coordinadoras* and *asambleas de barrios*) mushroomed, and many rejected the clientelist patterns of old and joined either the PRD or became independent.[4]

The collapse of the stock market in October 1987 and the following 40 percent devaluation of the peso made matters worse. The CTM filed thousands of strike petitions and threatened to hold a general strike on December 15, if the government did not grant an immediate wage hike. In 1988, the PRI, which had historically won 75 percent of the vote, proved unable to win a simple majority without resorting to widespread electoral fraud. The PRI's share of the presidential vote shrank to 50.7 percent. Traditional labor leaders failed to deliver the rank and file's vote. Workers, averse to the PRI's neoliberal agenda and no longer believing in the ability of their elected leaders to deliver benefits, voted for the opposition. This crisis of representation was evident in the fact that a number of elite labor candidates failed to win elections, and 30 of the 101 candidates for the Chamber of Deputies representing the Labor Congress affiliates lost. Lorenzo Meyer notes that labor suffered more legislative losses than any other sector, because voting workers punished union bosses who were congressional candidates.[5]

De la Madrid's team had not foreseen the PRD challenge. Electorally, the PAN was viewed as the greatest challenge but not a threat to market reform since business backed the neoliberal agenda. The PRD's impressive electoral show in 1988 prompted a rethinking of the entire reform strategy. The PRI's worst losses had come in districts with heavy concentrations of working voters.[6] One study of electoral results in cities with a high concentration of working class voters (Tijuana, Moncloa, Ecatepec, Tlalneplanta, Cuernavaca, Coatzacoalcos) showed Cardenas had won an average of 51.4 percent of the vote, compared to only 30.3 percent for Salinas. The CTM was particularly hard hit, with only thirty-four of fifty-one candidates winning seats, and the organization failed to win a senate seat for the first time since 1940.[7]

After 1988, not only were union leaders unable to deliver the working class vote, but they became openly critical of the PRI's economic program.

Salinas realized that top-down reforms without the support of organized constituencies—particularly labor—could not be sustained. Anti-inflation pacts could not be enforced without the support of organized labor; wage cuts and adjustments would be more difficult to implement without a loyal labor leadership. Scores of workers had voted for the PRD, and if the PRI maintained its current course, the official labor leadership and high ranking progressive party officials would be tempted to defect as well to Cardenas's splinter group. A change in the regime's mechanisms of control was needed. Salinas would embark on a strategy of "New Unionism" designed to reduce the importance of organized labor within the party state apparatus, while still relying on loyal labor bosses as middlemen to insure industrial peace.

Divestiture and the Labor's Response

Privatization under de la Madrid proceeded rapidly, and workers suffered enormously. From 1986 to 1987, the government crushed all the important strikes and in one case (at a Ford plant) ended the strike and dismissed 3,200 workers. De la Madrid took a hard-line position vis-à-vis top labor leaders. He rebuffed every economic proposal presented by Fidel Velazquez, seriously eroding the leader's credibility. The closing of the Fundidora Monterrey in May 1986 and the elimination of fifteen thousand jobs showed how the government was abandoning its historic prioritization of jobs. The number of SOEs and public investment funds dropped from 412 in 1982 to 232 in 1992. Salinas carried out the largest and politically most difficult privatizations of strategic public enterprises, including banks and investment houses, telecommunications, air transportation, mining companies, steel producers, sugar mills, and port facilities. In preparing SOEs for sale to private investors, the government often forced upon workers significant cuts in wages and fringe benefits, which substantially reduced unions' influence in enterprise affairs. By 1990, there remained 286 SOEs, and the public enterprise sector had been reduced to 11.8 percent of GDP.[8]

State officials rebuffed labor's threats to withdraw. In early 1984, the CTM threatened to call a general strike to secure an emergency wage increase, but, despite a wave of strike petitions filed by individual affiliates, no national mobilization occurred. Tight controls on labor mobilization and continued government intransigence prevented leading labor organizations from winning significant policy concessions. In 1985, the CTM changed its position. Rather than merely opposing the government's austerity measures, the confederation began to promote an alternative policy that would both protect workers from the effects of inflation and reaffirm its historical role as an advocate of egalitarian development. The CTM demanded more material benefits. Realizing no significant policy change was coming, labor had decided to negotiate within the alliance's parameters rather than threaten to leave. The CTM subsequently declared its support for the government's program of divestiture and SOE restructuring, echoing the official line that the objective was to strengthen the state's economic leadership role. Even when it became clear that divestiture meant massive layoffs, the CTM defended privatization as necessary to eliminate inefficiencies. Because of this failure to take strong positions against divestiture, confederations lost union support and became weaker.[9]

Labor leaders did, however, denounce the PAN's demands to completely overhaul the historic state-labor alliance. Unionists realized that some state elites were sympathetic to the PAN's calls for a "new political order" that would completely exclude labor from the ruling coalition and abandon workers to the discipline of market forces. While they disliked the neoliberal reform agenda, labor leaders feared the exclusion proposed by the PAN even more and wanted to defend their position in the coalition and to protect their right to bargain from within the governing coalition. They could threaten to withdraw from the alliance, but in reality they could not actually withdraw. Despite occasional strikes and rising rhetoric, as the 1988 election approached, Mexican labor leaders chose to work within the existing corporatist framework, trying to influence the choice of the PRI's presidential candidate for the 1988 elections and preventing Salinas, head of SPP, from receiving the PRI nomination. When that failed, the CTM did not abandon the state-labor alliance but changed tactics again.

Given the declining standards of living and the fall in real wages in Mexico (which was nearly twice as severe as the Latin American average),[10] Mexican labor's timid response has puzzled many: why was Mexican labor so accommodating to economic measures that eroded its power, while elsewhere in Latin America labor forcefully mobilized against such reforms? The "official" Mexican labor movement's reaction to the economic reversals and reform policies of the 1980s was significantly less confrontational than the responses of organized labor in other large Latin American countries. Argentina's Confederacion General de Trabajo (CGT), for example, led eight general strikes between December 1983 and early 1987 in opposition to the Alfonsin government's austerity program and reformers' attempts to remove resistant leaders from major unions.[11] Even in Brazil, where organized labor's support for the transition to civilian rule in 1985 made unions more reluctant to challenge the newly installed democratic government, labor organized general strikes in 1986 and 1987 in protest of sharp price increases and higher unemployment. How did the Mexican corporatist bargain make remaining in the alliance a more attractive option for labor leaders than defection to opposition parties, as in other countries? And relatedly, how did Salinas's team regain the confidence of alienated rank-and-file workers? By the end of Salinas's term, privatization had been achieved, and labor was still a partner—legitimating the regime's reforms. Salinas had simultaneously weakened labor but also strengthened labor's ability to deliver votes.

Privatization and the "New Unionism"

The "New Unionism" was Salinas's attempt to reduce the influence of organized labor in national politics and ensure effective labor mobilization for the PRI without much reliance on traditional corporatist structures.[12] The 1988 elections had shown that labor leaders' quiescence to de la Madrid's economic policy did not insure consent of the rank and file. Salinas claimed that the "New Unionism" would make unions more representative. Labor's alliance with the state would be maintained, although with increased autonomy for unions; and labor-management relations would be based on greater cooperation and communication, with workers recognizing the primacy of increased productivity. This new system was meant to further Salinas's political aims as well as his economic program: by making unions more representative, it was hoped they would be able to gain greater rank-and-file support internally, which could in turn deliver more political support and votes for the PRI than had the traditional oligarchic unions. Salinas would use different institutional mechanisms to weaken and extirpate etatist unionists, to strengthen pro-reform leaders, and to reach out to rank-and-file support side-stepping the traditional power brokers.

The PRI historically maintained industrial peace by delegating control to unions themselves and granting them a degree of freedom not available to Egyptian unionists. Accommodationist labor leaders were given significant power in managing internal affairs of a union. Despite requirements that unions inform the government of any change in their constitutional bylaws or leadership, they were legally free to prepare their own statutes and internal regulations, elect their offices, and formulate union policy. While consistent with democratic unionism, these provisions allowed for labor leaders to limit dissent from workers, especially since there were no legal requirements regarding the use of secret ballots in union elections. Historically, unionists were used as agents of social control. But for Salinas, this setup was no guarantee of the broader support he needed. The Economic Stability Pact (PSE) put in place by de la Madrid had called for a sharp reduction in government deficit spending and public consumption subsidies and instituted wage controls to limit inflationary pressures; and while workers in the CTM and CT affiliates benefited from the increased subsidized foodstuffs, worker housing, and financial credits, these amenities failed to compensate workers for declining wages.[13] Salinas thus moved against anti-reform leaders by targeting the rank and file and negotiating separate agreements with individual unions in such key sectors as telecommunications, education, and electrical power generation.

Weakening Charros

To root out corrupt charros and weaken senior labor leaders, Salinas began to dismantle the decades-old institutional setup that had granted top unionists tremendous power. With the notable exception of La Quina, head of the oil workers union, most charros did not stand up to Salinas's neoliberal agenda or anti-corruption measures. After Salinas arrested La Quina, the union's new leader, he quietly consented to a major restructuring of Petroleos Mexicanos (PEMEX) that resulted in the firing of more than thirty thousand workers. Salinas thus demonstrated the limits of permissible opposition to privatization and indicated to the rank and file that dissidence in unions run by caciques would be welcomed by the government. So in the following months, several other powerful union caciques were confronted by massive protest demonstrations, legal actions filed against them, and defeats in union elections—led by dissident unions encouraged by Salinas.[14] Salinas directed resources toward these politically alienated workers and the local community affected by job losses.

Mexico's economic restructuring program affected the traditional corporatist system in different ways. At the confederation and union levels, economic reform deepened divisions within the labor movement, making control through a single national labor organization almost impossible. Reform also undermined rank-and-file support for charro leadership and the PRI. Salinas exploited these schisms. He supported pro-reform unionists, fomented dissent among disgruntled rank and file, and used forced privatization to solve intractable labor disputes. Deliberate government attacks on charrismo, along with rising unemployment, inflation, and widespread layoffs, left organized labor in disarray.

The Strike Legality Law and Worker Demand Forums

De la Madrid and Salinas also quelled labor resistance using laws regarding the legality of strikes. The de la Madrid administration made frequent use of the *requisa*, a constitutional provision (Article 112) that allowed the government to intervene in a strike, annulling the collective agreement and forcing workers back to work. The provision was supposed to be used only in very unusual circumstances, such as when the security of the country was threatened, but reformers evoked it in less urgent situations, for example, to crush the strikes at AeroMexico and Fundidora Monterrey. Another mechanism used by both de la Madrid and Salinas to put down worker unrest was rulings, or threatened rulings, by the Board of Conciliation and Arbitration on the legality of strikes. The legality of strike activity is ruled on in accordance with the 1931 Labor Code. The Federal Labor Law allowed the state to regulate strike activity that undermined the mobilizing capacity of unions. To be recognized as legal, a strike had to be supported by the majority of workers and preceded by a formal petition specifying the goal and time of strike action. Even if allowed to proceed, the state could still insist, by law, that the parties to the conflict were required to participate in conciliation efforts led by labor authorities; and employers could also ask the authorities to declare the strike "nonexistent" within seventy-two hours of the strike's initiation.

This institution was repeatedly used during the economic restructuring of the 1980s and 1990s. De la Madrid declared many strikes started by SOE workers nonexistent. On average, his administration approved 1.8 percent of the strike petitions filed in federal jurisdiction economic activities between 1983 and 1988. So even though the volume of strike petitions remained high, the number of legally recognized strikes actually fell during the worst period of economic recession, from a historical high of 675 in 1982 to 230 in 1983. The number of strikes fell again between 1986 and 1987, even though the number of petitions increased sharply during 1987, the year that registered the highest annual inflation rate since 1917.[15] The government also used force against strikes or simply forced their suspension by declaring them "illegal." In addition to control over strikes and union formation, state officials also used the forums for "worker-demand articulations" to enforce a wage ceiling on a case-by-case basis, which helped make the Pact work. Tripartite conciliation and arbitration boards had long been the state's principal administrative channels for the resolution of individual worker grievances not settled in private negotiations between workers and employers. Pact and wage-price agreements between state, capital, and labor succeeded thanks to these preexisting forums.

The Exclusion Clause

One significant party-union linkage used by unionists to control the rank and file was the exclusion clause ("closed-shop clause"), included in most collective contracts of SOE unions, which made it necessary to be a member of the union in order to keep one's job. The clause of exclusion was reinforced by "clauses of inclusion," which required management to hire exclusively from the union. Such clauses operated in conjunction with the Labor Code requirement that all unions must be registered with the Ministry of Labor to receive the benefits of that code. Since only one union is recognized in each enterprise, state and party authorities had the ability to empower cooperative unions over uncooperative ones, allowing the union leadership to easily rid itself of uncooperative workers by dismissing them from the union.[16] Labor leaders favored by the regime could also negotiate special protections against worker dissent. In addition, by linking union membership to employment, these clauses restricted the options of voice and exit for workers.

The clause of exclusion also allowed state officials to bypass unionists and go directly to the rank and file. The Federal Labor Law gave the state the right to intervene in disputes between groups of workers vying for the control of a collective contract. Workers had the right to ask the labor authorities to conduct a survey to determine which group was supported by the majority of workers and thereby entitled to a contract. Labor authorities had the power to decide whether the survey would be taken and controlled the process by which the responses were collected and counted.[17] Like the controls on union formation, this mechanism gave the PRI the capacity to wrest membership and negotiating power away from unions that stepped out of line. In addition, the provisions of the LFT and the PRI's dominance of the political system enabled the ruling party to expose previously protected labor leaders to voice and exit by workers. Burgess describes how the PRI could retain the loyalty of CTM leaders: "The threat of worker dissent worked paradoxically to reinforce the CTM's loyalty at the expense of its workers. The PRI could thus reach directly to base and turn rank and file against leaders." The institutions of Mexican corporatism could be used to protect unionists from the rank and file, bypass them if they were recalcitrant, or even empower and lure disaffected workers.[18]

Union leadership in Mexico had a variety of rewards with which to sanction workers. Unions were the ones who distributed company benefits to workers—benefits such as housing, scholarships, promotion, appointments to new jobs, loans, vacations, and transfers. De la Madrid used the leverage of social programs to gain support for the Pact, which as a formal institution was crucial to successful wage negotiations. To secure labor support, de la Madrid enacted constitutional reforms that formally recognized the union-owned enterprises and guaranteed workers access to adequate housing and health care, and through the Pact, he recognized and expanded the PRI's "social sector," measures that persuaded the CTM and the CT to endorse the pact. So the PRI, until 1993, pursued a dual strategy of reducing the CTM's influence while granting sufficient concessions to gain the CTM's cooperation on key issues.[19] A pattern, in fact, emerged whereby the PRI would compensate the CTM for declining wages by creating new social programs that allowed CTM officials to channel benefits to their union members, and although this did not improve the lot of most workers, it did maintain the loyalty of unionists, who, in exchange for these programs, continued to support the state-labor alliance despite the regime's reneging on historic commitments.

Because of government subsidies, in the 1991 midterm elections, the PRI experienced an electoral turnaround. The ruling party won over 60 percent of the vote. The PRD lost over four million votes, and PAN did not go beyond its "historic limit" of 18 percent of the national vote. The PRI had the resources to reward and sanction workers and leaders, extending and withdrawing inducements as Salinas saw fit. Salinas's technocrats in fact had granted new programs to the CTM leadership for distribution to rank and file but simultaneously retrenched programs already in the CTM's hands as a way to weaken these leaders. The loyalty of Mexican labor leaders in1991 showed that they were in an institutional context that made staying with the PRI the most rational choice; while some workers found it more rational to defect, leaders opted to stay, defend their threatened organizational and political prerogatives, and fight for their position in the governing coalition. Salinas eventually rescinded his threats to reform the Federal Labor Law and Article 123, and his technocrats pursued other mechanisms for deregulating relations between labor and management. As long as the Labor Code was not altered, the CTM agreed to support NAFTA and production restructuring on the shop floor. By insuring that patronage kept flowing, albeit selectively, and the Federal Labor Law—the structural source of labor's power—was preserved, Salinas succeeded in making "exit" an unattractive alternative for unionists and even for the rank and file.

And many unionists drew a distinction between the economic program that Salinas was set on pursuing and that they could grudgingly accept and the political or structural aspects of the new unionism, which they opposed as a fundamental threat.

Disorganizing Labor

Reformers successfully used rents, institutions, and force to divide and weaken labor elite. Many labor leaders moderated their demands and controlled the rank and file in exchange for legal, financial, and political benefits from the state. The opportunity to hold electoral office was critical in insuring the loyalty of the CTM's leadership. While posturing radically then moderately for wage increases in de la Madrid's reform package, the CTM was also negotiating for more party candidacies for the midterm elections of July 1985. Realizing the importance of these political benefits to the control of labor, de la Madrid rejected some of his advisors' calls to do away with party sectors; to maintain the state-labor bargain, he granted the CTM a greater share of candidacies. These selectively distributed rewards helped prevent collective action against reform.

Mexican state elites' administrative control over union formation allowed for the exclusion, isolation, and control of dissident unions and in some cases the reorganization of unions into newly established confederations. Salinas was not soft on recalcitrant unionists. He crushed strikes and purged unionists who were anti-reform, whether they were genuinely pro–rank-and-file or simply charrista power brokers. Salinas manipulated the labor movement. He favored rival confederations (CROC, CROM, Revolutionary Confederation of Workers and Peasants, and the Mexican Regional Labor Confederation) in their unionization drives. In exchange, these confederations opposed the CTM's general labor strike proposal, accepted wage increases smaller than those sought by the CTM leadership, and publicly endorsed the state's reform agenda.

In 1990, Salinas appointed the pro-reform Hernandez Juarez to head the new Federation of Unions of Goods and Services Companies (FESEBES), a national organization that was to form the organizational nucleus of the new unionism. Accomodationist unionists were placed in the newly formed FESEBES, and the organization was used to counter and weaken the older labor centrals. Although Fidel Velazquez personally attacked the fledgling federation as having no right to exist and accused Hernandez Juarez of trying to divide the Labor Congress (CT), there was no unified response from organized labor to the "new unionism." The Labor Congress was internally divided over how and if leaders should defend rank-and-file interests.[20] The "New Unionism," with its emphasis on union representativeness, threatened the charros and their undemocratic privileges and control of benefits. Many leaders knew their political clout would diminish if the labor struggle shifted from the national federation level to the firm level.

As mentioned, during the Salinas sexenio, the CTM and other labor confederations in the Labor Congress abandoned the militant rhetoric of the de la Madrid era and moved to a more cooperative stance under Salinas, acquiescing to economic policy and focusing their energy on impeding any measures that would challenge the structural power of labor, particularly any effort to change existing federal labor law or to eliminate labor's privileged position as a sector within the ruling party. The state's administrative controls on union formation and strikes played a critical role in controlling the labor elite, but so did the PRI's extraordinary co-optive capacity. An analysis of the PRI structure—with its myriad institutions and rents—can also help explain why Mexico's leading labor organizations failed to oppose structural adjustment more aggressively.

Party Reform and Neoliberalism

For a moment, Salinas considered replacing the long-standing system of corporatist interest representation, based on the official labor and peasant organizations, with a territorially based system that strengthened the PRI at the state and local levels and that sought to build a more direct relationship between the PRI and individual citizens. In reality, deep institutional reforms were needed to increase the party's legitimacy and insure a popular support base. Thousands of new cadres were needed to organize members at the grassroots level, to develop new registration and membership lists, to build linkages to new (unincorporated) groups and community-based organizations, and to make the candidate selection process at the local level more competitive. Since reformers were not capable politically or financially of such far-reaching reforms, they undertook more limited reforms of party mechanisms and electoral rules again to weaken unionists and draw the middle classes to counter labor's clout. Salinas's team tried to reform the PRI's structure on three fronts: in its internal structure, support base, and recruiting patterns.[71] Under the new territorial strategy, local party officials gained more voice in the selection of lower- and mid-level candidates and functionaries, although candidates for federal deputies, senators, and the presidency were still selected in Mexico City by high-ranking PRI and government officials.

Electoral reform was undertaken along with internal party reforms to make the party competitive and to broaden its support base. Since the PRI was established in the 1930s, Mexico had changed from a rural to an urban society. Myriad urban constituencies including the middle class and informal worker groups were excluded from the party sectors and demanded political inclusion. Like his predecessor, Salinas did briefly ponder a plan to decorporatize the party altogether and move from a sectoral to a territorial organization. State officials were considering whether to completely exclude labor or reform the state-labor bargain to alter the terms of inclusion. In 1992, incoming PRI president Gerrardo Borrego Estrada announced a reorganization of the ruling party, which would have dramatically reduced the importance of organized labor. The purpose of this restructuring was to broaden the base of the support for the party and to make the party attractive to the middle classes. The sectoral groups of the PRI (the worker, peasant, and popular sectors) would be replaced by three "great movements": the Popular Territorial Front, the National Citizens' Front, and the Worker-Peasant Pact. Not only would the labor sector no longer be one of the main organizations of the party, but it would be merged with the peasant sector. Obviously, proposals were strongly opposed by labor.[22]

Salinas's technocrats realized party democratization could weaken the influence of unions, but they also knew that the PRI could ill afford to lose the support and cooperation of labor. Since the PRD was the greatest threat to their project, Mexican reformers tried to shape a party system in which the PRI would find its greatest electoral challenge and opposition in a regionally based PAN; reformers could then loosen the PRI's links to labor but not risk a mass defection of workers to the PRD and a derailment of the neoliberal project. In drafting new electoral laws, state officials wanted to insure a PRI victory, with the PAN coming in second. The reformist faction of the PRI agreed to cooperate with factions of the PAN to neutralize the PRD. Both sides supported neoliberal reform and believed in political liberalization only insofar as it did not endanger economic liberalization. The new electoral reform law reflected this perspective. So long as the PRI remained the largest party and could win at least 35 percent of the vote, the new electoral law did not threaten its dominance.

The 1994 Election

After chipping away at the CTM's power and weakening charros through much of his tenure, as the 1994 election approached, Salinas, expecting to rely on the confederation's ability to deliver votes, began to restore privileges and benefits he had withdrawn. Privatization, after all, had been successfully achieved despite labor's protest. And political support was now needed from labor. The CTM's leaders had also calculated accordingly and not "exited" but kept defending their organizational benefits knowing that the PRI would not abandon its labor allies with a presidential succession on the horizon. In 1993 and 1994, as elections approached, the PRI retreated from its plans for an "alliance restructuring" and began to shore up the old corporatist bargain. Major plans to reform the PRI were abandoned. The party structure could not be sacrificed for the unpredictable game of democracy, particularly since the technocrats' political survival rested on the PRI's hegemony. An internal struggle within the PRI or among rival parties could jeopardize Salinas's political-economic project.

So despite announcements of plans to "citizenize" the party through a major restructuring of its organizations, the PRI ended up not only reaffirming the role of the sectors but reinstating some of the privileges withdrawn in 1990. Patronage was again deployed strategically. Just weeks before the PRI assembly, the CTM negotiated an accord with the president's office to appoint a close associate of Fidel Velazquez as the gubernatorial candidate in Nayorit, thereby restoring the CTM's quota of three governorships per sexenio. At the PRI's XVI Assembly in March 1993, the ruling party accepted a CTM proposal to reinstate the sectoral posts that had been eliminated from the PRI's Executive Committee in 1990.[23] The CTM was slowly regaining its hegemonic position within the labor movement.

As the election approached, Salinas also distanced himself from the FESEBES and sought the support of more established organizations like the CTM. Despite the loss of some political influence, the CTM still claimed a membership of five million workers organized into eleven thousand affiliated unions, and, to a degree, control of the election process depended on labor's support. The Chiapas rebellion and the assassinations of 1994 made labor's collaboration even more important for the succession process. Thus, during the 1994 elections, CTM leaders closed ranks with Salinas and the PRI. In accordance a with decades-old practice, the CTM and its affiliates offered financial incentives for workers to attend PRI rallies, threatened CTM members if they failed to vote, and published an ad in the national media encouraging workers to support the PRI's candidate, Ernesto Zedillo. Soon after he won, Zedillo appointed the CTM's secretary of education, Juan Millan, to the position of secretary general of the PRI, the highest position in the ruling party ever held by a labor leader.

It is important to note that while maintaining the PRI's basic traits and structure, Salinas did introduce reforms to increase the PRI's electoral competitiveness and enhance the legitimacy of the election results. In 1993, legislation increased the size of the federal Senate and guaranteed that opposition parties would control at least half of its seats. The legislation also placed limits on campaign financing and permitted independent verification of voter registration procedures and national election observers. With the Chiapas rebellion, Salinas came under greater domestic and international pressure to further political liberalization, and in May 1994 new reforms were enacted limiting direct government and PRI influence over the Federal Electoral Institute, banning the use of public funds and government personnel to benefit the PRI, allowing foreign visitors to witness federal elections, and establishing a special prosecutor to pursue those accused of electoral fraud. The electoral reform laws introduced in 1990, 1993, and 1994 were intended to establish a more balanced playing field for intraparty competition, but in practice the PRI retained considerable advantages over opposition parties.[24] And state officials and PRI elites still had control over nonelectoral forms of mass participation with institutions like Pronasol.

The National Solidarity Program: "An Institutional Innovation?"

Pronasol has been described as an "umbrella organization aimed at developing health, education, nutrition, housing, employment, infrastructure, and other productive projects to benefit the 17 million Mexicans who live in extreme poverty."[25] The program was the linchpin of Salinas's coalitional strategy aimed at enlisting lower and middle class support for economic reform. The political objective of this enormous antipoverty bureaucracy was two-fold: to reverse the PRI's declining electoral strength and to develop new linkages between the government and the urban and rural poor who had voted for Cardenas in 1988. As mentioned above, while rewarding and protecting loyal unionists, Salinas was also wresting control of social programs from resistant unionists and delivering the benefits directly to workers. The benefits were often delivered via Pronasol. When PRI officials resisted his economic policies, Salinas used Pronasol's state and local committees to circumvent the PRI, going directly to voters and asserting the president's authority over the party's machinery as well as state governments. Pronasol tried to reshape state-society relations and to expand the state's social base by gaining the vote of low-income urban and rural countries where the PRD and leftist independent popular movements were gaining control. As head of the SPP, Salinas had realized that the traditional methods of federal government spending in poor areas were not generating sufficient support for the PRI and that the links between government agencies and different social groups had to be tightened. Through Pronasol, Salinas's team sought to draw in the lower middle class and urban informal sector into the PRI's coalition, even to incorporate groups and political elites sympathetic to Cardenas. Pronasol delegates often pressured independent urban and rural popular organizations to join the PRI.

Pronasol is an example of how state elites can use institutions to alter the policy preferences of citizens and gain the control and support of alienated constituencies. While a number of scholars have analyzed the objectives and functions of Pronasol, few have described the institutional origins of this "institutional innovation." How was Salinas able to establish such a massive bureaucracy seemingly overnight? Did he make use of preexisting institutions? Given Pronasol's success in mobilizing lower class support for economic reform, this question is laden with implications for other countries; in particular, why have state elites in Egypt been unable to create a similar patronage machine? The conventional wisdom holds that Salinas realized the need for a welfare policy to compensate groups hurt by adjustment and founded this huge bureaucracy on the first day of his presidency to fund regional development programs in four strategic areas—food support, production, social services, and infrastructure. According to Salinas, by November 1993, Pronasol had over 150 thousand local committees throughout Mexico, and Pronasol projects had been started in more than 95 percent of the country's 2,378 municipalities.[26] But this depiction of Pronasol as an overnight creation is inaccurate. An analysis of the institutional lineage of Pronasol shows this successful program to be the result of two decades of institutional engineering; Salinas built upon administrative reforms introduced by Lopez Portillo and de la Madrid and utilized the PRI's corporatist sectors and the Mexican state's local and municipal branches.

Pronasol and Privatization

Pronasol helped forge a new base of support for the regime and its economic program. Since labor was among the most adversely affected by privatization, Pronasol directly channeled its "compensatory flows" to workers and poor consumers in an effort to tie the disaffected citizens to the state rather than to other political organizations. Salinas expressly sought the support of alienated workers and anti-reform unionists by claiming that money from privatization would be used for Pronasol; in 1991, he claimed that funds from privatization would provide one billion dollars for antipoverty spending.[27] He tried to gather support for the sale of Mexicana de Aviacion by saying proceeds from the sale would be used to provide electricity to five hundred thousand residents of Mexico's poorest regions.[28] Thus not only did Pronasol generate support for economic reform, but divestiture is what insured the functioning of Pronasol. Much of the funding for Pronasol came from revenues generated by privatization and tax reform and Salinas's contingency fund, also established from SOE sales. While government austerity had sharply reduced the resources that could be pumped through the PRI's national patronage system, Pronasol delivered more than fifteen billion dollars in benefits to some twenty-five million Mexicans.[29] Pronasol channeled patronage to the electorally crucial urban slums where Cardenistas had won much support in 1988, helping the ruling party recoup votes lost. In contrast to its 1988 performance, in 1991 the PRI won overwhelmingly in 121 out of 123 municipalities. In 1988, the PRI had lost all subdistricts; in 1991, it won all back.[30]

Unlike previous subsidy programs to which all citizens had access, Pronasol employed a more selective, targeted system partly because of fiscal stringency but also reflecting the regime's strategy to incorporate select groups. One aspect of Pronasol's modus operandi that generated local support was Salinas's insistence on local participation in projects, working with "natural representatives" at the community level. Salinas understood that participation not only insured Pronasol's "accountability and effectiveness" but also helped generate political support for government-sponsored programs and larger economic projects.[31] This coalitional strategy of *concertación* with independent groups proved crucial to the PRI's recovery. These organizations surrendered a degree of autonomy in being incorporated, but they gained institutional recognition and a channel to express their demands.

Pronasol helped mobilize support for market reforms in the agricultural sector. The National Indigenous Institute, which distributed Pronasol funds, helped garner support for the 1992 reform of Article 27, which called for the privatization of ejido land, the tenure system that was at the heart of the state's postrevolutionary bargain with the peasantry. The institute organized meetings between peasant leaders and Salinas, with the understanding that Pronasol funds would be forthcoming if they supported the proposed land reform.[32] As with labor, reformers weakened and bypassed corporatist peasant organizations. By reducing services to the rural sector, Salinas's technocrats weakened the National Confederation of Peasants and strengthened independent peasant organizations, undermining the support of CNC leaders in the eyes of the rank and file.[33] As with divestiture, these reforms imposed great hardship on Mexican peasants, especially those in the southern regions of Mexico who lost access to state subsidies. Procampo was another program associated with Pronasol, established in 1993 to shore up support in rural areas, and it also tried to "weaken the old corporatism" by disrupting preexisting alliances between bureaucratic actors and different social groups and building new ties between the state and societal actors.[34]

The Origins of Pronasol

The origins of Pronasol's supposedly fifteen thousand newly established solidarity committees used to distribute benefits and provide incentives have not been sufficiently explored. Pronasol actually built upon the infrastructure of previous welfare programs, redirecting preexisting state and party institutions to reach different constituencies. Discussing the structure of Pronasol, Guevara Sangines notes that Pronasol "relied on a complex network of relationships among different government levels and social organizations" and granted decision-making power to authorities at the municipal and community levels that "had been virtually neglected over time despite their constitutional powers."[35] But Pronasol differed from previous welfare programs, such as Echeverria's Caminos de Mano de Obra and de la Madrid's General Coordination of the Plan for Depressed Zones and Marginal Groups (COPLAMAR) which distributed benefits at various levels of the hierarchical state-party and trade union structure. Pronasol linked local communities directly to the presidential office—"unmediated by corporatist structures."[36]

Analysts have overlooked the continuity between Pronasol and its direct precursors from the 1960s, National Company of Popular Foodstuffs (CONASUPO), Integrated Rural Development Program (PIDER), and the Mexican Food System (SAM) and COPLAMAR. Alan Knight has rightly observed that "one of Solidarity's successes . . . has been its capacity to cover its trail, to deny its political paternity,"[37] and that "Pronasol—as a federal government initiative not necessarily welcome to local elites—thus has a long pedigree."[38] Those stressing the program's "newness" point to Salinas's personal commitment and frequent visits to Pronasol centers as a distinction between him and de la Madrid. But de la Madrid performed similar tours distributing land titles and inaugurating urban services in low-income settlements. Luis Echeverria had his "open-door policies" aimed at building support for the presidency rather than welfare agencies.[39] Likewise, Pronasol's system of coparticipation touted as innovative was also not new. As early as 1971, government programs, such as Operacion Hormiga and Ejercito del Trabajo, which installed water and sewage system in the state of Mexico, collaborated with municipalities and made use of residents' labor. Salinas's team, it seems, deliberately presented Pronasol as a break from the past, a radical antipoverty program that bypassed the country's corrupt patronage machine and aimed to help the poor and gain their support. Scholars have also cast doubt on the claim that 150 thousand Solidarity committees were "created" by November 1993. As Varley observes, "The most credible explanation for 150,000 such committees . . . is that many of them existed on paper only or that they represented a grafting of the solidarity label onto existing organizational structures."[40]

Unlike its predecessors, Pronasol circumvented established institutional routes for welfare programs and was run directly from the president's office. But like the technocrats who used the party to restructure the party, Pronasol officials also made use of PRI sectoral institutions. While it dealt directly with independent groups, Pronasol often funneled resources through loyal Pristas in municipal governments. Pronasol funds created the Solidarity Institute to produce more reform-minded peasant and worker leaders. Pronasol was also distinguished by its urban bias—despite its declared focus on rural and indigenous groups. The successive programs of the '60s and '70s were essentially rural programs. If Pronasol was a strictly anti-poverty program and not an electoral/coalitional strategy, a rural bent to the program would have been expected, given that 70 percent of extremely poor households in Mexico were in rural areas. But in practice Pronasol had an urban tilt: this was the result of Salinas's realization that between the '60s and '80s Mexico had become urbanized, and the PRI, which had presented itself as a "party of the rural population," had been doing poorly in urban areas, whereas the opposition parties were doing increasingly well in cities; a similar dynamic was occurring in Egypt, except that the NDP never had active electoral support in urban areas, only passive quiescence. Critics now concede that although the program gained votes for the PRI in targeted areas, it did not reincorporate all the rural poor who had left the CNC in disaffection. Pronasol funds did not compensate for the withdrawal of benefits and technical assistance, the drop of international coffee prices, and the end of ejido land tenure. Local peasant leaders and their followers simply left the CNC and set up their own peasant organizations. Upon assuming office, Zedillo replaced Pronasol with Progresa, a program targeting the very poor, also believed to have been used to pressure poor rural voters to vote for the PRI in the 2000 election.[41]

Bureaucratic Reform and Pronasol

Pronasol would not have been possible without reforms within the state bureaucracy. The early 1970s saw the establishment of a coordinating structure called the Committees for the Socioeconomic Development of the States (COPRODES) that consulted federal and state agencies in the formulation and implementation of plans. Later, another agency, the Convenios Unicos de Coordinación (CUC) was introduced to coordinate pacts between the federal, state, and municipal authorities about project priorities and means of financing. The Ministry of Planning and Budget (SPP), established later, also used the CUC committees to funnel money to state governments—carrying out federally dictated projects. As Secretary of SPP in 1981, de la Madrid reformed the coordinating mechanisms further placing COPRODES (renamed COPLADES [Planning Committees for State Development]) under the coordination of state governors. As secretary of SPP, Salinas strengthened various interagency programs that Lopez Portillo had administered out of the presidency. Salinas grouped these programs into a "regular budget line" called "Regional Development," which had "programmatic elements that later evolved into Solidarity."[42]

By 1988, the SPP had emerged as a powerful agency handling budgets and, through its control of CUC-COPROME, wielding influence over the state and local governments. Pronasol, established in 1988 by Carlos Rojas in the SPP, was an offshoot of Regional Development and was partly administered through the SPP's field offices in the states. As Alan Knight remarks, "many existing programs (e.g. road-building) have simply received the imprimatur of Solidarity."[43] Among the Pronasol programs that were preexisting and simply altered for Pronasol's purposes were Alimentacion y Abaasto (Food and Supply), Electrificacion Rural y Urbana (Rural and Urban Electrification), Urbanizacion (Urbanization), Vivienda (Housing), Infrastructura Educativa (Education Infrastructure), and Agua Potable (Potable Water). Pronasol technocrats came from the team and budget apparatus led by SPP and had experience with grassroots-oriented programs from Regional Development. Salinas chose Carlos Tello, head of SPP under Lopez Portillo, to be Pronasol's first coordinator. Pronasol, in short, did not appear overnight with Salinas's ascension to power but was the product of two decades of administrative reform and institution building.

Pronasol served as a new "neo-corporatist" mechanism for political negotiation that often sidestepped labor and peasant organizations and was intended to go directly to the base—to replace the state institutions. Recent studies affirm Pronasol and Progresa's success in currying electoral support but are less sanguine about the effectiveness of such targeted programs in reducing extreme poverty and regional disparities. Laurell concludes that targeted programs like Pronasol and Progresa that reflect the neoliberal belief that states should only intervene when market and family networks fail, and should do so selectively and in response to community demands, proved less effective than Mexico's previous social programs that were run out of public institutions (not out of the president's office) and were broadly available to poor citizens. The Pronasol budget, for instance, was relatively smaller than that of earlier programs. Pronasol's budget increased from 0.3 percent of GDP in 1989 to 0.8 percent in 1994, but that was still less than the sum allocated for poverty alleviation in 1983; the crisis of 1994–95 would lead to a further 15 percent cut in social expenditures.[44] As the ejido system was dismantled, inequality increased, and Pronasol did little to reverse entrenched poverty. More significantly, some studies now show that correlations between regions with high poverty indices and regions receiving Pronasol funds are "very low"; in some cases an "inverse correlation" appears between Pronasol resources and the HDI (Human Development Index) by state, indicating that Pronasol funds tended to concentrate in states with a high HDI. Some scholars explain this fact noting that the most organized and vocal Mexican groups were not necessarily the poorest, while others see this as further evidence that Pronasol was intended primarily as a means of political control and electoral patronage, rather than a poverty reduction program.[45]

The financial crisis of 1994–95 and the political turmoil following the devaluation of the peso (the Chiapas uprising and the assassination of PRI presidential candidate Luis Donaldo Colosio) triggered the largest plunge in Mexico's GDP since the Great Depression of the 1930s and led to a widespread repudiation of Salinas's economic project.[46] As it became evident that market reforms had not reduced poverty, generated employment, or sparked growth (comparable to the rates achieved from the 1940s through the 1970s), members of Congress, organized labor, and other groups grew loudly critical of Salinas's economic project, pointing to the increased income inequality, violence, and insecurity and the corruption and lack of transparency in the privatization process. Critics noted that some of the privatized enterprises were less productive and efficient than when they were state owned; the government had to step in and bail out insolvent enterprises in the mining and sugar sectors.[47] Salinas's institutional maneuvering and the Solidarity discourse had contained dissent and persuaded important sections of the Mexican population to support economic reforms, which many had hoped would bring a higher standard of living. But the financial meltdown dashed these hopes and had a devastating impact on the PRI's electoral performance. The PRI lost its majority in the Federal Chamber of Deputies in 1997 and would subsequently lose control of the presidency in 2000. The PAN emerged from the 1997 race with six state governorships, and PRD candidate Cuauhtémoc Cárdenas would go on to win the mayorship of Mexico City. Following the 1997 debacle, prominent PRI leaders left the ruling party to establish their own movements.[48]

The crisis also eroded labor's support for the regime. Several labor unions declared their opposition to neoliberal policies. Some unions left the Labor Congress, claiming it was controlled by the state, and joined FORO (Trade Unionism Facing Crisis and the Nation), a new umbrella organization that declared independence from both the state and the party. In 1997, a larger organization, the National Union of Workers, emerged uniting breakaway unions and calling for labor rights, greater autonomy, higher salaries, and an end to corporatism.[49] Because of declining support from labor, Zedillo after 1997 stopped using political pacts for fear that labor might not abide by the Pact's stipulations and undermine business confidence. The privatization of the ejido system, at a time when peasant groups were hoping for the redistribution of land, similarly undermined rural support for the state and led to political violence. The reform of Article 27, seen widely as the government's reneging on its protection of peasant rights, combined with the fall in international coffee prices and the withdrawal of technical assistance from the state coffee institution, INMECAFE, all helped spark the political violence in Chiapas, Oaxaca, and Guerrero.[50] Pronasol's targeted assistance proved woefully inadequate in reducing poverty, or compensating peasant hurt by reforms.

If the crisis of 1982 led to the Mexican state reversing course—from import substitution to export-led growth—the 1994 crisis led policy elites to forge ahead with neoliberal reforms. As *Privatization International* reported in early 1995, "Mexico's currency crisis has given new urgency to the government's plans to privatize several key infrastructure areas."[51] Zedillo's emergency plan, unveiled in January 1995, called for further divestitures, including the privatization of Mexican toll roads, railroads, airports, and seaports—by selling operating rights to the private sector.[52] But while deepening privatization, Zedillo also began to pursue political reforms in an effort to defuse public anger. The reforms introduced in 1996, which made the Federal Electoral Institute independent of the government, paved the way for the PRI's defeat in 1997. That defeat in turn led to even greater pressures for political liberalization, and in 1999 Zedillo did away with the practice of the *dedazo*, whereby an incumbent president could appoint his successor, and the presidential candidate Francisco Labastida Ochoa was selected through a primary process. Political liberalization unleashed greater opposition to Zedillo's economic policies. Since 1988, the PRI had held a majority in the Senate and House of Deputies, which by and large endorsed the privatization process. But the crisis had galvanized opposition in Congress to press for further political reform. In trying to privatize PEMEX petrochemical companies, the government faced resistance from PEMEX workers, the PRD, and even PRI congressmen. At the seventeenth PRI convention, delegates issued a resolution against the privatization of PEMEX petrochemical companies, proclaiming the party's intention to defend the entire oil sector.[53] The government had to back down from offering investors an 80 percent stake in PEMEX to 49 percent, foregoing up to $1.5 billion in revenue.[54]

But the financial crisis and the political backlash did not threaten the state's economic project. Zedillo pursued political reforms to distance himself from Salinas's administration, to gain the support of a public dispirited by Mexico's declining economic fortunes and the Chiapas uprising, but also because he was confident that the economic opening and neoliberal policies were not at risk of reversal; trade liberalization had been locked in by the NAFTA agreement, and the regime had the support of PAN and the business community, so that granting Congress some influence over economic policy was not risky. Despite the House's tinkering with Zedillo's proposed budget and value-added tax cut and labor and Congress's successful blocking of the divestiture of the electricity sector, political reforms, as Shadlen states, did not derail or reverse "the general thrust of the neo-liberal economic model."[55] Despite the political violence and labor discontent, the public sector had been restructured, labor flexibilization achieved, and the regime's coalition reconstituted post-factum to include the private sector and a weakened labor movement.

Mexico's experiment with state reform and economic restructuring proved more far-reaching and transformative than elsewhere in Latin America. In Argentina, state officials between 1989 and 1995 managed to contain worker and Peronist opposition to market reforms, but as unemployment reached 18.4 percent in 1995, labor protest spread. A general strike occurred in 1996 protesting structural adjustment, followed by two more general strikes in 1997, after which Peronist politicians demanded a government response. Unlike their Mexican counterparts, Argentine reformers lacked the institutions with which to co-opt, contain, and manipulate opposition; in fact, efforts at co-optation backfired since "the regime's strategy of labor containment afforded collaborationist labor leaders sufficient input into the policy process that they were able to stall labor flexibilization and alter other reforms such as social security."[56] Reform continued in Mexico despite the crisis and backlash: "Between 1994 and 2000, Mexico continued to lead the developing world in privatization, opening up basic infrastructure such as natural gas, the generation of electricity, satellite communications, ports, airports, and railroads to private investment."[57]

In conclusion, Mexican corporatism granted labor a position different from that inherited by organized labor in Egypt (or in other Latin American countries) that made it more rational for many unionists and workers to work within the parameters of the historic alliance than to defect to opposition arties. While some union leaders opposed neoliberalism and confronted the state calling for greater autonomy, most union leaders cooperated strategically with Salinas, accepted neoliberal policies, but defended the labor law and fought to preserve the old political structures. This decision on the part of labor leaders allowed state elites to neutralize labor opposition. The Egyptian ruling party never made labor an institutional stakeholder in the same way, and workers in Egypt would be able to paralyze the privatization drive, not because of their organizational strength or because, as Bianchi argues, organized labor "captured" the very corporatist institutions meant to control it, but because Nasserist incorporation never engendered the institutional linkages that state elites could use to mobilize worker support for reform or, at least, contain opposition.

Mexican corporatism, in short, had granted organized labor a position within the ruling coalition that made it more rational to work within the system than to "exit," a decision that ultimately enabled reformers to neutralize labor opposition. This situation is different from Egypt where labor had a different historic position that made it more rational for workers to "exit" the state-labor alliance when the reform process began. As the following chapters illustrate, Egyptian labor was never made an institutional stakeholder as in Mexico, and ironically when reforms began, the Egyptian state's passive inclusion of workers proved ineffective as a mechanism of control.

As in Mexico where some technocrats and PRI figures considered shedding the corporatist sectors and completely excluding labor, a similar debate is now taking place in Egypt with NDP officials considering ways to tighten or loosen organized labor's links to the state-party organization. Some Egyptian reformers think that the incorporation of labor was never complete and that labor needs to be brought in as an active partner and institutional stakeholder. Others envision a refurbished, less generous corporatist bargain, while others are calling for the total exclusion of labor from the ruling coalition and allowing the market to decide prices and wages. But Egyptian elites lack the economic and institutional resources of their Mexican counterparts (the ETUF, for example, does not command five million members like the CTM), so rather than rely on moribund corporatist institutions, state elites are trying to use electoral mechanisms to reshape the political landscape, to insure the NDP's dominance, and to allow for the implementation of reforms, even if it that means excluding labor. Mubarak's technocrats have also attempted to build an Egyptian Pronasol, but the Mexican program has a long institutional genealogy that, as Egyptian technocrats are discovering, is not so easy to replicate. Pronasol made use of a preexisting institutional context that does not exist in Egypt. Pronasol also boasts an urban bias, while the Social Fund in Egypt is more rural in focus. The Egyptian Social Fund for various reasons will not be able to reshape state-society relations the way Pronasol did. Mexican reformers were also able to enlist the support of an estranged private sector and overcome the resistance of small and medium businesses and their allies within the state.

6

Bureaucratic Reform and State-Business Relations

While containing labor opposition, Mexican officials realized that their economic project could not succeed without the support of capital; the private sector's backing was needed in the provision of public goods, particularly public investment. An acute fiscal crisis prompted Mexican reformers to reach out to private capital and to pursue policies that would gain businesses' support. In this chapter, I explain how reforming elites in Mexico would draw the support of big business for privatization through strategic institutional reforms and by accompanying the divestiture program with price-wage controls and trade liberalization.

If privatization required reformers to relegate labor to a secondary position in the ruling coalition, Salinas's rapprochement with big business similarly involved reducing the role of small and medium business, which, as a coalition partner, had historically relied on state protection. State officials in effect used big business as intermediaries to control the behavior of less powerful business actors. The organizational capacity of Mexican business associations, particularly big business's ability to coordinate sectoral and regional interests through peak associations and to monitor the compliance of small businesses, facilitated the implementation of the Pact. The strength of Salinas's coalition-building project was not only that he managed to gain the support of big business and foreign capital for an economic program that gored the interests of his erstwhile coalition partners—labor and small and medium business—but that he managed to retain the support of these groups and when necessary could rely on their leadership as political intermediaries to help implement policies.

Market reforms cannot be implemented by a state without the reform of key bureaucratic institutions. This chapter also shows how underpinning the rapprochement between the Mexican state and private sector was a process of administrative reform and a centralization of power within the bureaucracy, which allowed reformers to impose their policy preferences on the rest of the state. Like economic reform, bureaucratic reform is a contentious process that creates winners and losers both in civil society and within the state apparatus. The process of bureaucratic reform in Mexico spanned three presidencies and involved a protracted institutional struggle between the Ministry of Finance and the Ministry of Programming and Budget (SPP), on the one hand, and the Ministry of Commerce (SECOFI) and the Ministry of Energy (Mines and Parastate Industry [SEMIP]), on the other. External rents play an important role in these battles: as long as bureaucrats in the statist camp were controlling state revenues, such as oil earnings, they could impede divestiture. But as loans from foreign banks became a significant source of revenue under Echeverria and Lopez Portillo, officials negotiating with foreign banks became more influential and gained leverage within the state. Increased access to funds combined with administrative reforms and a recruitment strategy, which brought in more market-oriented bureaucrats with ties to the private sector and IFIs, allowed the neoliberal technocrats to trump the statist camp. Bureaucratic reforms also helped strengthen the Mexican presidency and concentrated power in agencies that shielded elite technocrats from anti-reformist pressures within the state and society. The ruling party's institutional resources again proved crucial: reformers used the party structure to protect themselves from societal groups by diverting interest group pressures away from the state bureaucracy and into the party.

Mexico has been touted as an exemplar of "neoliberal" reform and praised by reformers across the developing world. Yet recent analyses of that country's adjustment experience show that the state intervened aggressively in the economy, disorganizing labor and distributing rents to political allies. The Mexican state's "embeddedness" allowed it to intervene extensively in the economy, subcontracting the provision of public goods and even the implementation of privatization to allies in the business community. The Mexican state's maneuverability was aided by the institution of the *sexenio*—the sexennial turnover of political elites—and the *dedazo*—the president's right to appoint a successor. Both of these institutions played a role in the initiation and continuation of bureaucratic reform and in checking popular opposition to Salinas's economic restructuring program. The elections, albeit flawed, combined with the regularized turnover of political elites provided the authoritarian regime with a degree of democratic legitimacy, but more importantly, flexibility and responsivity that allowed the regime to restructure the economy with the collaboration of powerful social actors.

State-Business Relations on the Eve of Reform

On the eve of privatization, relations between the Mexican state and the private sector were anything but harmonious. Mexico's ISI strategy, as in Egypt, had created a small, dependent private sector that relied on the state for protection from imports and subsidies for water and electricity and subsidized credit through NAFINSA, the state development bank. Small and medium businesses were part of the PRI's coalition benefiting from subsidies and protectionist policies and lobbying successfully for policies that often ran against the interests of big business. Labor elites, who had benefited from ISI, often sided with small business leaders in opposing trade liberalization. Relations with big business were particularly strained. From the 1940s onward, the government and private sector did cooperate, but by the 1970s this alliance came under stress as a balance of payments problem developed. When the oil crisis of 1973 began to slow Mexico's economic performance, the private sector protested state expansion. Business responded to Echeverria's devaluation of the peso in 1976 with capital flight.

The windfalls from the oil boom of 1976–82 only exacerbated Mexico's economic problems. The government used oil funds to maintain growth rates and stability, but by 1982 Mexico had an enormous debt, a balance of payments crisis, a debt-ridden public sector, and an uncompetitive manufacturing sector. When the oil boom ended, business began to transfer capital abroad, criticizing the government for excessive public spending and overly generous contracts to labor. In response to business's "antisocial" behavior, Lopez Portillo nationalized banks in September 1982, hoping that the government would be able to stem capital flight and regain control over the national financial system. But the bank nationalization further alienated big business, and massive capital flight followed.

When de la Madrid assumed office in December 1982, Mexico signed an austerity agreement with the IMF to reduce inflation and rectify the balance of payments and to fundamentally restructure the economy so as to reduce the country's dependence on petroleum exports, liquidate the public sector, and promote exports. By the mid-1980s, Mexico's public deficit averaged 13 percent of GDP, and debt service rose to half of government revenue. Oil revenues constituted more than a third of the government's revenues, so that with the sharp fall of oil prices in 1986 the Mexican state suddenly found itself without the funds needed to maintain its expansionary policies.[1] Efforts by the government to boost private sector confidence, though, could stem neither capital flight nor the PAN's growing electoral appeal among business and middle class constituencies. The government borrowed heavily from Mexican banks to cover deficits, but the state could not play the economic leadership role it had played historically, and state officials realized they would have to rely on the private sector for investment.

The Mexican private sector is not homogenous. It is made up of small and medium industrialists from the valley of Mexico who have historically been pro-regime and the larger business groups of Monterrey. The small and medium business interests, which emerged after the Great Depression and the Second World War, were represented by the National Chamber of Transformation Industries (CANACINTRA), which has always been pro-regime and for state intervention. The Monterrey group, which emerged before the Mexican revolution, is made up of large financial and industrial conglomerates and has always been critical of state intervention and the regime's pro-labor policies. The Monterrey businessmen were represented by the Business Coordinating Council (CCE), which was established in 1975 to protest Echeverria's policy of state expansionism. The Monterrey businessmen were also represented in the Employers' Confederation of the Mexican Republic (COPARMEX), the Confederation of Industrial Chambers (CONCAMIN), the Confederation of National Chambers of Commerce (CONCANACO), and the Mexican Bankers Association.

Businessmen were historically excluded from party politics as a formal sector, but their organizations, namely CONCAMIN and CONCANACO, were legally considered "consultative organs" of the government. All business associations, with the exception of CANACINTRA, which represented small and medium firms, opposed the bank nationalizations of 1982. In protest, businessmen began to lend their support to the PAN, starting with the elections of 1983 and 1986. CANACINTRA, in turn, called for reforms in the PRI and the creation of a business sector within the PRI.[2]

Although de la Madrid tried to regain business confidence by partially reversing the bank nationalization decisions and returning bank-owned stock to their owners, his anti-inflation measures displeased the private sector. Mexican business protested that it could not compete with foreign businesses since there was little credit available and interest rates were too high. In 1986, the industrialists of Monterrey—and the small and medium firms of CANACINTRA—threatened a moratorium on their payments to the Mexican banks if more credit was not made available. Mexican officials realized that for economic liberalization to succeed, reforms would have to be put together in a way that would attract business support; privatization was thus presented as part of a package that included trade liberalization and price-wage controls.

Privatization, Trade Liberalization, and the Pact

Representatives of small and medium-sized business were opposed to trade liberalization, but large industrialists represented in the CCE supported a gradual opening and slower removal of industrial protection. Big business also demanded changes in the 1970 Labor Code, including a fifteen-day limit on strikes followed by obligatory arbitration, a reduction in vacation time, greater flexibility in carrying out layoffs, and the abolition of the forty-hour week. The CCE argued that flight capital would only be reversed with the privatization of strategic public enterprises.[3] Privatization thus became a critical measure with which to restore the confidence of big business.

To gain the support of the private sector and impede collective action on the part of industrialists opposed to reform, state elites introduced the institution of the PECE, which used rents to alter the preferences of actors in the private sector. The functioning of this pact illustrates Mares's argument that leaders can use institutions to raise barriers to collective action and block opposition to government policies. By presenting trade liberalization and divestiture as part of the stabilization program that would reduce inflation and stabilize the economy, reformers split the private sector, marginalizing smaller and medium businesses and closing ranks with large industrialists and business organizations whose cooperation was crucial in monitoring compliance to the Pact's conditionalities.[4] *Concertación*, which involved regular meetings between business elites, state officials, and labor leaders to discuss policy implementation, was critical to the success of the Pact because it institutionalized information sharing, created channels of communication, and helped build consensus around reform.

Crucial to concertación's success was the strength and organization of the Mexican private sector. Business associations were pivotal in implementing neoliberal policies and enhanced the state's capacity for social control. The Mexican private sector was organized with the CCE, serving as an umbrella organization and coordinator for sectoral and regional organizations, and was big business's main representative in the Pact. The Pact coordinated expectations and responsibilities between representatives of the state, labor, and business; but, as analysts have observed, labor had little influence, and business had little choice but to participate.[5] Participation in the Pact was officially voluntary, but most firms participated because if they did not sign on their unions would not be bound by the terms of the Pact. Using the PRI's control over CANACINTRA, Salinas was able to impede small producers from mounting collective action or even expressing their opposition to neoliberal reforms.[6] The state signed numerous *concertación* agreements with large firms, groups of firms, or associations and created the tripartite Price and Monitoring Commission, which met weekly and relayed information from business to the state. These associations representing cement, retail, chemicals, and the auto industry were crucial in insuring the compliance of smaller businesses; for instance, the National Association of Self-Service and Department Stores controlled 35–60 percent of the retail market, and they bought only at prices authorized by the Department of Commerce. The state relied on large-scale retailers to monitor the pricing behavior of their suppliers. The cooperation between the Ministry of Commerce and ANTAD was critical. The channels of communication the Pact created between the state and powerful business elites helped in policing constituents and reduced the incentives to cheat on individual prices and wages.[7]

When faced with resistance from producers and retailers, state officials threatened leaders of smaller and medium-sized businesses with sanctions, audits, and loss of government contracts. The central role assigned to the CCE in negotiating the Pact was significant because it magnified the interests of large financial-industrial groups that were able to absorb the costs of economic liberalization. As Kaufman and coauthors write, "because power was concentrated within the business sector, the cooperative bargains struck by the business elites tended to restrict the economic and political options of their less powerful counterparts."[8] The state sometimes compensated the businesses hurt by trade liberalization: the NAFIN program, for instance, offered subsidized credit to select businessmen, and FICORCA provided exchange rate protection. But overall the way reform policies were packaged in the Pact tended to neutralize potential opponents in the private sector whose anxiety about a rapid trade opening was outweighed by their fear of inflation and their desire to build a positive relationship with the state.

The Pact's sharing of information helped business know the government's plans and in turn helped business with planning and investment. The Pact served as the institutional basis for rebuilding relations with the private sector, but the cementing of the state-business alliance also depended on informal, behind-the-scenes contacts between business leaders and bureaucratic elites. Salinas established close ties with leaders of the alienated Monterrey group, who benefited handsomely from the privatization process. His team established links with top representatives and jointly drafted proposals for the privatization of banks and the ejido sector, which also benefited the Monterrey businessmen. The then CCE president, Agustin Legoretta, boasted that despite the signatures of labor and peasant leaders the Pact was an accord between "the president in a presidential system with a comfortable little group of 300 people who make the economically important decisions in Mexico." He added that authorities understood that if inflation was running close to 1,000 percent, they risked losing power: "Since holding on to power is of paramount importance to them, they agreed to the conditions imposed by the 300 people comprising the business elite."[9]

The Pact gave big business a prominent role in politics. The private sector led many of the negotiations with the United States regarding NAFTA and even led the propaganda campaign for the free trade agreement in Mexico. State bureaucrats often relied on data and research gathered by the COECE (Coordinator for Foreign Trade Business Organizations) and member associations. Business leaders subsequently cooperated with the government on price control policy and trade liberalization. Salinas in turn allowed the private sector to invest in petrochemical products, the agricultural sector, the postal system, railways, the construction of roads, bus transportation, and airport and seaport services. During the reform process, business also gained a role in the PRI, with some claiming that Salinas had added a fourth sector—the entrepreneurial sector.

Luring Big Business

State elites pursued a number of policies to induce business support. De la Madrid used state funds to bail out indebted private enterprises. The Monterrey businesses benefited from the Trust for Foreign Exchange Protection (FICORCA), a program created in 1983 to provide subsidies to businesses facing exchange risks triggered by the external debt. Big business also appreciated the state's ability to deliver labor and supported the National Accord to Increase Productivity and Quality (ANEP) of 1992, which diminished labor's bargaining power by eliminating industry-wide labor negotiations, forcing labor to negotiate at the plant level and linking future wage raises to increases in productivity.[10] Divestiture, in general, was critical to securing the political and economic backing of the private sector: Salinas's privatization of 80 percent of 1,155 SOEs brought in more than twenty-one billion dollars, opening up sectors previously closed to business and increasing their market share in others. Salinas wooed foreign investment with high interest rates and a newly reformed foreign investment law in 1989. Between 1987 and 1991, private investment increased by more than 10 percent per year.[11]

As with the signing of the Pact, the process of privatization was exclusive, including only the representatives of the very large firms and conglomerates. Despite the Ministry of Finance's insistence on the transparency of the process, critics spoke of irregularities in the sales of AeroMexico (where the company was illegally declared bankrupt) and the Cananea Copper Mine (which was sold to Jorge Sarrea, whose offer was not the highest made in the public bidding). The directors of the Research Center for Free Enterprise (CISLE) denounced the "high-tech political clientelism" that governed the privatization process.[12] Thus, the process of privatization itself was used as a tool to build support. Preferential sales and market shares to cronies in the private sector helped garner business support but also allowed state elites to maintain control, if indirectly, over policy areas from which the state had withdrawn. Valdes Uglalde observes that "state power was also used to increase the weight and influence of certain segments of the bourgeoisie through preferential privatization. . . . Several SOEs were sold below market value or were relinquished by the state even when they operated in the black in order to induce long-term investment."[13]

Divestiture also led to an astonishing concentration of wealth. A small number of powerful businessmen, sometimes in partnership with foreign capital, bought most of the SOEs sold.[14] According to one report, by 1992, nine entrepreneurs accounted for 39 percent of nonbanking SOE purchases. Another account notes how one group in the financial sector got 83 percent of the shares of the SOEs.[15] Small and medium business protested the lack of transparency surrounding the sell-offs. CANACINTRA openly charged that the government was practicing favoritism and that smaller-sized firms were not able to make the purchases they wanted and demanded anti-monopoly policies. Leaders of big business responded that financial concentration was necessary for the success of export-led growth. Smaller business leaders through CANACINTRA also bemoaned the dearth of credit and the exclusivity of the privatization process. Salinas addressed their concerns by creating the Programa Nacionale de la Micro, Pequena y Mediana Industrias, in 1991, which provided aid to smaller businesses and is believed to have helped gain CANACINTRA's support for NAFTA.[16]

Discretionary presidential power, in short, proved critical to splitting the business community and preventing oppositional collective action. Heredia argues that "collective action by industrialists against the government proved extremely difficult to organize and sustain because government policy tended to exacerbate differences that naturally exist among private firms due to size and sectoral or regional location."[17] Bureaucratic reform also helped weaken the opposition of protectionist business groups. The weakening of SECOFI, which was historically an important channel for firms wanting special treatment and concessions from the state, is crucial to understanding business's inability to organize a strong opposition. As described below, de la Madrid's sexenio saw a reduction of pluralism within the upper echelons of the government and the monopolization of the "commanding heights" of the executive branch by technocratic elites drawn from public financial institutions. The rise of the SPP and the neoliberal technocrats clearly helped rebuild business confidence, but the emergence of this pivotal agency was the culmination of years of administrative reform and institutional struggles.

Bureaucratic Reform and the Centralization of Power

Robert Kaufman has demonstrated that development policy shifts occur only when there is a major concentration of state power.[18] On the eve of reform, the Mexican bureaucracy was divided between statists and neo-liberals, and the presidency's policy-making power was hindered by the policy inputs of myriad state agencies and their societal allies. But under de la Madrid and Salinas, a centralization of power took place within the presidency; the planning and finance sector gained prominence in the bureaucracy, and a homogenous elite sharing the same economic outlook rose to lead the state apparatus. To understand the centralization of power that took place, it is important to stress that Mexican "presidentialism" was the result of the country's revolution and reflected the exigencies of the founding moment, when the head of state had to battle warlords and antirevolutionary forces. Cardenas had concentrated enormous power in the presidency to build the Mexican state and enshrined this power in the constitution. The Mexican constitution thus granted the president vast powers: for example, regarding the national political economy, Article 27 gave the president the capacity to intervene and regulate property relations according to the public interest; Article 123 gave the president the right to arbitrate relations between capital and labor.[19] Under Salinas, the presidency would become even more powerful.

To centralize power in the Mexican presidency, de la Madrid and Salinas built upon bureaucratic changes and recruitment patterns initiated by Lopez Portillo and Echeverria. Most of the early presidents had risen to power through the ranks of the ruling party, and state expansionism was carried out by presidential initiative in collaboration with the PRI's old guard. Echeverria was the first president who moved to sideline the PRI and to concentrate power in the presidency. Despite constitutional provisions, before Echeverria's tenure, the president did not have ultimate control over economic policy. Before Echeverria took office in 1970, the president was institutionally constrained: the Minister of Government (Gobernacion), along with the Ministry of Labor, the ruling party, and state governments controlled the state security apparatus and managed the appointment of governors, state and city authorities, and corporatist leaders, while the Ministry of Treasury (Hacienda), along with Banco de Mexico and NAFINSA, controlled the budget and fiscal policy and tried to promote investment and economic growth. Treasury's policy preferences were often blocked by Gobernacion, its rival ministry. Treasury would decide how much funds a state would get in the upcoming fiscal year, but Gobernacion would decide how the money would be disbursed. In the 1950s, Lopez Mateos tried unsuccessfully to curb the power of the Ministry of Treasury and to gain control of the budget. Maxfield argues that Treasury was strong and could resist reform because of its long-standing relationship to the private sector and the Bank of Mexico.[20]

When Echeverria assumed office, Mexico was in the midst of a crisis, and further measures to prune the state were introduced. The president's etatist policies prompted administrative reforms. Between 1970 and 1976, the number of SOEs increased from eighty-four to one thousand. This expansionist policy was in part an attempt to shore up the regime's legitimacy following the 1968 student revolt. By recruiting loyalists, Echeverria hoped to build political support and gain greater control over the bureaucracy. The number of public servants subsequently grew from 610 thousand in 1970 to 3.3 million in 1983.[21] The Bank of Mexico and Treasury, which prioritized fiscal balance and surplus budgets, were vehemently opposed to Echeverria's expansionism. Echeverria thus began to bring financial policy under the control of the presidency and away from the Treasury's influence; he refused to share power with Treasury and declared that "economic policy is made at Los Pinos." Lopez Portillo introduced additional reforms in 1976, centralizing control over policymaking and increasing the power of the presidency and the agencies closest to the president. The government also began to show a greater commitment to planning by releasing the Basic Plan of the Government 1976–82, the National Plan for Development of 1978, and the Global Development Plan of 1980. These decrees were later codified by constitutional reforms in 1983 that helped strengthen "planning."

The "Superagency"

To consolidate the president's power over economic decision making, in December 1976, Echeverria created the Ministry of Programming and Budget (SPP), which held all the planning responsibilities that had previously fallen under the purview of the old Secretariat of the Presidency, Treasury, SEPANAL, and the statistical office of the Ministry of Commerce. SPP's greatest strength, though, was its control of the budget, which had previously been under the Ministry of Treasury. As Centeno observes, Lopez Portillo realized that "it was imperative that those in charge of programming also have control over the budget. This would not only give the new institution the power with which to enforce the new planning system but it would also liberate government expenditures from the limits placed by fiscal policy."[22] Lopez Portillo removed the control of expenditure from the Treasury ministry, limiting its responsibilities to taxation and fund-raising. External rents played a role in shifting the balance of power within the state. Echeverria was able to circumvent Treasury and pursue his expansionist policies because of his access to oil revenue and public borrowing. Lopez Portillo also had access to loans through public borrowing (which constituted 25 percent of the federal budget by 1975) and oil revenues (which accounted for 25 percent of the state budget in 1982), which gave him the economic werewithal and political space to introduce reforms.[23]

The SPP subsequently became a very powerful ministry (similar to the Ministry of Finance in Japan), responsible for the design of development plans, the budgeting of federal and public sector expenditures, and the training of public personnel. Additional administrative reforms were carried out in 1983 and 1986: the Ministry of Commerce was expanded, gaining greater control over industrial policy; SEMIP was granted greater control over public enterprises and energy policy; Treasury continued to manage revenues and the debt, while the Bank of Mexico was responsible for monetary policy. These four agencies were supposed to coordinate policy with the SPP through the Council of Economic Advisors and the Economic Cabinet, which was under the Secretariat of the Presidency. The SPP thus emerged as a powerful pilot agency that could dictate policy to the entire bureaucracy. De la Madrid further expanded the SPP by establishing a new network of planning offices throughout the country, coordinating regional programs and maintaining tight control over local expenditure. Because of their access to the budget, the area representatives of the SPP became more powerful than the representatives of Gobernacion.

Throughout Lopez Portillo's sexenio, the Mexican state had been divided between officials based in Commerce, SEMIP, and SEPAFIN, favoring state expansionism and arrayed against the fiscal conservatives, and those based in the Ministry of Finance and the Central Bank, who called for privatization and a reduction in the fiscal deficit and inflation. SEPAFIN (the Ministry of Natural Resources and Industrial Development), responsible for state-owned enterprises, had an etatist outlook and close links to the public sector and to small and medium business interests dependent on state support.[24] The Finance Ministry's monetarist views, in turn, were shaped by its relationship with the IMF dating back to the 1940s when the fund pushed for currency devaluations during a balance of payments crisis. Administrative reforms helped close this rift. Upon taking office, de la Madrid purged the government, removing statists from high positions in the bureaucracy. Cabinet responsibilities were reorganized to diminish the power of SEPAFIN, which was the base of the statist camp. Industrial development, previously under SEPAFIN, was assigned to the Ministry of Commerce and Industrial Development (SECOFI), and SEPAFIN became the Ministry of Energy, Mines, and Parastate Industry. Finance emerged stronger than SEMIP, as it assumed duties previously under the latter's jurisdiction. SPP gained control of the budgeting, evaluation, and approval of all state investment, including that of the public enterprises—a responsibility previously assigned to SEMIP. Moreover, a new ministry, the Ministry of the Comptroller General of the Nation, was created to reduce the public deficit by instituting greater controls over public expenditure. Control over revenue collection and expenditures was centralized in the upper echelons of the state bureaucracy.

Economic Reform and Bureaucratic Politics

Despite these administrative reforms, there was still disagreement among ministries regarding the pace of reform. The statists had allies and constituencies outside the state, and the neoliberal technocrats upon rising to power also began building external alliances to counter their rivals. The Ministry of Finance and the SPP, who were involved in debt negotiations and the formulation of macroeconomic policy, favored a faster pace and wanted to reduce the deficit and meet the inflation targets set by the IMF. As the debt negotiations got going and the IMF and World Bank gained more leverage, the Ministry of Finance became stronger. As head of SPP, Salinas staffed the agency with like-minded neoliberals and pushed for swift structural reform, but SECOFI and SEMIP insisted on a slower process. The statist camp did manage to slow down privatization. The established procedure for divestiture required the secretaries of Finance, the SPP, and the Comptroller's Office to present to the Intersecretarial Expenditure and Financing Committee (a bureau established in 1979 to coordinate the three financial ministries) a list of SOEs listed for sale. The statists, however, often hedged in providing such lists. De la Madrid changed this procedure in 1985: under the new system, the Ministry of Finance was responsible for the implementation of privatization decisions, a procedure codified in the 1986 Law of Public Enterprises.[25]

Despite resistance from state managers in charge of SOEs, the Ministry of the Comptroller General that allied itself with SEMIP, technocrats in the finance sector were gradually winning the power struggle over divestiture. Between 1983 and 1985, privatization occurred slowly. De la Madrid initially did not fully support divestiture in "priority" areas such as steel, mining, and fertilizers, but he relented as the technocrats closest to Salinas prevailed in the institutional battle with SEMIP. By the end of 1988, the state had withdrawn entirely from the production of consumer durables and significantly reduced its production of capital goods. Once within-state opposition had been defeated, Salinas forged ahead with privatization. In late 1989 he had all SOEs in sectors not labeled as "strategic" in the constitution slated for divestiture. He then proceeded to privatize the banks nationalized by Lopez Portillo.

In 1992, Salinas merged SPP and Hacienda under Pedro Aspe. Salinas's decision-making circle became even more exclusive. Salinas excluded SEMIP from the economic cabinet, because the ministry had a broader view of what constituted "priority activities" and wanted mining and steel to remain in the state's hands, while the president, the SPP, and Finance wanted to privatize these sectors. With the exception of the Labor Secretary, party veterans were also excluded from the cabinet. Salinas made additional changes to the privatization process. In 1989, technocrats managing the privatization process were placed in an institution called the Unit Responsible for Divestiture (Unidad de Disincorporacion). This team, one scholar observes, was "accountable only to the president and the relevant minister [and] designed and implemented policies without being subjected to the ebbs and flows of political battles in Mexican Congress or in the press."[26] The Unit Responsible for Divestiture received information and expert consulting from private consulting firms, and the Bank Divestment Committee allowed the private sector a voice in the process, all of which shows that Salinas's gaining of business support not only broadened the regime's support base but enhanced the state's technical capacity and ability to privatize. (Under Zedillo, in fact, the state partnered with private firms, offering them contracts to restructure the operations of railroads and the building of a private highway.[27])

Organizational changes in 1992 further centralized power in the hands of Salinas. The SPP was eliminated and its responsibilities transferred to the Ministry of Finance. Salinas had, in effect, gone beyond de la Madrid in centralizing power in the Mexican presidency and took unilateral action as he saw fit. He designed the major policy initiatives of his sexenio, launched preemptive strikes to weaken opponents, removed more governors than any Mexican president in history, and established Pronasol as a base of support independent of the PRI. Pronasol, which Salinas established, was also part of this centralizing effort; it marginalized state and local governments and was under the control of the presidency. But the financial crisis of 1995 led to a backlash against such discretionary presidential power, and between 1997 and 2000, the process of privatization would be expanded to include input from a broader number of state agencies and officials, not simply the President and the Minister of Finance, but also the ministers of Commerce, Industrial Development, Labor and the Ministry of the Comptroller.[28]

Electoral Reform and Coalition Building

The reform of electoral institutions was central to de la Madrid and Salinas's coalition-building project. The economic crisis and adjustment measures had politicized elections (which were historically, in the words of one analyst, "peripheral to the real business of Mexican political life"),[29] making them an important indicator of the opposition's strength and the president's willingness to reform. Reformers would use the electoral mechanism to meet challenges from the left and the right. In his study, *Political Reformism in Mexico*, Morris draws a useful distinction between "positive" and "negative" reforms, with positive reforms referring to "any moves that enhance the legitimacy of the regime or the reformer's credibility, or that broaden or strengthen the regime's supporting coalition," and negative reforms alluding to measures aimed at maintaining political control; as he writes, "exemplified by corruption, electoral fraud and repression, negative reforms reduce the reformer's credibility and the system's legitimacy."[30] De la Madrid and Salinas repeatedly tinkered with the PRI's internal operations—trying to strengthen the party's district structure so as not to rely on the traditional corporatist sectors—and with election laws to co-opt actors and movements outside the party's purview. But the state also periodically resorted to fraud to win elections.

The economic crisis of 1982 found the PRI faltering. The electoral reforms of 1977 had allowed opposition parties to organize and gain legal status and reserved at least a quarter of the Chamber of Deputies' seats for opposition parties. By 1982, opposition parties had cropped up and were challenging state policies. Between 1976 and 1982, the ruling party lost almost 20 percent of its votes, most going to the PAN. The PRD, made up of former PRI elites marginalized by the rise of neoliberal technocrats, presented Cauhtemoc Cardenas as presidential candidate and called for a mixed economy and a suspension of debt payments. The breakaway of the Cardenas faction undermined the cohesion of the PRI's elite. In the 1985 midterm elections, PRI leaders had to use fraud to win. If in 1982 the PRI had lost votes to the rightist PAN, in the 1988 election the PRI lost votes to the left. The official results, viewed as fraudulent by many observers, showed that Salinas had gotten 50.4 percent of the popular vote, while Cardenas got 31.29 percent, and Manuel Clouthier, the PAN candidate, got 17.7 percent.[31] The deteriorating standards of living had led many workers to vote against their union leaders and the PRI and for the PRD, which had united numerous popular movements that had arisen in the 1980s. The PRI's failure to win labor's votes in 1988, or more specifically the failure of corporatist sectors to deliver workers' votes, highlighted the need for institutional reform.

State officials wanted a measure of political liberalization to appease the opposition and diffuse the growing economic and political crisis. Several political reforms were undertaken with this in mind. To reduce the importance of the labor sector in the PRI, in 1990, state elites did away with the long-standing obligatory collective membership of a union in the PRI; membership was made voluntary. To expand the PRI's electoral base and weaken the regime hard-liners, that same year Salinas also democratized candidate selection. Anyone running for office in the PRI would thereafter require a certain percentage of district-level votes to get the party's nomination. This measure weakened the labor sector whose nominations declined; the fall in representatives from the labor and peasant sectors helped Salinas's team expand its support base, because the reforms led to an increase in representatives from the popular sector, mostly Salinas supporters in state and federal governments and members of the local business communities.[32] The number of deputy and senate seats allocated to labor leaders was also reduced,[33] and the state began reaching directly to the popular classes through Pronasol. After centralizing power in the presidency, Salinas began to assert control in the party apparatus. He removed potential challengers and placed 114 state party leaders under the control of Luis Donaldo Colosio, who was chairman of the PRI's National Executive Committee. Salinas also replaced more governors than any president since Cardenas, removing governors who did not deliver the vote in 1988 and could not guarantee local support.

As the state repaired its relations with business, a rapprochement occurred between the PAN and the PRI with the aim of marginalizing and weakening the PRD. To neutralize the PRD, in 1989, Salinas introduced electoral laws that made it difficult for the PRD to form a coalition similar to that of the FDN in 1988. Salinas wanted to prevent a PAN-PRD alliance. Cardenas had proposed such an idea in advocating a broad-based National Democratic Accord. But such an alliance was forestalled by Salinas's electoral reform package passed in 1989 with PAN support. The newly introduced "governability clause," as it was called, reduced to 35 percent the vote needed to guarantee a majority of the seats in the Chamber of Deputies and increased proportional representation for the PRI and smaller parties. Salinas co-opted leaders of small leftist parties like the Popular Socialist Party (PPS), the Authentic Party of the Revolution (PARM), and the Cardenist Front for the National Reconstruction Party (PFCRN), which had been part of Cardenas's FDN coalition, granting these politicians prestigious political positions. At the same time, the government tolerated the PAN's electoral victories. Salinas defied local authorities on several occasions, overturning election results sometimes in favor of the PAN and selecting particular candidates over others.

Salinas began earnestly negotiating with the PAN following his dubious victory in 1988. Eighty-five PAN members in the Congress had refused to recognize his victory, and the PAN only agreed to recognize him as president if he agreed to carry out economic reforms through an agreement called the National Commitment for Legitimacy and Democracy. Salinas used market reforms to restore business confidence and political reforms to draw the private sector into the ruling party, which some termed the PRI's "entrepreneurial sector." Representatives of big business were included in the PRI's Committee for the Financing and Consolidation of Resources, responsible for raising money for the PRI, which also provided a forum for business leaders to meet candidates and express their policy preferences.[34] As big business was gradually brought into the PRI's fold, business leaders began to run for office under the PRI banner. In crucial states, the PRI used local business leaders such as Eduardo Villaseñor in Michoacan to counter the threat of the PAN and the PRD. Businessmen and many members of the middle class—some former PAN supporters—voted for the PRI, such that support for the PAN fell in 1991. But Salinas's strategy of reconciliation with the PAN also split the conservative party in 1992, as top PANistas left to form the Partido Foro Democratico, denouncing the PAN's newfound support for the government. Salinas brought most business interests back into the PRI's political fold, but many small and medium entrepreneurial interests gave active support to the PAN in the 1992 elections.

While in office, Salinas changed the electoral law on a number of occasions. The 1990 electoral reform increased opposition parties' presence on the Federal Electoral Institute, called for a new voter registration list, and created a forum to examine charges of fraud. In 1993, Salinas introduced proportional representation to the Senate, increased the opposition's role in monitoring elections, called for equal access to the media, and set a limit on financial contributions. In pursuing political reforms, state elites made use of preexisting institutions and often grafted new institutions atop others. As Morris observes, "though recognizing the importance of the old institutions, the leaders still promoted reforms that 'added' to the party's corporate foundations and coalitions."[35] The electoral and bureaucratic reforms, however, could not have succeeded without the institution of the sexenio, a strong presidency, and unstinting U.S. support, all of which aided the reformers' statecraft enormously.

Sexenio and Elite Circulation

The Mexican rule of no reelection and regularized turnover of elites every six years gave the regime stability and flexibility. By institutionalizing presidential succession, Mexican state builders had solved the crucial problem of succession and contained intra-elite conflict. Mexico is in fact the only Latin American state that has not seen a violent change of government since the 1920s. Rather than trying to overthrow the system, political elites could wait for the end of the sexenio to assume office. The sexennial system offered the opposition an institutional opportunity to challenge the ruling party's dominance; the regime and the ruling party were also vulnerable to crises during this transition process. A historical analysis of Mexican reforms reveals two patterns: since the sexenio provided governments with a honeymoon stage, with new space and legitimacy, most reforms are attempted at the beginning of every term; but crises also often occur at the end of each six-year tenure. The end of Echeverria's, Lopez Portillo's, de la Madrid's, and Salinas's tenures in office all ended with crises.[36]

Most importantly, the sexenio allowed presidents to institutionalize and insure the continuity of their policy measures by selecting like-minded successors. In 1933, following the Great Depression, Calles selected Lazaro Cardenas from the populist-agrarian wing of the PRI to address labor and the peasantry's demands, which Cardenas did through his policies of land reform, oil expropriation, and increases in workers' wages. Cardenas, in turn, selected Miguel Aleman in 1946 to continue his policies of industrialization. The institutions of the sexenio and the dedazo, both of which exist in Egypt, allowed presidents since Lopez Portillo to select a successor that was not only a committed reformer but also from the same bureaucratic faction. This institutional guarantee permitted de la Madrid and Salinas to pursue bureaucratic reform and divestiture. Toward the end of his sexenio, de la Madrid helped his successor by privatizing the larger SOEs, allowing Salinas to focus on electoral and institutional reforms. De la Madrid also devalued the peso in November 1987, before Salinas came to office to avoid a foreign reserves crisis following the stock market crash and to help facilitate the implementation of the stabilization program put in place in December.[37] Salinas, in turn, chose Zedillo as his successor and the latter became the third consecutive president to ascend to the presidency after heading the SPP.

The sexenio also allows for change by regularly bringing in new personnel; in attempting market reforms, the regular turnover of the Mexican ruling elite allowed the new president to bring in loyalists and purge or co-opt opponents. Incoming presidents also had an enormous amount of patronage to dole out to supporters in the form of positions in the party, federal bureaucracy, legislature, and local and state governments. Peter Smith holds that during each presidential term approximately two-thirds of high national offices have been held by complete newcomers to the elite circles.[38] Presidential power and the turnover of elites allowed presidents to recast political coalitions and, through personnel change, to strengthen control over the bureaucracy. Thus, upon assuming office, Zedillo launched an ambitious project of administrative reform to transform the federal public administration and combat corruption, described as the Program for the Modernization of Public Administration, 1995–2000 (PROMAP); and while his efforts to create a federal civil service may have stalled, Zedillo did make "significant progress" in establishing a more independent Central Bank.[39]

The sexenio also contributed to the cohesion of the Mexican political elite, because even when not in power elites had a stake in the system. Hansen argued decades ago that the Mexican system's ability to contain elite conflict is a key reason for the regime's stability. Mexico boasts an elite cohesion unheard of in Latin America; and although defections have occurred, as with the Cardenista splinter group in 1988, the political elite has remained unified in its support for the regime. Another related institutional advantage that Mexican reformers had involved the marginal role of the military. Mexican reformers inherited a system where the military was marginal and the state had, via the party, numerous channels of communication by which to mobilize and guide social actors. If the electoral mechanism failed, then the state would resort to repression. The regime's adaptability led Mario Vargas Llosa to describe the Mexican regime as a "perfect dictatorship," its authoritarian colors masked by regular elections and elite circulation.[40]

International Actors and Economic Reform

External pressures and international circumstances were crucial to shifting the balance of power within the state, weakening statist ministries, and strengthening the reformist camp. Opposition to restructuring came from SEMIP and SECOFI, both of which were allied with business interests. It was SECOFI after all that had vetoed Mexico's entry into the GATT, stating that greater investment was needed to help national industry modernize. But SECOFI was weakened by international developments. External shocks strengthened the position of the bureaucrats from Finance who led the debt negotiations and were responsible for macroeconomic policy. The fall of petroleum prices in 1985, which produced a loss of $330 million in foreign exchange and an inability to meet debt payments, enfeebled the etatiste camp. The subsequent sidelining of statists from decision-making circles was partly the result of international pressures and financial assistance, which strengthened the neoliberal camp. While the statists were controlling state revenues, they could impede divestiture. But as bank loans became a source of revenue under Echeverria and Lopez Portillo, those negotiating with foreign banks became more influential. Debt negotiations spurred the process of privatization. After months of negotiation, sectors previously labeled "priority" were opened up for divestiture on the eve of the signing of the 1986 agreement.

Mexico's debt situation and the protracted negotiations with the United States and the IFIs made the financial ministries central actors, which aided the privatization process. In 1989, Mexico signed the Brady Plan with the United States, which offered a reduction of debt in return for reforms aimed at promoting privatization, foreign investment, trade liberalization, and further cuts in the public deficit. This plan was backed by the World Bank and the IMF. A separate deal was signed with the IMF in 1989 providing funds for debt reduction, and the World Bank provided three separate loans of $500 million each for assistance with structural change in the industrial, public utility, and financial sectors. The NAFTA talks also strengthened the neoliberal technocrats since IFIs put pressure on Mexico to open up its energy sector, especially petroleum, and provided Salinas's technocrats a way to divest of petroleum without seeking a constitutional amendment.[41] The finance-related ministries, SPP and Finance, with the support of the presidency, in turn pushed for privatization seeing divestiture as one way to alleviate the country's public deficit. And, in effect, by 1991 revenue from the sale of TELMEX and a few banks turned the public deficit into a surplus, and funds from privatization were used to pay off external and internal public debt.[42] By 1992, funds from the sale of SOEs represented the most important source of government revenue, and in that year Mexico paid $7.2 billion of its debt in 1992, using cash from SOE sales.[43]

Morris has argued that the Mexican regime had more international support than other authoritarian regimes in Latin America or Eastern Europe that were attempting reform. In 1992 Mexico was the largest recipient of the World Bank's nonpoverty lending. Mexico also received large amounts of aid from the United States, including emergency loans to stabilize the currency and prevent a run on the peso, following the 1988 election and then the 1994 crisis. Aggarwal reports that in the negotiations between Mexican officials and private American banks in 1983, Paul Volcker, then chairman of the Federal Reserve, sided with the Mexicans and pressured the American banks to make concessions.[44] Mexico was the first to receive debt relief under the Baker Plan in the mid-1980s and then the Brady Plan in

1989 and the first developing country to sign a free trade agreement under Bush's Enterprise for the Americas Initiative. The U.S. Treasury pressured commercial banks in the 1989 negotiations to accept the Brady Plan and agree to new loans for Mexico.[45] Mexico was also the largest recipient of aid ($1.2 billion) under the General Sales Management (GSM) program of the U.S. Department of Agriculture and the largest recipient of loans from the Export-Import Bank finances (getting 25 percent of loans disbursed in 1992). Mexico also obtained economic and food aid from USAID, including $40.6 million in economic aid and $27 million in food aid in 1992.[46]

After the 1988 election, the Federal Reserve Bank of New York offered Salinas two billion dollars to cover short-term payments. The United States supported Salinas as a reformer, offered him aid, and encouraged investors to do business in Mexico. PRD leader Cardenas put it bluntly: "The economy of Mexico is being saved thanks to a political decision of the United States."[47] The United States also endorsed Salinas's "democracy within reason" approach. Since the rise of Cardenas in 1988, Washington did not pressure the Mexican leadership to democratize. Reagan had spoken in support of the PAN and called for free elections in 1985–86, but neither Reagan nor Bush called for democracy following Salinas's rise to power.[48] Teichman observes that, compared to other Latin American countries, Mexico received the strongest and most steadfast support from the United States, so that Mexican reformers had "greater leeway in policy reform and allowed it to go forward at a more leisurely pace" than their Chilean or Argentinean counterparts.[49] Mexico, like Egypt, had a special geostrategic importance for Washington. American officials were very supportive and more "lenient" in pushing for reforms for fear that economic and political instability could trigger mass migration to the United States.[50] President Clinton in fact approved a bailout package in 1995 following the peso crisis, despite opposition from Congress. Thus, the image of Mexico as a reformer subject to the hard budget constraints of private lenders and IFI conditionalities is belied by the special treatment and support Mexican reformers received from Washington. Like Egypt, Mexico has a political ("soft constraints") relationship with the United States, the logic of which often overrides market rationality.

Mexico: "A Neoliberal Model?"

By 1983, the Mexican state's role in the economy—measured as a percentage of GNP—began to fall, for the first time since 1977. Public sector investment in manufacturing, oil, infrastructure, and agriculture continued to decrease in the 1980s along with welfare spending. Salinas cut federal spending from 31 percent in 1987 to 21 percent in 1990, resulting in a surplus by 1991. International observers were highly impressed. Secretary of State James Baker declared Mexico a model for reform in Eastern Europe and the former Soviet Union. Even after the 1994 peso collapse, investment banks and the IMF would continue lauding Mexico's "fundamentally sound economic policies." The World Bank praised Mexico as one of the most successful reformers in the world along with Korea and Chile.[51] J. P. Morgan, Chemical Bank, and Swiss Bank Corporation called for a credit-rate upgrading for the country, and Mexico rose rapidly in country-risk tables.[52] Officials in the Clinton administration eager to sell NAFTA also lauded the Mexican miracle, noting that Mexico, unlike Chile, had restructured economically in a democratic context, ignoring the deeply authoritarian nature of the Mexican political system. But was the new Mexican state the minimal "nightwatchman" state envisioned by the Washington consensus, and was Mexico the success it was billed to be? The "Mexican model" means different things to analysts on different sides of the debate on the state's role in the economy: neoliberals who believe the state should play a minimal "nightwatchman" role and more interventionist economists who think the state should play a guiding role and underline that there are different models of development and state-market engagements.

Starting with the question of the "Mexican miracle," at a macro level, Mexico's reform policies were considered a "success" in luring investment, liberalizing trade, and cutting the public deficit; but in terms of living standards, the record under de la Madrid and Salinas was negative; as wages declined, the average Mexican's caloric intake decreased, and infant mortality increased from 1982 to 1988.[53] The minimum wage by 1991 had lost two-thirds of its purchasing power since 1982. The peso collapse of 1995 and the subsequent austerity measures plunged Mexico into a severe recession. In 1996, the economy shrank by 6 percent.[54] That same year real wages in manufacturing were only 64 percent of their 1980 level, and real wages among maquila production workers were only 54 percent of their 1980 level.[55] Critics note that it was not only the devaluations and subsequent rounds of austerity measures but the policies of free trade and privatization that led to the declining living standards and that the Mexican economy grew substantially more during the eras of (state-led) "conservative developmentalism" of the 1950s and the "populist developmentalism" of the 1970s. Between 1955 and 1970, real economic growth was an average of 6.5 percent, while from 1983 to 1999 the growth average was a mere 2 percent.[56] Under Zedillo, capital flows resumed, and certain sectors benefited from economic liberalization, but the benefits were not evenly distributed; the buying power of the Mexican worker declined by 47 percent with real wages falling to pre-1980 levels; and by the end of Zedillo's sexenio, economists' estimates claimed that over 45 percent (some say 75 percent) of Mexico's hundred million people lived in poverty, and real wages had declined to pre-1980s levels.[57] Most of the descriptions of Mexico as a star reformer ignored the falling living standards and rising inequality.

The second question is whether the reformed Mexican state was a "minimal state" or an "interventionist state"? In a speech in 1982, de la Madrid declared, as if explicitly rejecting the neoliberalism of the minimal nightwatchman state, "We defined a state . . . with the capacity to be the rector of national, political, economic and social development."[58] He underlined the state's role in managing the economy and guiding the private sector: "We must regulate, orient, and induce the development of the private sector so that it supports national priorities and state policy."[59] Mexican technocrats often spoke of "rectorship," saying the government would not control the economy or own production but would supervise the market, aiding and disciplining economic actors. Pedro Aspe, a leading "neoliberal" technocrat, underlined that privatization was not simply about the liquidation of SOEs but was to be accompanied by measures that included disciplining private enterprises through the withholding of subsidies and the threat of tax audits and getting them to pursue state-determined goals. Mexican economists Aguilar Camin and Lorenzo Meyer contend that both de la Madrid and Salinas distanced themselves from neoliberalism. Salinas, they argue, was against the large, behemoth state of the 1970s but believed in "un Estado rector" (a rector state) that would not intervene or nationalize but would promote.[60] Salinas repeatedly proclaimed that the new Mexican state would practice a "socially determined interventionism" and that his vision of the state drew on social liberalism, which he distinguished from neoliberalism: "Neoliberalism minimizes the state and responsibilities of the state, marginalizing it from national life. . . . Social liberalism assumes that unregulated markets create monopolies, making social injustice worse and resulting in diminished growth. . . . Social liberalism proposes a promotional state that supports [private] initiative but with the capacity to regulate economic activities firmly."[61]

Privatization may have downsized the Mexican state (in terms of GNP and public employment), but the state was redeployed into other areas and remained involved in managing economic development. It was declared that the state would no longer own enterprises; reformers never renounced the state's duty to "regulate and manage" national development. Richard Snyder's compelling study of the Mexican coffee sector shows that instead of "freeing the market," neoliberal reforms in the coffee sector led to re-regulation and "new institutions of market governance" as "the governments of Mexico's coffee-producing states sought to establish subnational regulatory frameworks and essentially reregulate what federal law had deregulated."[62] The Mexican state also had to reintervene to rescue the roads and ports that had been subcontracted to private actors. These "concessions"—as these public-private deals were called—often failed. For instance, in August 1997, the state was forced to rescue twenty-seven of these "privatized" toll roads, most of which were financially insolvent; state officials immediately reduced tariffs to make the roads functional again. Invoking the public interest, the state would "reincorporate" fifteen other highways and bridges that had been subcontracted to the private sector. As economist Aguilar Quintero would observe, Zedillo was forced to (re)incorporate three thousand kilometers into state ownership and absorb 18,5000 in debt.[63]

Another way in which privatization actually strained the state's capabilities and budget was in the public insecurity that followed economic liberalization. The crisis of 1994 had a devastating effect on employment and real wages and, along with NAFTA, which removed tariff and trade barriers, pushed a large number of Mexicans into the informal sector, triggering a boom in illegal activities, crime, and public insecurity. The cash-strapped state was hard-pressed to fund adequate security services. The demand for private security led to an explosion of private security forces in Mexico City, which escaped and challenged the government's control. In 1994, the Ministry of Public Safety created the Private Security Services Registration Department to monitor these firms; that year the government counted 2,122 "registered" private security forms in the capital—by 1998, the number had grown to 17,132.[64] This illustrates that the Mexican regime had the ability to push labor and capital toward its developmental goals but was struggling to provide security to its citizens and was trying to bring the new private security firms under state control.

Centeno argues that Salinas was emulating the East Asian interventionist state that directed the market and "governed the economy." The Pact is a clear example of this kind of interventionism. The state, in effect, pressured the private sector and labor confederations to accept the new economic project. The policy package underpinning the Pact included orthodox neoliberal measures like budget cuts and trade liberalization but also a wage-price freeze meant to check inflation, which required technocrats to intervene in the functioning of the market. Salinas overvalued the exchange rate by maintaining a "crawling peg" and a strong peso, which made foreign debt cheaper for big business. Lustig and Ros note that, during the era of structural reform in Mexico, "industrial policy continued to be an active ingredient of Mexico's trade regime."[65] Salinas also intervened to protect the banking sector, shielding reprivatized banks from competition. Kessler, in a survey of Mexican financial policy since the 1950s, observes that the "Salinas administration seems the most schizophrenic of those examined. . . . On the one hand, it deregulated and reprivatized the banks and liberalized and internationalized capital markets. On the other hand, it protected the banks from both foreign and domestic competition and artificially propped up the value of currency through exchange rate intervention."[66]

The privatization of banks showed how the political calculus of coalition building often overrode market rationality: Salinas sold financial institutions to his allies in the private sector while assuring the new bank owners that financial liberalization would be delayed. Despite pressures from U.S. negotiators, the terms of NAFTA restricted foreign investment in Mexican banks for an extended period, and it was only in 1998—following the 1995 financial crisis—that the Mexican state did away with restrictions on bank ownership, and Mexico's most important banks were subsequently bought by foreign interests.[67] In his study of economic reform and coalition building in Mexico, Argentina, and Chile, Hector Schamis similarly argues that center-right coalitions may be smaller than populist coalitions, but they are also distributive, granting rents and subsidies to the propertied classes rather than the popular classes.[68] The Mexican government intervention was clearly titled toward upper class interests, and it appears that de la Madrid, Salinas, and Zedillo accepted the neoclassical tenet that capital accumulation was more important than concerns for welfare and social justice and that the best way to achieve social justice and equality was by promoting efficiency and economic growth.

Some economists think the 1994 crash was a result of the contradictions of pursuing neoliberal policies along with interventionist policies. The interventionist, neopopulist strategies, the argument runs, failed to produce growth and led to the 1994 crash because Salinas kept the currency overvalued to attract foreign capital, which was financing his coalitional strategy (i.e., Pronasol), and to retain the support of the middle class, which consumed imports; but this policy would eventually lead to a current-account deficit, a savings-investment gap, and eventual financial collapse. With the collapse of the banking system in 1995, Zedillo—who as director of FICORCA had absorbed billions of dollars of debt of Mexico's largest conglomerates, intervened, this time as president, to rescue private firms and banks that had lost billions of dollars because of the devaluation. The privatization of banks between 1991 and 1993 had earned the state $12 billion, but the cost of rescuing the privatized banks, absorbing their debt, and restructuring operations cost an estimated $115 billion, almost ten times the revenues received from the sell-offs.[69] The soft-constraints thesis often applied to Egypt can thus also describe the Mexican political economy: the Mexican government prevented big business from failing, just as Washington prevented the Mexican economy from going under.

Imitating the Mexican Model

Long before the ascendancy of neoliberalism and IMF-sponsored development programs, countries in the Middle East have imitated Western states. During the reforms (*tanzimat*) of the 1840s, Turkey's Ottoman rulers borrowed commercial and legal codes from France; in the 1930s, Ataturk would reform the Turkish bureaucracy in imitation of Germany's bureaucracy.[70] Between Latin America and the Middle East, in particular, there has been political imitation at least since 1922 when a group of German-educated Brazilian military officers known as the Young Turks and inspired by Mustafa Kamal launched a series of revolts that shook the Brazilian state.[71] Historians have also noted the influence of Nasserism on General Velazquez's "revolution from above" in Peru and his ensuing policies of land reform and state expansion.[72] The populist ideas of Castro, Vargas, and Peron all exerted influence among Arab state builders after gaining independence. Today Latin American political ideas—from Mexico's Pronasol program to Peruvian economist Hernan de Soto's theory of releasing wealth from "dead capital"—still resonate in the Arab world. (I describe in the next chapter how, on the basis of studies carried out by the Lima-based Institute for Liberty and Democracy in partnership with the Egyptian Center for Economic Studies, Egyptian technocrats have used Hernan de Soto's argument to push for legislation, including a new mortgage law and a property titling program, which would purportedly create funds by bringing to life the dead capital of irregular [nontitled] real estate.[73])

Political scientists have described how this process of policy diffusion and emulation is driven by a combination of factors—external pressures, symbolic or normative imitation, rational learning, and cognitive heuristics.[74] Regarding external pressures, Barbara Stallings has argued that since the end of the cold war, different models of capitalism—Japanese, European, and American—have gained sway in different parts of the developing world, in various "spheres of influence"; the Japanese model is popular in East and Southeast Asia; European models are important in Eastern Europe and North Africa; while "the U.S./IFI model" is dominant in Latin America, the United States' historic sphere of influence.[75] Analysts note that as the United States deepens its presence in the Middle East, Arab states, like their Latin American counterparts, will begin to adopt neoliberal or Anglo-American variants of capitalism. (One scholar has observed that Chile under Pinochet was the first case of American-sponsored "neoliberal state formation," and the same (neoliberal) economic-political formula is now being prescribed in Iraq.)[76]

If Nasser was impressed by Brazilian and Argentine populism, military rule, and aversion to party politics, Sadat and Mubarak appear more drawn to Mexico's economic-political formula. A number of World Bank officials and IFI-affiliated Egyptian technocrats have lauded Mexico and recommended some aspect of the "Mexican way." Neemat Chafiq, the World Bank's vice-president for private sector and infrastructure development, explicitly recommended liberalization as implemented in Mexico (preferable to Chile and Argentina.) Yousef Boutros Ghali, Minister of Economy and Commerce and formerly an IMF official, claimed to have studied the impact of economic liberalization on the "similar experience" of Mexico.[77] The Word Bank dispensed funds to build the Social Fund for Development in imitation of Mexico's National Solidarity Program.[78] But as Weyland notes, in emulating foreign models, policy makers often misunderstand, "distort," and "overinterpret short stretches of success as proof of the intrinsic superiority of the new model."[79] And in effect, in imitating Mexico, Egyptian technocrats were following prescriptions based on IMF and World Bank interpretations of the Mexican model, which ignore the Mexican state's institutional interventions and the path dependence of that country's experience. And curiously, scholars in the Arab world were looking to replicate Latin American reform strategies at a time when scholars of that region were noting that market reforms had yielded disappointing results in terms of economic growth, social equity, and quality of democracy.[80]

While the international community was presenting Mexico as an exemplar of neoliberalism and Egyptian policy analysts were trying to imitate Mexico's "free market" policies, scholars were also showing that Mexican policy makers were inspired by the interventionist policies of the East Asian NICs. "The model [for Salinas] was Taiwan or South Korea, not Friedman Chile," writes sociologist Miguel Centeno. [81] Critics have also underlined the different representations of Mexico put forth by the Mexican government, which showed one face—"the Washington Consensus face"—to the United States, IFIs, and international business groups, and a "discretionary and subsidizing face" to domestic constituencies who received export credits, tax incentives, price controls, and poverty alleviation programs. These arguments not only challenge the neoclassical belief that privatization "shrinks" the state and that "the best way to limit rent-seeking is to limit government"[82] but lend credence to scholars from Foucault to Joel Migdal who point to "the often anomalous relationship between image and [state] practice, even when practices tend to reinforce the myth of the state."[83] In actuality, Mexico is a hybrid case, an example of a regime that combines traits of a participatory and authoritarian regime, and a state that, as one economist said, demonstrates the "unimportance of the private-public distinction," that is, of "a regime combining certain features of interventionism with others of a free market."[84] In Egypt, as will be demonstrated, limited market reform was accompanied with institutional interventions, but any growth achieved and investment lured was presented as due to free markets by IFIs and Egyptian policy makers, while scholars were pointing to the Egyptian state's not-so-invisible hand and reformers' preference for "recombinant" property arrangements.

In summary, with Washington's support, reformers in Mexico pursued an eclectic policy package that included orthodox measures but also populist, interventionist policies. De la Madrid and Salinas carried out administrative reform to protect technocrats from protectionist pressures and to create linkages between them and pro-reform business groups; political reforms, in the form of the Pact, election laws, and party restructuring were also undertaken to include the private sector—all the while keeping labor and the peasantry in the PRI's fold, though in a weaker position. The new pro-privatization coalition thus marginalized statist bureaucrats, subordinated labor and the peasantry, and rested primarily on the support of big business, neoliberal elite bureaucrats (in the finance ministries), and their international allies, specifically the U.S. government and international financial institutions. Salinas's efforts to build a pro-reform coalition were similar to the coalition-building measures used by Cardenas in building the Mexican state five decades earlier, with state officials reaching out to constituencies lying outside the PRI's coalition to serve as a counterweight to anti-reform groups. The PRI provided a crucial organizational space into which support could be mobilized, lower classes organized, and intra-elite settlements negotiated.

Big business's support would prove crucial in buying up SOEs, and domestic capital would become an important source of public financing as the state tried to reverse capital flight. The large business federations also enhanced the state's capacity for political control. Comparing Egypt to Mexico, there is no denying that the size and organizational strength of the Mexican private sector surpasses the capabilities of the Egyptian business class. But as far as privatization is concerned, the problem in Egypt is not an absence of buyers; foreign companies were always interested in buying up ailing SOEs, even if Egyptian businessmen would not or could not. And divestiture was in the interest of the state; selling off SOEs, often to cronies, as a way of paying for the public deficit serves the regime's interests. But when divestiture implies mass layoffs, the Egyptian state lacks the institutional capacity to contain labor discontent. For this reason, the Egyptian regime often backtracked on sales even after deals had been struck with foreign buyers.

State-Labor Relations and Public Sector Reform

Heba Handoussa, director of the Cairo-based Economic Research Forum, has observed that "Egypt has always had the political will for reform, but it has dragged on for decades."[1] Reform has "dragged on" because of the state's limited control over society, particularly over urban popular sectors that have repeatedly brought the process to a halt. Despite pressures from IFIs and local business groups, privatization, since it began in earnest in 1996, has proceeded at a glacial pace largely because labor opposition has thwarted or threatened to thwart divestiture. To counter the opposition of labor and other urban groups, Mubarak is reaching out to the propertied classes and trying to build a pro-reform coalition using the National Democratic Party.

Workers in Egypt have managed to derail the privatization process not because, as some have argued, labor leaders—though co-opted and insulated from the base—are vetoing privatization policy but because the labor elite cannot insure the quiescence of the rank and file. The Egyptian Trade Union Federation (ETUF) leadership has repeatedly stated its support for privatization, but it cannot deliver the base. The state corporatist system of Egypt insured labor docility for decades with no general strikes or widespread work stoppages (with the exception of 1977 food riots), but Egyptian leaders never developed a control capability vis-à-vis the working class, nor did they eliminate workers' ability to resist. Egyptian labor was economically included and politically demobilized, that is, neither fully included as in Mexico nor fully excluded as in the bureaucratic-authoritarian regimes of Latin America. Egyptian labor lost the right to strike but was not banned; in fact, labor's political cooperation remained crucial to the stability and legitimacy of the postrevolutionary regime. But as one Egyptian scholar writes, "Despite the corporatist arrangements imposed by the state on all associations of civil society, there are no established mechanisms for negotiation and bargaining between capital, labor, and the state—hence the danger that relatively minor disputes could get out of hand and develop into widespread disturbances—as happened in 1977 over very modest reductions in food subsidies."[2] What the Egyptian case illustrates is that state corporatism's stymieing of autonomous union activity combined with the criminalization of strikes deprives state elites of various institutional mechanisms available in party corporatist systems through which workers can participate, policies can be negotiated, and support can be mobilized.

"System accessibility" is thus a key difference in explaining the different reactions of Egyptian and Mexican labor. Egyptian workers simply do not have the access to the state that their Mexican counterparts enjoy. The institutional carapace of the ETUF does not allow for much turnover of personnel or upward mobility from the base and does not give mid- and upper-level unionists incentives to take up positions and issues favored by the rank and file. More broadly, "structures of contestation" in Mexico— the corporatist and electoral system—led most labor federations to opt for a with-in system response to reform, whereas the corporatist and electoral system in Egypt has led workers to seek alternatives outside the system. As in Mexico before the 1986 elections, Egyptian leaders are relying on elite-level negotiations with labor and focusing on maintaining the loyalty of high-level unionists, a strategy that is leading to the loss of rank-and-file support. As the Egyptian regime uses legislation, fraud, and patronage to insulate loyal NDP-affiliated upper-level unionists from rank-and-file pressures, the privatization process has stalled, and workers are gravitating toward other organizations. Unlike the Mexican regime, the Egyptian state cannot control the rank and file or recoup lost votes; the state can neither provide incentives to retain workers' support or incorporate the new groups that have appeared to defend labor's interests. The Egyptian regime's response to the current upsurge in labor protest—what has been described as "the longest and strongest wave of work protest since the end of World War II"—has been repression, as attempts at co-optation have failed.

Since the early 1990s, Egyptian reformers have tried to incorporate sectors of the labor and peasant movement into the ruling party. Today party reforms appear to have secured the loyalty of the union elite but are politically excluding the majority of workers. The regime, as the next chapter illustrates, is gradually drawing the private sector into the ruling coalition, but populist groups are leaving or are being excluded by new electoral laws. Unlike Mexico, where, as Edward Gibson has shown, reformers relied on the rural ("peripheral") coalition for electoral support while reconstituting the PRI's "metropolitan areas" that provided the regime with organizational and ideological support for the economic reform project, in Egypt, the regime's alliance with rural notables helped maintain peasant quiescence when liberalizing agriculture, but rural electoral support did little for the NDP's overall declining fortunes; moreover, Egyptian state elites lack the corporatist institutions and middlemen to reconfigure their "metropolitan" base.[3] The state is responding to labor and urban discontent by restricting participation in both legislative and trade union elections and demoting labor's position as a coalitional partner.

Finally, in response to the argument that Egyptian leaders are not reforming because of access to external rents, one can observe that economic reform proceeded on various fronts (e.g., trade and price liberalization), and privatization went forward whether external funds were flowing or not—and stopped when labor protest increased. In fact, it is not clear how the pace of privatization is linked to external flows into Egypt: often the process went forward when IFIs and donors were funding early retirement schemes, but the process also proceeded when such funds dried up; the process often stopped in face of labor agitation regardless of whether aid money was flowing. The relationship, if any, between external rents and the ability to maneuver domestically is a complex one. Despite aid and pressure from different international actors, Egyptian leaders could not lay off half a million workers and maintain stability as Mexico did.

Crisis and Reform

As in Mexico, Egyptian state builders opted for a centrally planned economy and embarked on a strategy of ISI. The state's commitment to labor was enshrined in the 1956 constitution, specifically in Article 52, which stated that work was a right for all Egyptians and guaranteed just wages, work hours, vacations, and insurance.[4] The strategy of ISI required the importation of technology and other material for production and was initially financed by Suez Canal fees. But the cost and the inefficiency of this development model became evident as Egypt found itself in a balance of payments crisis, with imports consistently outstripping exports. Also, an expensive subsidy system had developed to keep the prices of consumer goods and industrial inputs (for the public sector) low. Sadat's *infitah* policy in 1974 was intended to speed up economic liberalization by attracting foreign, particularly Arab, capital. But rather than boosting exports, *infitah* led to a four-fold increase in imports and a boom in construction and real estate due to windfalls from oil exports. During this period, Egypt grew immensely dependent on external revenue. By the end of the 1970s, remittances from Egyptian workers in the gulf and capital from Arab countries reached three billion dollars, and aid from the United States (following the Camp David Accords) and Europe totaled two billion dollars a year.[5] As revenue from loans, tourism, and labor remittances flowed into Egypt, state elites delayed the necessary structural reforms, though widespread food riots in 1977 had already led the regime to abandon reform measures.

The Egyptian economy grew by about 8 percent every year from 1974 to 1985, and per capita income doubled from $334 in 1974 to $700 in 1984. The public sector expanded during the Sadat era and the early Mubarak years from 34.4 percent of GDP in 1975 to 43 percent in 1990. But this growth was really a result of increased worker remittances and tourism and a rise in the price of oil. With the end of the oil boom and the fall in oil prices, Egypt was faced with high levels of unemployment (15 percent) as workers returned from the gulf. Between 1981–82 and 1986–87, Egypt's earnings from oil exports dropped from $3.3 billion to $1.4 billion, a drop that led to a shortage of foreign currency and a recession as the country's current accounts deficit reached an unprecedented high of $5 billion in 1986.[6] By 1990, Egypt's foreign debt had reached $50 billion with an annual debt service of $6.6 billion.

In November 1991, Egypt signed a structural adjustment agreement with the IMF and the World Bank. A deal with the Paris Club granted Egypt twenty-eight billion dollars in debt relief contingent on successful economic reform (and in exchange for Egypt's supporting the Gulf War effort). Egypt accomplished many of the macroeconomic objectives set out by the IFIs, including the reduction of state subsidies, the liberalization of interest rates, the introduction of a new sales tax, and a single unified exchange rate. Satisfied with the stabilization process, in 1993 the IMF began a three-year Extended Fund Facility calling for structural reforms. When Prime Minister Kamal al-Ganzouri took office January 1996, another two-year agreement was signed with the IMF. The agreement accompanied the U.S.-Egyptian Partnership for Economic Growth and Development, signed by Mubarak and then Vice-President Al Gore, and outlined far-reaching structural reforms: the acceleration of the privatization process, the reduction of civil service employment by 2 percent, and the elimination of subsidies in gas, oil, and electricity. Between 1991 and 1998, as subsidies were removed on energy products and the prices of agricultural and consumer goods liberalized, inflation fell from 20 percent to 4 percent, the budgetary deficit was reduced from 15 percent to 1.3 percent, and foreign exchange reserves increased from six billion dollars to twenty billion dollars; in exchange for this progress, Egypt received more loans from the IMF and had more debt forgiven.[7] By mid-1999, Egypt was being lauded as a "success story" and called "the IMF's model pupil."[8]

The Privatization Drive

Law 203 of 1991 was passed to facilitate public sector restructuring. Sixteen independent holding companies were created to handle divestiture; 314 public companies with an official book value of 90 billion Egyptian pounds (EGP) and debts of 77 billion EGP were listed for sale. Between 1991 and 1993, over 1,500 small state-owned enterprises (SOEs) at the local level were sold. Between 1991 and 1996, divestiture progressed very slowly in Egypt, with only three companies being completely sold to the private sector, and sixteen were partially liquidated (5–10 percent divestiture) through the stock market.[9] After the cabinet shuffle in 1996 and with increased IMF pressure, the pace of privatization accelerated as the government made public a list of one hundred companies whose shares were up for sale, including the Egypt Aluminum Company and several shipping companies, previously considered "strategic." Between 1993 and 1998, Egypt' privatization drew in $3.3 billion.[10] In 1998, an IMF report ranked Egypt among the top four countries in the privatization drive.[11] But then the process came to a halt. The recession and liquidity crisis that began in 1999 was worsened by the post-9/11 global economic downturn and the Iraq War, which cost Egypt an estimated $2 billion in exports to Iraq under the Oil-for-Food program. Despite the pressure from IFIs who counseled that further sell-offs could bring in needed currency, the process came to a standstill until late 2005.[12]

There were several reasons for the halt: resistance from SOE managers with vested interests in the public sector, the lack of accurate evaluations of assets, and the dearth of investors willing to buy ailing SOEs. But the greatest obstacle was how to deal with labor during privatization. One study by a British consulting group found that 30 percent of the labor force in SOEs was redundant; 40 percent of the workers had a second job; and 40 to 45 percent were under- or unqualified. Yet shedding the excess labor through divestiture was politically explosive. The government began offering workers a plan to buy shares in companies being privatized and, with the help of USAID, started a program of employee buyouts modeled after the American Employee Stockholder Associations (ESAs), whereby workers could buy up to 10 percent of company equity through an ESA at a 20 percent discount of the market price. According to the Public Enterprise Office, by 1998, fifteen companies had been sold to their respective employee stockholder associations. The government retired sixty thousand employees in this fashion and paid their compensation with an estimated LE1.467 billion.[13]

The strategy reformers pursued was to privatize slowly, trying to rid SOEs of "excess labor"—often through early retirement—before selling them off to the private sector, who would then negotiate wage and employment policies with unions under a new labor law. But this proved insufficient: investors demanded even more "flexibilization," and the government was unable to lay off more workers or to mobilize workers' support for reform. Labor activists opposed early retirement programs since such schemes shrank union membership and weakened unions. They argued that privatization would diminish union membership, which for decades had been mandatory with membership dues deducted from salaries, but would become voluntary in the private sector. Despite media campaigns and numerous conferences (twelve in 1998 alone) organized by the Public Enterprise Office, claiming that wages would rise after privatization, the government was ineffectual in mobilizing support for the process.

Labor protest gradually picked up speed. In April 1993, the shop floor leaders of different branch unions established union committees for the Defense of the Public Sector and of National Industry in Helwan and Mahalla al-Kubra; in November of that year other shop floor leaders, in opposition to their federation and union leaders, established a National Committee Against Privatization. In 1996, the National Progressive Unionist Party (NPUP) and the Nasserist Party also filed a lawsuit on the basis of the constitution's reference to the public sector as the foundation of the Egyptian economy. A survey of six thousand public sector workers conducted by *Al-Arabi* newspaper in 1996 found that 91.2 percent of the workers opposed privatization; of the 8.8 percent who supported the process, 80.6 percent were opposed to the sale of SOEs to foreigners, and only 35.5 percent supported the sale of the SOE where they were employed.[14] In May 1999, the Center for Human Rights and Legal Aid in Alexandria organized a conference for representatives of different labor unions to discuss the "crisis of the trade union structure," "the unresponsive nature of the trade union system," and labor's relationship to the National Democratic Party.[15]

Before the start of the privatization program, strikes were rare. In 1988 and 1989 only thirty-seven incidents of labor protest took place in response to cuts in wages and bonuses, and they often took the form of sit-ins, demonstrations, petitions, or refusals to accept paychecks.[16] Strikes died down after a brutal crackdown in 1989 but became more frequent as the reform process progressed, with eight strikes occurring in 1990, twenty-six in 1991, twenty-eight in 1992, sixty-three in 1993, and culminating in the bloody strike at Kafr al-Duwwar in 1994.[17] Between

January 1998 and December 1999, 287 protests, including ninety strikes, were recorded in what was then described as a period of the most labor agitation in Egypt since the 1952 revolution.[18] The protests were against cuts in wages, bonuses, workplace services (such as free transportation to and from work), forced early retirement, eviction from homes owned by former employers, arbitrary dismissal, and the relocation of workers to different branches of the company.[19]

In 2000, the government backtracked on its offer to sell off its 47.9 percent stake in Helwan Cement Company and TeleCom Egypt because the foreign investors were concerned about the "excess labor," but with rising protests, the government could not lay off more workers.[20] An attempted privatization of the Egyptian Company for Chemical Industries (KIMA) in 2002—wherein 2,300 workers would be shed with 1,000 being reemployed in a new oil project in southern Egypt and the remaining 1,300 receiving agricultural land to reclaim—was also blocked by worker opposition. (As one report put it, "The main force behind the government's decision to keep KIMA operating is angry workers.")[21] The government also went ahead with the partial sale of assets in Alexandria Cooling, the Bags Factory at National Plastic, the Liquid Batteries Factory, and the Medical Amoules Factory at Al-Nasr Glass and Crystal Company. Meanwhile, economic liberalization proceeded in other areas; the floating of the Egyptian pound on January 28, 2003, for instance, led to a 6 percent price increase in basic commodities. Foreign direct investment increased from $2 billion in the financial year of 2003/2004 to $3.9 billion in 2004/2005 and reached $3.3 billion in the first half of 2005/2006.[22]

Between 1992 and 2004, 142 SOEs (of the 314 slated for sale) had been partly or totally privatized. The state under Law 203 still owns 172 companies and holds stakes in 695 joint venture companies.[23] In early 2004, Public Sector Minister Mokhtar Khattab announced a three-year plan to sell off an additional 114 loss-making or low-profit SOEs.[24] When privatization resumed in 2004, so did the protests: there were 267 protests that year.[25] Critics of the reform process observe that in late 2004 there were still 172 companies employing some 401,000 individuals that had yet to be sold. In 2005, there were 43 strikes and 159 protests (sit-ins, gatherings, and demonstrations). That same year, striking workers at the Egyptian Fish Company successfully blocked efforts to privatize their company. Workers who led a sit-in at the Torah Cement Company a few days before the deadline of an offer by the French multinational Cement Français to buy the company ended their protest only when the government decided to turn down the multinational's offer.[26] One account notes that efforts to privatize textile enterprises led to an "unprecedented wave of wildcat strikes," which since 2004 have spread to other sectors; "in late 2006 and 2007, the strike wave has reached a particularly high crest."[27] Labor's ability to resist was also seen in the resistance to the new labor law.

Opposition to the Unified Labor Law

Labor opposition delayed the passing of the new Unified Labor Law for ten years, from when it was first proposed in 1993 to when it was finally adopted by the parliament in 2003. For a decade, state officials, unionists, business leaders, and ILO representatives grappled over the details of the new labor law, particularly over the right to strike and worker dismissal. The business community staunchly opposed a guaranteed right to strike. The ETUF wanted the right to strike guaranteed but wanted control over when strikes would be called, as high-level unionists were wary of granting greater space for autonomous factory-level activity. ETUF leaders insisted on the right to strike—at least on paper—partly because opposition union activists were threatening to form new unions independent of the ETUF, which would insure that right. Opposition activists noted that the high constitutional court had twice ruled that workers had the right to form independent unions.[28] To lobby against the new labor law, the National Committee in Defense of Workers' Rights was formed, encompassing a coalition of five opposition parties and three workers' groups, and in one of its first public statements it threatened to campaign against all parliamentarians who supported the legislation during the November 2000 elections.[29]

The Unified Labor Law finally passed in 2003, granting workers the right to strike but under restrictive conditions and banning all wildcat strikes; employers were allowed to dismiss workers for economic reasons but only after negotiating with labor unions. While Clause 192 of the new law states that Egyptian workers are guaranteed the right to strike in accordance with the Egyptian government's obligations under international conventions, the conditions of the clause seriously limit this right. The new law grants workers the right to strike only if two-thirds of the ETUF board give their approval. Union leaders are expected to inform employees and state officials with a written notice two weeks ahead of the strike. The new law thus further strips the base—the plant level, where opposition to privatization is most intense—of decision-making power. Clause 192 says that Egyptian workers—including local union representatives—have no right to strike without ETUF permission and without specifying a strike's duration, conditions that activists say in effect negate the right to strike.[30] The law also prohibits strikes during arbitration and in vital service sectors.

Labor activists see the new law as a step back. Under the preexisting labor law, public sector workers were guaranteed lifetime employment, and employers could only dismiss workers if the latter commited violations such as assaulting a manager, or for absenteeism, alcoholism, or revealing company secrets; the new law makes it considerably easier to dismiss workers. Labor activist Kamal Abbas of the Center for Trade Union Workers' Services (CTUWS), a Helwan-based NGO, criticized the new labor law for this reason, pointing to "Clause 69 of the law which stated that a worker may be fired of she or does 'does not perform [her or his] essential duties.' It [the clause] provides no definition of 'essential duties,' opening the door to the arbitrary sacking of staff." The new law also does not distinguish between public and private workers and does not specify the rights of workers in public-private ventures.

It is worth emphasizing that the delay in the passing of the labor law was not because of ETUF opposition, whose top leaders backed the legislation. In early 1999, Aisha Abd Al-Hadi of the ETUF's executive council told an Egyptian weekly, "Our position remains in favor of the law and we continue to call on the government to send it through the parliament."[31] But state officials, cognizant that the support of the labor elite did not guarantee rank-and-file docility, tried to enlist mid- and low-level labor leaders by raising the pay for union representatives and workers elected to the boards of companies to an estimated LE30,000 a month. This elite-based approach to dealing with labor succeeded in getting Law 203 and the recent Unified Labor Law passed, largely because the base was shut out from decision making. But the ETUF leaders' public support for privatization and the new labor law further alienated workers. After the new law went into effect, strikes erupted partly over its unfulfilled promises. In February 2005, ESCO textile workers went on strike to protest the government's sale of the factory to a private industrialist. The workers wrote to the attorney-general questioning the legality of the sale, stressing that although the new labor law stipulates that workers are partial owners of the plant—with a 10 percent equity stake—they were not informed of the sale. The ETUF's refusal to defend the workers' further eroded its credibility. "The GFTU [ETUF] takes its orders directly from the authorities. They tow the official line and support privatization," declared Mohamed Awad Nahran, one of the striking workers. "We reject this so-called union and what it stands for."[32]

Reformers have used different strategies to neutralize labor opposition, including repression. State authorities' attempts to break up a sit-in at Kafr al-Dawwar in 1994 left four dead. A strike in January 2000 at Helwan Hastings Company was crushed by the police; five workers were arrested, sent to a military prosecutor, and then sent to a military camp.[33] The state also uses more subtle means of coercion, such as forcibly "persuading" workers to take early retirement. Reformers have also used the structure of the ETUF to check labor opposition and preempt protest. In 1995, an amendment to the trade union law was passed increasing the trade unionists' tenure in office from four to five years and allowing trade union officials to maintain their position on union boards after the official retirement age. The new law required candidates aspiring for a position on the federation board to have served at least one term in the office of a plant-level union, and candidates for a plant-level union position must have held union membership for at least a year. The 1995 law further increased the ETUF's stranglehold over plant-level unions and widened the distance between workers and unionists. Workers on fixed contracts had the right to vote in union elections but were not permitted to seek candidacy in such elections, and they would be the first to be dismissed in reforming the public sector. Law 203 also changed the relationship between the state and labor in the 314 SOEs listed for sale: workers hired on short-term contracts were not necessarily entitled for a renewal or extension of their contract; those hired on permanent contracts were not insured the benefits generally granted to public sector employees.

Labor's Crisis of Representation

A crisis of representation existed latently in the ETUF long before the economic crisis of the 1990s, which, straining the state's patronage sources, exposed the fault lines within the union movement. Since its establishment, the ETUF was under the control of the state. The regime had the right to appoint the entire executive board of the ETUF, and the minister of labor had the power to dissolve any union that did not toe the regime's policy line. Since the ETUF's 1961 convention, there had been a problem of representation: sixty-five federations had been formed, but only twenty-one individuals had positions on the confederation's executive committee, so that in effect forty-four other federations had no representation at that level. In 1964, a law changed the number of federations in the ETUF from sixty-five to twenty-seven. Many mid- and lower-level unionists protested that this made coordination and collective action difficult by placing together unrelated industries and unions.

Unionists likewise disliked the indirect electoral system introduced by the 1964 law wherein rank-and-file workers chose members of their own local board, which then appointed representatives to the federation convention. This impenetrable setup was exacerbated by the practice of *jam'*, whereby loyal upper level unionists were allowed to hold several positions at different levels of the union hierarchy at once. An amendment limited the number of positions senior unionists could hold to two, but upper level unionists still held positions in the ETUF and government at once. Throughout the 1960s, the state was able to influence the selection of candidates in trade union elections by making membership in the ruling party, the Arab Socialist Union (ASU), a prerequisite for candidacy. When the ASU was abolished in 1977, the Socialist Public Prosecutor was introduced to control the candidate selection process.

Since Sadat's bureaucratic purges of the early 1970s, there has been very little turnover at the top union leadership. Federation presidents have rarely been replaced by electoral challengers. Adli Rouman has described in detail the tensions and schisms existing within the ETUF, between the leadership and rank and file, among the leaders of different federations, and among confederation leaders and federation leaders who resent their superiors' increasing powers.[34] The structural constraints affecting the ability of lower level unionists to articulate their constituencies' opposition to reform became a source of contention in the 1990s. In the singular pyramidal structure of the ETUF, leaders of a federation have to receive the approval of confederation leaders, and local leaders require the permission of federation officials before they can act on plant-level issues. But as the debate over the new labor law showed, federation and confederation leaders largely support reform, even when large numbers of workers are affected. In Mexico, senior unionists did not constantly defend rank-and-file interests when it came to national issues, but union leaders used the party's structure and the state's resources to deliver workers' support in exchange for targeted benefits; as in Egypt, top Mexican unionists were co-opted, but scores of unionists at different levels were also given myriad incentives (and disincentives) to support reform.

Labor was unable to use the legislature to defend its interests either. The 1964 law reserved 50 percent of the Egyptian parliament's seats for workers and peasants, but these seats have rarely been occupied by workers and peasants and are more often taken by wealthy individuals who can afford to run for office. On the eve of the 2000 legislative elections, Ahmad Harak, the assistant secretary-general of the ETUF, put it candidly: "From the very beginning, the [1964] law defined 'worker' and 'peasant' too loosely, and as a consequence it was never really implemented . . . the upcoming parliament will be dominated by businessmen. Very few genuine worker and peasant representatives are running. We at the [ETUF], which represents over four million organized workers, will have only one member of parliament in the next parliament. He is Sayed Rashad, head of the EFTU, who won in the first round. We have no candidates standing in the third."[35] Unlike Mexico, where turnover occurs with every *sexenio*, there is little circulation in Egypt trade union hierarchy. The turnover that takes place in the ETUF's structure is often at the lowest level, where workers can monitor elections. At the middle and higher levels of the union and federation elections, unionists are insulated from electoral competition and rank-and-file pressure, a practice that was reinforced by the 1995 legislation. In Mexico, lower level unionists have recourse and opportunity for upward mobility via the PRI, the CTM, and alternative federations.

Unionists continuously bemoan the lack of representation for public and private sector workers. An activist at the Center for Trade Union Services cites the example of the 10th of Ramadan City home to "more than 600 factories and 90,000 workers, and only 18 union committees."[36] Workers have gone on strike and pressured for institutional reform within the ETUF but have been obstructed and told that the "unity of the trade union movement" must be protected. Regime elites were thus particularly disconcerted by the protest at Mahala al-Kubra in December 2006, which culminated in a rally of ten thousand workers in downtown Cairo; the protesters presented a petition to the General Union of Textile Workers demanding the impeachment of the Mahala local committee and the holding of new elections. The workers invoked Law 35/1976 to impeach their trade union representatives and began sending individual letters of resignation from their union with the aim of creating an independent parallel organization. While this conflict has yet to be resolved, the protests have spread to other areas, with thirty thousand workers in the Nile Delta and Alexandria staging similar demonstrations. This overt challenge to the leadership of the ETUF is worrisome to the regime, as the confederation often turns out workers for pro-regime demonstrations.[37]

Calls for the elimination of the trade union structure and the establishment of a more competitive trade union system are growing louder but sill have an uneven appeal. These leaders believe a plurality of independent unions would better articulate and defend workers' interests.[38] Labor historian and activist Amin Izz al-Din argues that the existing system of obligatory membership may increase a union's constituency and financial resources, but if mandatory membership were done away with, workers could use their right not to join to gain bargaining power and extract concessions over labor and state leaders. But critics retort that trade union pluralism would deprive workers of state subsidies and allow employers and state elites to employ divide-and-rule tactics, and they argue that a democratic restructuring of the current trade union system and an end to government interference would better serve workers.[39] One indication that state corporatism is losing control over labor is Egyptian workers' ability to form alternative organizations and to express their interests outside of the ETUF. If the corporatist system is neither containing nor articulating labor discontent, neither is the ruling party; but before analyzing party-labor relations, it is instructive to see how the Egyptian state, frustrated by urban opposition, was able to override rural opposition and liberalize agriculture.

Liberalizing Agriculture

In 1992, the NDP pushed through parliament Law 96, amending Law 18 of the 1952 land reform and raising the maximum rent from seven to twenty-two times the land tax for a five-year transition period, after which rent could be unregulated and tenants evicted. When the law went into effect in 1997, it led to a wave of protests. The new law affected approximately 905 thousand tenant farmers: an estimated 432 thousand became landless, 12 thousand were given land by the government, and the remaining farmers renegotiated tenancy or moved to land they already owned. The Ministry of Agriculture set up a credit fund of thirty-three million dollars to help tenants purchase land, but this was simply not enough given the projected cost of thirty-five thousand dollars per acre.[40] Despite the lack of funds to compensate all farmers affected, the state forged ahead with the liberalization program violently repressing protests and relying on rural elites to maintain order. The NPUP, which is supposed to defend labor and peasant interests, was unable to block the land reform legislation in parliament. The "official" party of the left may have lacked the clout to impede legislation, but as critics point out, the NPUP and other satellite parties could have pushed for an amendment to the legislation or provided services to their peasant constituency, but they did not. Like workers affected by privatization, peasants did not have a corporatist channel for representation or mobilization. The regime used coercion and NDP-affiliated rural allies to contain peasant protest. In 2004 alone, 49 farmers died, and 429 were arrested.[41] As NGOs stepped in to help affected peasants, the government in 1998 passed a law restricting NGO advocacy, in part to prevent groups such as the Land Center for Human Rights from lobbying for the displaced peasants.

Despite the swiftness of agricultural liberalization, the regime cannot effect similar policies in urban areas leading to the layoff of hundreds of thousands of workers; state and party control exercised through rural elites is what allowed for such drastic measures and contained rural protest. Urban popular discontent is stronger and more destabilizing than rural opposition, hence the regime's inability to implement Peruvian economist Hernan De Soto's proposed plan to create wealth from "dead capital"; the Egyptian state simply could not move thousands of urban squatters as planned. The regime's greater political control in rural areas rests on the support of rural notables and their ability to use the party institutions to contain dissent and deliver the peasant vote.

Labor and Party System

To understand ETUF-NDP relations today, it is helpful to return briefly to 1962, when Nasser formed the Arab Socialist Union, his third attempt at creating a party mediating relations between state and society. Nasser tried to attach the labor confederation to the ASU. The ASU was created and developed partly with the objective of monitoring elections at all levels of the ETUF. This party had a larger membership, a decentralized structure with bases throughout the country, and a presence in all the major work-places. When Sadat came to power, he ordered elections throughout the ASU, which had been demobilized after 1967, and the labor confederation. He then divided the ASU into different political parties and created the NDP, which, by design, had no ties to labor. Labor leaders were apprehensive of Sadat's project of multipartyism and feared that their benefits would be infringed upon. In November 1976, the ETUF declared that it would not align itself with any of the newly established political platforms and called for the establishment of an independent workers' party. Sadat had no intention of linking the ETUF to a party and rejected such calls for fear of losing control of the working class. In 1976 he altogether delinked the ETUF from the ruling party. But following the riots of 1977, he created new positions for the ETUF's elite at the top of the union bureaucracy and tried to lure the labor elite into publicly defending his regime's move toward capitalism by increasing their powers and privileges, further centralizing power at the top.

In 1981, Sadat passed a law that tightened the control of the federations over the locals and extended the term in office of all unionists at all levels to four years. He changed the ETUF leadership and reduced the number of federations down to sixteen. Sadat was in effect rebuilding the Egyptian state, and he needed labor's support; the reforms were intended to dilute labor's veto power and suppress the opposition of the base to the regime's new capitalist direction. Sadat needed labor's backing for his policies, particularly his new position toward Israel and the United States and to marginalize the leftist Tagammu party (NPUP), which had grown out of the ASU's leftist plank and gained the support of thousands of workers.

The ETUF gradually shifted its position regarding economic liberalization. If throughout the 1970s and 1980s the labor confederation had opposed Sadat's attempts at public sector reform, in May 1989 the ETUF issued a joint declaration with the Egyptian Businessmen's Association calling for price liberalization and reforms in the operations of the public sector.[42] Although this declaration did not endorse privatization, the fact that the ETUF was meeting with business leaders represented a significant turnaround in the confederation's stance—or at least of the leadership that had theretofore opposed public sector reform. The ETUF did not oppose Law 203 of 1991, which introduced the bureaucratic and managerial changes necessary for divestiture. The ETUF expressed some opposition to privatization after the 1991 trade union elections, during which the NDP lost a lot of votes at the base, but the ETUF backed down in 1994 when Sayyid Rashid said he supported privatization provided, as Mubarak promised, workers' rights would not be violated. The Electrical, Engineering, and Metal Workers' Federation (EEMWF) was the only federation that publicly opposed the law and rejected it at a federation congress. In March 1996, the ETUF declared its strong support for privatization.

Regime elites see labor's quiescence as necessary for implementing wage policy, price liberalization, and structural adjustment but are also aware of organized labor's veto power, which they have tried to diminish by manipulating the legal mechanisms and electoral institutions in the trade union hierarchy and the parliament. The regime's loyal and handsomely rewarded labor elite though cannot deliver their constituents' support for privatization. As El Shafei observes, "Today, Egyptian unions neither lead workers in struggle as their proper role would seem to require, nor manage to contain workers as the state would like," adding that when reform began "even middle and lower-level trade union representatives lost support of the workers."[43] Elite-level negotiations have enlisted the backing of the ETUF's bigwigs, but the rank and file, who oppose privatization, have yet to be incorporated into the NDP or the party system writ large. In some cases, when thousands of workers went on strike, as in Mahalla al-Kubra in December 2006 and September 2007, they poignantly rejected the mediation efforts of the NDP and called for the impeachment of the local union committee, which reports to the ETUF.

Political parties in Egypt are weak for various reasons, including state-imposed impediments to party formation, electoral rules that favor independent candidacy, and the parties' financial dependence on regimes. The practice of independent candidacy by which non-NDP candidates can win as many seats as the opposition and then join the ruling party hampers party formation, because it hinders the development of distinct party programs and the formation of constituencies. But it is the legal impediments restricting party formation that lead candidates—often from the outlawed MB—to run as independents. The leaderships of different parties' proximity to the government have stripped opposition parties of legitimacy in the eyes of workers. Thus, the NPUP was founded to defend farmers, and workers saw its membership decline from 240 thousand in 1976 to 30 thousand in 2002, largely because of its secretary-general Rifa'at El-Said's "pro-government leanings," which critics say shifted the party from far left to "governmental left."[44] Observers have also noted the deleterious effect of "incomplete parliamentarization" on party development, wherein unelected upper houses can censure governments and obstruct elected representatives.[45]

Access to the state is becoming more restricted. Before the Unified Labor Law went into effect, labor activists often used the courts to address grievances; workers would take their complaints to the Labor Office, then to the courts of first instance, and then finally to the appeals court. (In fact, in 2004 the Coordination Committee to Defend Worker Rights obtained a court ruling stating that the ETUF elections of 2000 were invalid.) But the new labor law has impeded workers' access to the courts by having petitions go to a five-member committee and then to the appeals court—of which there are only eight in Egypt—instead of the courts of first instance; this has deprived workers of an "important stage of arbitration" and led to a massive backlog of cases.[46] The weakness of the legislature and political parties, combined with the myriad laws restricting access to courts and NGOs, has led workers and other popular groups to find noncorporatist channels to express their demands. Historically, alternative avenues of protest have been the aforementioned workers' representation in management (WRM), which Nasser introduced to counterbalance the ETUF, and Voice of the Worker (*sawt al-amil*, VOW), created by workers in the mid-1980s. VOW activists often provided the leadership to plant-level protests that occured outside the union structure and set up a Center for Union Services in Helwan and Shubra al Khayma to provide assistance to workers.[47] While these alternative organizations still exist, NGOs and Islamist groups are becoming the most popular and effective conduits for labor protest today.

Labor and NGOs

Advocacy NGOs are increasingly articulating and defending the interests of Egyptian workers and farmers. If the NPUP could not prevent the reversal of the 1952 land reform or provide services to affected peasants, the Land Center for Human Rights (LCHR) would step in, providing services and legal aid to peasants who had lost homes. Likewise, while the leftist parties did little for workers adversely affected by privatization, the LCHR and the Center for Trade Union and Worker Services (CTUWS), founded in 1995 by a veteran unionist, defended workers' interests. Upon its founding, 135 workers appealed to the CTUWS for legal assistance when the regime prevented them from running in union elections.[48]

The growing importance of NGOs is a result of the weakness of the party system and the legal impediments to party formation. Law 40 of 1977 stated that all applications for the establishment of a party had to be signed by at least fifty people, half of them workers or peasants, and then submitted to the Committee for the Affairs of Political Parties.[49] In 1992, amendments to Law 40 made it even more difficult to establish a party. Individuals wanting to establish a new party had to submit a formal application but could not act or speak in the name of their political group until the Political Parties Committee (PPC) recognized the new party as legal. Out of the fifty applications submitted in the Mubarak era, the PPC only approved the establishment of the National Union Party in 2000; and out of the eleven parties legalized in the Mubarak era, ten gained legal status because of a ruling by a higher administrative court. Party development was also impeded by the PPC's stipulation that each party should represent a distinct political idea and that the organizations may not alter their philosophy or risk being dissolved for "deviating" from originally stated principles. This restrictive legal context leads activists to establish NGOs, which state elites find less threatening than political parties with their mobilizing capacity.[50] Many Egyptian NGOs also receive funding from Western-based organizations, so they are financially less dependent on the regime and have historically had more freedom to maneuver.

But state elites are limiting the space within which NGOs can operate. Article 11 of the 1998 NGO law drew a distinction between associations, which must be nonpolitical, and political parties. An association may not have political objectives, thus an opposition group like Kifaya cannot gain NGO status; more importantly, an NGO is prohibited from having ties to any political party. Unable to establish formal links with NGOs, which provide services at the grassroots level, parties are impeded from developing a social base. But the NDP has ties to many associations and relies on such groups to turn out the vote. Moreover, the labor corporatist sector was linked to the state bureaucracy, not the party (especially after the ETUF was delinked from the NDP in 1976), yet the trade union movement's upper echelons are dominated by leaders closely linked to the regime and with high positions in the NDP. (Currently twenty-one of the twenty-three federation heads are members of the ruling party.) While NGOs are forbidden from building ties to unions, the NDP also has semiofficial links to trade unions and openly courts workers' votes. In May 2005, Sayed Rashid, head of the ETUF, publicly enjoined workers to back Mubarak for another term and even asked the General Assembly of the Federation to applaud the president's achievements and demonstrate support for his candidacy;

in November 2005, NDP and ETUF bussed in poorly paid public sector workers to polling stations to stuff ballot boxes in support of the ruling party—and the ruling party still did poorly.[51] The regime thus prohibits both NGOs and opposition parties from developing ties to trade unions. This institutional hamstringing of political parties is a critical difference between Egypt and Mexico; in Mexico opposition political parties were free to develop and did develop ties to unions, NGOs, and different grassroots groups.

Links are nonetheless being forged between workers, NGOs, and opposition groups like Kifaya. The protests in the summer of 2005 leading up to the parliamentary elections saw mass protests led by NGOS and Kifaya, which tried to mobilize workers and unions. Kifaya bussed in demonstrators from over twenty governorates and specifically tried to mobilize workers. At one protest, Kamal Abbas of the CTWS denounced the ETUF's leader for endorsing Mubarak's reelection "on behalf of Egypt's 20 million workers." Opposition leaders are increasingly trying to attract workers' support to broaden the base of the reformist camp.[52] Labor activists in turn are trying to build ties with Kifaya and different NGOs to build a coalition for reform of the labor law. Activists are calling for the repeal of Law 35 of 1976, which allows the ETUF to control nomination and election procedures to trade union offices and prohibits the formation of independent local unions (a law that was deemed unconstitutional by the Supreme Constitutional Court). Clause 192 of the new labor law of 2003 is also proving to be a flashpoint because it states that workers cannot legally strike without permission from the ETUF, which must approve a strike with two-thirds majority. Badry Farghali of the NPUP has argued that independent unionism is the best response to privatization: "The government is privatizing the entire public sector at lightning speed and there is even talk of privatizing the Suez Canal. The time has come to privatize the unions. I propose we launch our own independent federation of trade unions."[53]

Islamists and Labor

Workers are also gravitating to different Islamist organizations. Some Islamist groups have protested market reforms because of their ideological commitment to labor; others have denounced privatization simply because they oppose the sale of Egyptian enterprises to the "neocolonial West" and Israel. The Muslim Brotherhood (MB), for example, is not known for its pro-labor sympathies and has a long history of opposing labor agitation dating back to the 1940s, when they clashed with the

Communists at the textile factory of Shubra al-Khayma, north of Cairo. The MB is better known for its bourgeois constituency, but, after opposing the left through much of the last two decades, in the late 1990s there was a short-lived alliance with the Labor Party, which saw the MB's leadership take certain pro-labor positions. Workers began gravitating toward the MB.[54] But when Adil Husayn, the Labor Party's Islamist leader, died in 2001, the Labor-Brotherhood alliance ended, and the MB reverted to its historic pro-business position.

But other Islamist organizations have emerged to advocate for workers. In 1992, a group of construction workers from the Cairene neighborhood of Imbaba tried to join the MB but were rejected for being "uneducated." The laborers instead joined the Islamic Group, a movement that had splintered from the Islamic Jihad in 1984 and moved from Upper Egypt to Cairo where it provided social services to the poor, found work for the unemployed, and mediated conflicts among workers, foremen, and contractors in Imbaba. Another pro-labor group, the Islamic Trend, appeared in the early 1990s fielding candidates in the 1991 trade union elections, calling for the right to strike and denouncing privatization and government meddling in labor elections.[55] Islamist social services associations have a significant presence in Egypt's urban areas, especially Cairo, among workers in large urban factories and rural migrants from southern cities. As James Toth observes, since the dismantling of the ASU, the urban underclass—which had expressed its interests through various ASU channels—did not have a channel for airing grievances until Islamic associations began appearing in the 1980s catering to the needs of the urban popular classes. Urban-based workers "joined more impersonal and anonymous trade unions and professional syndicates,"[56] whereas rural-born workers joined Islamist groups. As the adjustment process advanced, more and more workers began abandoning state-affiliated unions and syndicates for independent NGOs and Islamic groups.

The Islamist associations and progressive NGOs may have not been able to block the passage of the new labor law, but they did provide assistance to affected workers. And collective action on the part of workers—often backed by these groups—has derailed the privatization process. Different groups and Islamic associations are taking advantage of the state's limited control and splintering social base and seem to be having more success in incorporating the urban masses. The Egyptian state has been unable to override labor opposition or incorporate the organizations that defend labor's interests. The regime has responded to this challenge with exclusionary measures. State corporatism may have granted regime elites the capacity to manipulate different social groups in the 1970s, but today's reformers find that the institutions at hand do not provide the requisite flexibility and reach. After attempting liberalization, Sadat found that he lacked the tools to transform state-society relations and began moving toward repression and exclusion, shutting down channels of communication. Mubarak is continuing this policy of exclusion and disincorporation.

Elections and Exclusion

Structural adjustment has had a different impact on unions in different parts of the public sector. The public sector in Egypt includes the "public entities" (*hay'at 'amma*) such as the Suez Canal, other state-owned enterprises know as the "public sector" (*al-qita' al-'amm*), and the 314 companies that, since Law 203 of 1991, make up the "public business sector" (*al-qita' al-'amm li al-'amal*) slated for privatization. One reform measure that weakened unions was the fixed contract. In publicly owned enterprises, workers became union members automatically because their membership contributions were taken from their salaries. But this practice was not pursued in SOEs where workers were hired on temporary contracts. After 1995 most workers employed in SOEs were hired on temporary contracts and were not union members; the strategy, according to critics, was part of the state's attempt to "deunionize" workers. But the temporary contract was not used in the public business sector affected by Law 203, possibly because the new labor gave private sector investors considerable leeway in dealing with labor. The authorities created by Law 203 straddled the public-private divide and were partly intended to loosen ties and commitments to labor.

In 1995, rules were also altered to render unionizing in the private sector difficult. Consequently, the majority of workers in the private sector would not unionize and had little representation.[57] The ETUF decreed that to form a new union committee in a private sector company required 250 supporters—raising the minimum up from 50. This sector was made up of mostly small and medium-sized enterprises, so that not more than 10 percent of private sector workers were unionized. These measures in effect stripped workers of their rights. To stifle anti-reform activity, the government further tightened its control over the union movement passing laws, which took away decision-making power from the base, where activists could gain the most support. Law 12 of 1995 extended the terms of office for various union councils from four to five years, a measure that was retroactively applied to councils elected in 1991 and allowed senior personnel to stay in office past retirement. The law also allowed high-ranking executives, who had so-called "powers of employers" and were previously not permitted to join unions, to become members and to vote in union elections.[58] The right to vote was given to those in the upper tier of the ETUF, while those on the bottom were denied. Workers on fixed term contracts, who were the first to be affected by privatization and reform, could not vote at all and could not unionize. This was part of an effort to centralize control and amplify the voice of pro-reform unionists. The 1995 law further divorced the union leadership from the base by a new rule that allowed union leaders at the end of their terms to be reelected quite easily. The new provision did away with the preexisting rule that candidates for election to a higher union council—in the same year—first had to be elected to the council at the company or factory level. Loyal elite unionists were thus insured a longer stay in office, and there was consequently less turnover of personnel.[59]

In 1996 the ETUF decreed that any candidate for a union office had to receive the authorizing signature from the president of his branch union.[60] This function used to be performed by the socialist prosecutor. Now aspiring candidates had to receive authorization from the company and the local directorate of the workforce (*mudiriyat al-quwa al-'amila*) affiliated with the Ministry of Employment.[61] In his reading of the 1996 elections, Ibrahim underlines three features of the trade union elections: the lack of turnover in the ETUF's elite, the "bolting" of the ETUF's upper echelons from the organization's lower levels through electoral manipulation, and the continuing efforts to create a labor elite in favor of market reform.[62] In 1996, there was more turnover at the company level: 45 to 90 percent of the members of the union councils were replaced at every election, but no more than 30 percent were replaced at the branch level, and only 5 percent were replaced at the level of the federation, where change was generally due to retirement or death.[63]

After the elections, the ETUF council representing the twenty-three branch unions was made up entirely by NDP regime loyalists. In the four hundred seats of the councils of branch unions, there were barely any opposition figures. The regime also skewed elections through the practice of *tazkiyya*, which gave regime cronies elected positions in the administrative councils of the branch unions; around 45 percent were elected to office, but a large number of these positions were given to appointees because of a purported lack of candidates or competition. This absence of opposing candidates and competition was planned by outgoing union leaders who refused to provide signatures to potential candidates. Thirteen out of the twenty-three councils at the level of branch unions were "elected" in this fashion—by *tazkiyya*.[64] These councils thus kept their majorities. Finally, the regime's electoral engineering and organizing of the union movement by branch as opposed to geographic districts also inhibited collective action by making "physical mobilization" difficult. Authorities often divided companies into several constituencies so as to favor the regime's preferred candidate. These restrictions imposed on labor in the trade union elections allowed the state to maintain a consistent majority but prompted workers to seek alternative channels of representation.

Exclusion was also used in the trade union elections of November 2006. Boosted by its success in the 2005 parliamentary elections, the MB declared an interest in labor elections and in fielding candidates (many opposed to privatization) for 15 percent of seats allocated to company boards and 50 percent of the seats in the union hierarchy. The regime quickly resorted to administrative means to prevent Muslim Brothers from running for these positions by requiring candidates to produce two certificates—one from their workplace and another from the ETUF—before they could stand for office. Regime elites simultaneously moved to postpone municipal elections slated for 2006 to 2008 for fear of a string show by the Muslim Brothers. Labor activists complained that candidates were expected to get permission from union officials, who are often the incumbents they are running against, and in some cases, even if candidates did succeed in getting the required documents from the ETUF headquarters, they were told they would have to register in their local union offices the same day—a physically impossible task for candidates in regions distant from Cairo.[65] The elections of November 2006 seem only to have exacerbated labor's crisis of representation as many workers were barred by their superiors from running for office. The leadership of the ETUF council was in effect determined without elections. The results showed the NDP won twenty-two out of twenty-three ETUF council seats, while the Tagammu' (NPUP) won one seat.[66] A number of workers who were barred from running either by their unions or workplace administrations or the security forces are considering joining the Free Trade Union, an independent union in the process of being established by Nasserists and other leftist.

To many observers, the current situation is not sustainable. Hassan Fahmy, one of the leaders of the Mahalla campaign who tried to impeach their union officials, said the current predicament centers around union officials who have failed to represent the interests of their rank and file: "Three quarters of union officials are not elected by workers. They are appointed because the state security wants them, or else they are connected to management and work to protect management interests." One effect of the unprecedented wave of strikes of 2007, which spread from the textile industry to include transport workers, Cairo subway workers, sanitation workers, and even civil servants and real estate tax collectors, is that the elected strike committees of the tax collectors and the Mahalla textile workers have both in effect developed into organizational infrastructures for independent trade unions.[67] But the would-be founders of an independent trade union are still groping for political allies, given their reluctance to work with the Tagammu'—seen as a pro-regime force—and the MB.

The Muslim Brotherhood is historically not know for its labor sympathies, but recently, to the regime's chagrin, Muslim Brother MPs declared their support for protests at Misr Spinning and Weaving in Kafr al-Dawwar in February 2007 and for the strike at Arab Polvora Spinning and Weaving, which embarrassed regime officials since the enterprise had been privatized in the mid-1990s and held up as a successful model of divestiture. (When Polovora workers began protesting the elimination of benefits—paid sick leave, paid weekends—the government quickly blamed the MB for inciting the agitation.) Yet both the Nasserists and the Tagammu' (NPUP) have rejected the MB's overtures. The Tgammu', in particular, has been loath to form a coalition with the MB since the early 1990s, when under the leadership of Rif'at al-Sa'id, the party supported the regime's crackdown on the Islamist insurgency in southern Egypt and the urban slums of Cairo and Alexandria; this decision alienated the party from the grassroots struggle of the poor and working class.[68] At any rate, plans for a Free Trade Union have been considerably complicated by the regime's shutting down of the CTUWS in April 2007 on the charge that the center, while registered as a civil company, operates as an NGO and had incited workers to strike. Such exclusionary measures have also been used in parliamentary elections.

Labor and Parliamentary Elections

The People's Assembly in Egypt has little impact on legislation and usually simply ratifies laws introduced by the president, but an analysis of legislative politics can help gauge the support available for the ruling party and the opposition and illustrate how the regime uses elections to mobilize support. Since 1990, Egypt has been tinkering with electoral rules and interfering in elections to insure a majority that would support economic reform politics. If Egyptian leaders had the PRI's reach, they could reach out to workers and other urban groups who are voting against the NDP. The PRI bounced back following the electoral debacle of 1986 because of some effective institutional engineering; but lacking such capacity, Egyptian reformers are co-opting the labor elite and relying on coercion and exclusion to suppress rank-and-file opposition.

An examination of elections in Egypt shows that when relatively free elections were allowed in Egypt, starting in 1980 and 1984, the ruling party lost votes, and workers voted for the opposition. Bianchi's study of the relationship in different electoral provinces between the strength of the union

movement and electoral support for the NDP found "a persistently negative correlation in the parliamentary elections of 1976, 1984, and 1987 . . .
the strength of the negative relationship has increased with time and with
further advances in unionization."[69] The NDP's majority in parliament fell
from 88 percent in 1979 to 87 percent in 1984 and 77 percent in 1987, the
year when the NDP's official candidates won only 68 percent of the seats.
In 1990 a new system of constituency-based majority votes was introduced
to replace the preexisting system of party lists; this new practice would
weaken the opposition. The supreme court's constitutional decision to do
away with party lists was intended to liberalize elections, allowing anyone to run for office and ending the practice of "correction," whereby the
NDP would get the "leftover" votes.[70] The court ruled that the exclusion of
"independents" was unconstitutional and denied candidates a fundamental political right, and independent candidacies were thus allowed. With
the introduction of the new electoral system in 1990, the regime would
intervene, shamelessly rigging and manipulating elections. But despite
the use of fraud and appeals to the Emergency Law to dissolve opposition
meetings and arrest opposition figures, the NDP in recent elections has had
difficulty maintaining an electoral majority. With the introduction of the
majority lists system, the regime is no longer guaranteed the safe majorities it historically had. The heavy-handed manipulation and interference
in elections by the regime in 1990 and 1995 indicated the state's declining
control over party members.

Meanwhile, the adjustment process was alienating the regime's erstwhile supporters in the working class and eroding the state's social base.
Twenty-five years after its founding, the NDP still lacked a reliable base.
The ruling party was created in August 1978; by October of that year, its
membership numbered 900; it rose again to 2.2 million by October 1992
and was 3.6 million in October 1995.[71] But the NDP still lacked popular
support because the party provided few services or political opportunities.
Even during natural disasters, other political parties were more active than
the NDP.[72] The ruling party has yet to develop the popular base and infrastructure of the early Wafd, which boasted a wide institutional structure
to coordinate and lead the anti-colonial struggle and an electoral machine
that gained the support of the labor movement in the prewar era. The NDP
is also racked by internecine conflict. Al-Khawagga observes how Mubarak delayed the elections of 1995 because of infighting within the NDP
where local authorities in many districts resented the party leadership and
opposed the "parachuting" in of candidates chosen by the center in Cairo.
But the NDP is also the reformers' preferred tool for reconstituting the
regime's social base and governing coalition. As Kienle observes, "it was
only through this party that the regime created, re-created and maintained

its networks and clienteles, which, benefiting from the distribution of resources and favors from the top to the bottom, provided it with a limited but none the less real social base." The NDP's "limited" base was the product of the Nasserist state's aversion to parties, a historical legacy that Mubarak now has to contend with. Whereas in Mexico labor and ruling party have been historically linked, in Egypt a different situation has obtained: Nasser tried to have labor incorporated into the ASU but abandoned the effort; Sadat completely severed ties between the party and labor; and Mubarak is struggling with his predecessors' institutional legacies to build linkages between labor and the ruling party.

Party Reform

Following the 2000 elections and in anticipation of the 2005 elections, the NDP leaders began to focus on strengthening the party's ties to the grassroots. A six-hundred-member electoral college was established in every electoral district to select the local NDP candidate, doing away with the preexisting practice of informal selection by party notables. Party leaders also established procedures whereby members would elect the party's politbureau (fourteen members), general secretariat (twenty-five members), and chairman, a position for which party members could run. Five new secretariats were also added, so the party now boasts nine secretariats: for policies, financial and administrative affairs, political awareness, local municipalities, ethics and legal affairs, media, workers and farmers, women and the business sector. And to improve the party's finances in January 2003, membership fees were raised for sixty piastres to 2 EGP annually. To appeal to the youth, the NDP also began holding "town hall meetings" and "focus groups" to educate young people about the importance of political participation. The 2002 party congress described the new NDP as a "party for all Egyptians" and introduced its new slogan, "An Enlightened Vision and New Thought."

The party is being rebuilt in a neoliberal direction. Despite the emphasis on centrism, the party today offers more incentives and concessions to business than to the popular sectors. A new Public Business Secretariat has been established to encourage the private sector to join the party's ranks. The newly created Political Bureau has six committees reflecting the party's priorities: education, population and health care, economic direction, youth and participation, women's role in development, and "Egypt and the world." Yet while the economic directions section addresses the concerns of business groups and offers studies of taxation, industrial policy, and private sector investment in infrastructure, there is no comparable committee addressing labor or farmer interests. Even before the 2002 conference, the NDP was widely seen as not representing labor's interests. Labor activists observe that in 1994 the NDP Economic Committee had called for legislation to facilitate privatization: Unified Labor Law, Unified Investment Law, Housing Law, and Traffic Law.[73] The party's disregard for labor interest became more evident as the reforms deepened.

The party appears set on a neoliberal track, though increasingly frequent labor agitation forces the regime to make populist concessions. For instance, at its conference in 2003 to appease growing social discontent and to woo labor ahead of the 2005 elections, the NDP recommended that the government allocate an additional LE1.6 billion for food subsidies, to compensate the falling value of the Egyptian pound. In early 2005, Prime Minister Ahmad Nazif declared unequivocally, "The mistake of unconditional subsidies is over. We tried it for a long time and it failed. People have to earn their living. There is no free lunch. The government only interferes when there is a catastrophe."[74] But in July 2005, a few months after that declaration, Mubarak approved a 20 percent "social allowance" raise in the wages of government and public sector employees to diffuse labor discontent. These measures have not altered the party's commitment to market reform and seem designed to prevent civil unrest. (The government is now considering other—less drastic—ways of restructuring the subsidies program, either by revising the lists of ration card beneficiaries to exclude people deemed not needy or by replacing subsidies with cash payments.)

Despite party reform and Gamal Mubarak's insistence that the ruling party was introducing a "new social contract," where the state would grant rights in exchange for the citizens' participation in the country's development, the NDP still did poorly in the 2005 elections. The NDP won 311 seats, considerably less than the 404 seats it gained in 2000, and lost over a 100 seats. Although the NDP maintains a hold of 68 percent of the assembly seats, the MB tripled its presence by gaining 87 seats in the 454-seat assembly. The ruling party also failed to turn out voters. The turnout in 2005 was estimated at 25 percent. The party institutions being built in Egypt are still not reaching workers or urban areas. If, as Huntington wrote decades ago, a crucial aspect of party strength is "organizational complexity and depth, particularly as revealed by the linkages between the party and social-economic organizations such as labor unions and peasant organization,"[75] the NDP has yet to penetrate the lower levels of the labor movement and develop dense links with the popular sectors. The Egyptian state could establish Mexican-style channels through which urban working and popular classes can influence some of the allocational choices that bear on them and could create institutions like a tripartite wage and price commission to gain labor's quiescence. But while the Egyptian regime increased benefits to workers and set up a tripartite commission to negotiate the new labor law, it has not given workers much voice; the preferred strategy has been more exclusion, as opposed to Mexico's strategic inclusion. Instead of developing institutions to draw urban groups, the regime has tightened political control to manage a deteriorating economic situation.

The neoliberal reforms have inflicted tremendous hardship. Poverty increased, and living standards declined throughout the 1980s and through much of the 1990s.[76] Despite the taming of inflation, real salaries fell in the 1980s and 1990s.[77] The budget deficit was reduced by reducing subsidies on health, education, and various goods and through the passing of a regressive sales tax.[78] The depreciation of the Egyptian pound in 2000, combined with a widening fiscal deficit, led inflation to rise to 2.7 percent in 2002, 4.5 percent in 2003, and finally to 11 percent in 2004.[79] A study by Heba al-Leithi, a statistician at Cairo University, reported that the inflation rate on basic food items in 2004 was increasing at three times its pace during period of 2000–2. According to official Egyptian sources, unemployment rose from 8.9 percent in 1999 to 11.2 percent—that is, approximately, 19.3 million jobless—at the end of 2005, though many independent observers at the end of 2005 estimated unemployment at around 15–25 percent.[80] The Social Fund was created partly to deliver benefits to people hurt by market reform.

The Social Fund was established by a presidential decree in 1991. The World Bank granted the Social Fund $613 million for a program inspired by Mexico's Pronasol.[81] The state used the Mexican-inspired Social Fund for Development to channel benefits to affected communities in the areas of poverty reduction, job creation, and enterprise development. The SFD's main project though is the creation of small and micro businesses to generate jobs for recent graduates, unemployed youth, and workers laid off because of privatization. But with its limited budget, critics observe, the Social Fund cannot compensate for jobs lost or benefits cut and does not make up for a comprehensive social policy.[82] The projects are sponsored by an array of ministries and agencies (governorates, banks, NGOs, local community agencies, and public and private enterprises) that present proposals to the fund's top managers who then decide if a proposed project will be financed and then extend loans and draw up a repayment plan. The project is thus not run like Pronasol, from the president's office and serving as an antipoverty program and funding projects developed by local communities. Also, ever since it ceased financing early retirement schemes for workers, the Social Fund has become more focused on rural areas; some reports note that poverty in urban areas subsequently increased.[83] A recent study by the Near East Foundation praised the Social Fund's public works but warned that its projects contributed to urban growth and decreased agricultural land use.

More importantly, though, unlike Pronasol, the Social Fund lacks a discernible electoral strategy; projects are intended to combat poverty and diffuse social discontent but not necessarily mobilize votes. State elites may be unable to use the Social Fund for electoral or coalitional purposes because, while it was created by presidential decree in 1991 to help Egyptian workers returning from the gulf following the Iraq War, it is still financially dependent on various external donors including the European Union, Kuwaiti Development Fund, and various German and Japanese banks. This was different from Pronasol, which was funded by Salinas and, according to the official line, used revenues derived from divestiture, which further helped gain support for privatization by linking market reform to welfare policy. Sixty percent of the Social Fund's projects are public works done jointly with government organizations and implemented by private contractors, which again differs from Pronasol's modus operandi of rewarding pro-reform societal actors and incorporating popular groups.[84] Roger Owen has suggested that one way the Egyptian regime could try to reach the unincorporated population is by handing over the Social Fund from the World Bank to the NDP, which could then try and gain support in the poorest areas. But the Social Fund does not have the participatory dimension of Pronasol, and given the NDP's weakness and the Social Fund's relative youthfulness, it is doubtful if it can have the mobilizing effect of Pronasol.

External Rents and Privatization

While some scholars note that Egypt uses access to strategic rents to postpone a painful overhaul of the economy, others observe that IFI and U.S. funds are often contingent on economic reform. One could argue that international financial support is what jumpstarted the privatization process in Egypt. A debt relief deal of $4 billion was granted in late 1996, when the presumably reform-minded Kamal Ganzouri came to power. To alleviate the pain associated with privatization, in 1998, the Social Fund for Development received $672.5 million from international donors, of which $117 million was allocated to fund the early retirement compensation to fifty thousand laborers in thirty companies slated for sell-off.[85] In an interview with the *Washington Times*, even Mubarak acknowledged and expressed gratitude over how American aid had helped motor the privatization process.[86]

These scholars subsequently argued that the main reason privatization came to a halt in mid-1999 was because there was no money available to finance the early retirement schemes and pay off the debts of SOEs slated for sale.[87] This may be true, but the reform process went forward at other moments when external rents nose-dived, such as after the East Asian financial crisis that led to a decline in portfolio investment and Suez earnings, or following the Luxor terrorist attack in November 1997. I believe that no consistent causal relationship can be observed between access to rents and privatization, the latter process being ultimately more dependent on domestic opposition. It seems more likely privatization stalled in 1999 because the early retirement schemes strategy that had helped "shed" labor in SOEs subsequently sold was not useful in "shedding" labor in the remaining SOEs that were larger and required more layoffs. The Egyptian experience shows that when reformers have room to maneuver, they push ahead whether rents are flowing are not; on occasions external revenue directly aided the privatization process, but sometimes divestiture occurred even when rents were diminished or unavailable.

Starting in the early 1990s, the Egyptian regime began redesigning and restricting the boundaries of participation in both legislative and trade union elections to build support for pro-reform laws and policies. Unlike Mexico where state elites would reshape the political arena to absorb opposition from the left and the right, Egyptian leaders began using the NDP to mobilize the support of the "winners" of adjustment, but lacking the capacity to maintain the support of "losers," they are recasting the electoral landscape to include the middle and upper classes but exclude the populist sectors most opposed to adjustment. As in Mexico, the political backlash to market reforms has been the loss of support for the Egyptian regime, evident in the trade union and parliamentary elections. Despite the widespread fraud and manipulation of electoral rules, the Egyptian regime still has trouble maintaining a majority in parliament. As support for the Islamist opposition is growing, the state is scrambling to shore up its unraveling base. The regime is silencing critics, excluding opposition to reform, and giving political voice and patronage to the supporters of the reform process. Mexico, between 1982 and 1994, could politically manage the social tumult and electoral backlash unleashed by neoliberal reforms. The Egyptian state is not so nimble and has opted for exclusion and coercion. Amendments to the labor union law have restricted the participation of workers who would be affected by privatization, while strengthening the position of future owners and employers.

Like Mexico, Egypt is using electoral mechanisms to mobilize support and enlisting the support of business and the middle classes; but given its institutional limitations, it cannot insure the support of a demoted organized labor in the governing coalition and so is slowly excluding the working class. It appears the losers of the reform process are being politically marginalized in preparation for a more drastic economic exclusion and possibly a complete abrogation of the Nasserist contract, while the winners are granted political rights and an opportunity to join the ruling coalition. The exclusion may not be as extreme as in Chile under Pinochet, as the ETUF continues to exist and its politically compliant union elite continues to serve an important purpose of rubber-stamping regime policies. But with the implementation of neoliberal reforms, Egypt is becoming more authoritarian and state-society relations more polarized.

8

Shifting the State from Left to Right

In the early 1990s, Mubarak tried to rework the Nasserist political formula and craft a new bargain whereby he would grant a degree of political liberalization in return for acquiescence to an adjustment program, but the experiment was abandoned as opposition to economic reform mounted and Islamists exploited the opening. More than a decade after this political endeavor failed, and with privatization stalling, Egyptian state officials are reaching out to the private sector and strategic urban constituencies but also excluding groups seen as anti-reform. This chapter examines how Mubarak is trying to rebuild the state and shift the regime's social base from left to right, but without the pact-making or participatory programs used in Mexico; political liberalization, it is feared, would unleash organized opposition to economic reform and allow the Muslim Brotherhood to gain a foothold in the state.

The Egyptian state's isolation is the result of the regime's historical aversion to mass participation. Even when party organizations were created, wary of the competition posed by the Muslim Brotherhood, Nasser would check the participation of urban voters and rely on rural elites to deliver the rural vote. In the 1950s, Egypt's "problem of participation" was partially resolved by mobilizing the rural notables into the National Union and repressing strategic urban groups such as the Muslim Brotherhood, Wafd, and Communists. This type of detachment from urban constituencies served the regime well for a while, granting state officials a remarkable degree of autonomy and social peace as long as the boundaries of the postrevolutionary compact were not transgressed. But Egypt's participation problem rose to the surface with the fiscal crisis and initial attempts at reform. State officials are now realizing how participation can enhance their control and are becoming increasingly reliant on the National Democratic Party (NDP) as the main instrument with which to gain the support of propertied classes and to marginalize anti-reform Islamists and populist interests from the party and state apparatus. But, as in the 1950s, the participation is limited and selective.

The attempted democratic bargain of 1991 was also an effort to co-opt the Islamist "counter-elite" as new intermediaries between the state and society and to use members of the Muslim Brotherhood and other Islamic associations as middlemen to extend the state's reach. This failure to incorporate led state officials to adopt an exclusionary coalitional strategy, which has narrowed the regime's social base and resulted in the current standoff between the regime and the Islamist opposition led by the Muslim Brotherhood. Yet as the Egyptian state excludes and represses various social groups, establishing ties with business and rural elites (and to a certain extent, lower middle class groups), opposition to market reform mounts; the more the regime limits the channels of participation (outside the NDP), the more it loses the support of urban voters. These state-society struggles are being played out in the electoral arena and outside the corporatist system but also within the state, in battles between different bureaucratic factions and between the executive, legislature, and judiciary, with different state actors sensitive to the demands of particular societal interests.

To build support for market reform, the Egyptian state is also trying to introduce a new ideology and development discourse. Mubarak's attempt to ideologically reorient the Egyptian state or public can be seen in the NDP's new discourse of "active centrism," "market reform," and "equality." But in addition to its limited infrastructural capacity, the Egyptian regime also lacks ideological hegemony and coherence and has yielded significant ideological ground to the Islamist opposition. The Nasserist idea that the masses should refrain from politics in exchange for welfare benefits—that consumption, in Singerman's formulation, is a form of participation—is not sustainable as benefits are withdrawn. The regime is trying to introduce a new discourse and dialogue to overcome this "institutionalized apathy."

Several scholars have observed that the Egyptian regime is moving toward bureaucratic authoritarianism as reform is "deepened" and the popular classes are excluded. I argue that total Chilean-style exclusion will not occur. The ETUF still serves an important purpose, and top labor leaders are still crucial for the regime's legitimacy and control. Egypt is moving toward a soft kind of bureaucratic authoritarianism without the complete disbandment of parties and labor unions. As a state-business alliance is consolidated and propertied classes are brought into the NDP, Egypt is beginning to display the features of an authoritarian party corporatism, a soft bureaucratic authoritarianism with labor economically excluded and politically demoted from its already subordinate position as a junior coalition partner.

Crisis and Private Capital

In analyzing the Egyptian state's efforts to build an alliance with business, using economic inducements and administrative reform, it is important to note that the Mexican state never acted against the private sector—appropriating wealth and property—the way the Egyptian regime did. Nasser appropriated the capital of Egypt's European, "Egyptianized," and native business communities. The Mexican state was able to find allies for its reform project (in part because of Mexican business's organizational strength), while the Egyptian regime is still trying to find or build a business constituency for change. It is estimated that eighty billion dollars of capital are held by Egyptians overseas; the challenge is how to draw this capital back into Egypt.

In its Letter of Development Policy of September 1993, the Egyptian cabinet declared that "the government's vision of the economic future of Egypt is a rapidly growing private sector operating in a competitive and stable environment." Prime Minister Atef Sidqi told the People's Assembly that Egypt would move to export-led growth, exporting leather goods to the EU; textiles, foodstuffs, and pharmaceuticals to the Arab world; and cotton clothing to Japan and Holland.[1] Economic reforms were supposed to liberalize trade and promote exports, removing most nontariff barriers on imports and exports within two years and reducing high customs tariffs. The public sector and banking system were supposed to be restructured as well, liquidating unviable public enterprises and eliminating the soft-budget constraint for SOEs.

In the early 1990s, Egyptian regime did reach out to business, giving private entrepreneurs lucrative deals on SOE sales and setting up the investment promotion body, the General Authority for Investment and Free Zones. To promote private sector investment, the government also liberalized prices on cement and fertilizers and removed restrictions on the private sector's access to bank credit and foreign exchange. The Ganzouri-led government also weakened the Investment Organization (IO), which had been used to decide which private investment projects would be licensed; the IO now simply tracks and writes reports about new projects. Another incentive to investment was the Egyptian Trade Union Federation's Decree of 1996, which raised the minimum number of members needed to form new shop-floor committees in the private sector; it became very difficult to reach this number in the majority of private enterprises, which simply did not employ that many people. This decree is also significant because the Egyptian private sector employed 67 percent of the total workforce in the country and 36 percent of the nonagricultural workforce.[2]

Other legislation was passed to encourage investment. Law 230 was passed granting tax exemptions for projects promoting exports, technology transfer, and employment. Law 203 of 1991 restructured the public sector in preparation for selloffs. The Capital Market Law passed in 1992 helped establish the Egyptian capital market where shares of SOEs would be sold. The Banking Law of 1992 removed further restrictions on capital movement. In May 1997 the People's Assembly passed a new investment law (Law 8) that provided greater incentives for investment in sectors such as software, automobile parts, manufacturing, and infrastructure and provided tax holidays for projects in certain geographic regions. New guarantees protected enterprises from nationalization and the interference of administrative agencies in the pricing of products. The Ministry of Supply and Trade also drafted an antitrust law to oversee mergers, a couple of which took place in early 1997.[3] Business leaders were also granted positions on committees and consultancies with the state. The Federation of Egyptian Industries, the Egyptian-American Presidential Council (created in 1995), and the American Chamber of Commerce were all consulted more frequently by the regime.

Egypt has to some degree liberalized trade, considerably reducing barriers and eliminating export bans and quotas. The foreign exchange quota system for SOEs and the requirement of prior deposits for imports were also abolished. By December 1993, the state had eliminated almost all nontariff barriers. Egypt also signed a trade protocol with Israel establishing seven "Qualified Industrial Zones" (QIZs) where goods would gain free access to U.S. markets if 11.7 percent of their content originated in Israel (a deal that U.S. Trade Representative Robert Zoellick described as "the most important economic agreement between Egypt and Israel in two decades").[4] Joint ventures have also been established with Israeli companies: In June 2005, an agreement was announced whereby Israel would purchase $2.5 billion worth of Egyptian natural gas over the next fifteen years from East Mediterranean Gas Corporation, an Egyptian-Israeli consortium. Interestingly, while business interests have protested trade liberalization, labor has not opposed or felt threatened by the trade opening; more imports and exports do not necessarily violate the Nasserist pact.

Despite the progress made, critics note that the Egyptian economy still remains closed with high tariff barriers, an important source of revenue, and protects industries such as textiles from imports. And Egypt's trade balance has not been positive, primarily because of the weakness of the private sector. Much of the private economy is made up of micro-enterprises, many of which are based in the informal sector and lack the productive capacity, capital, and technology, and often even the legal status, to partake in export-led growth. Likewise, despite some improvement, FDI has not been as forthcoming as expected. From 1990 to 1998, revenues from privatization in the Middle East and NorthAfrica (MENA) made up less than 3 percent of the total revenue accruing to LDCs from privatization.[5] Scholars hold that MENA attracts little foreign investment because of the regimes's "illiberal" and "information-shy character," which drives away investors for whom the free flow of information is crucial.[6] Egyptian state banks also dominate the country's banking system. Businesses often complain about the lack of transparency and about rarely knowing the level of "capitalization" in the country's state banks. Egypt's capital market is also weak and undercapitalized. In 1993, Mexico's market capitalization stood at $139 billion, while Egypt's boasted $2.6 billion.[7] In May 2000 investors "fed up with the lack of clarity governing stock transactions," protested in front of the Egyptian stock exchange headquarters.[8]

More legal and administrative reform is needed to create the proper policy environment and to lure foreign and domestic capital. Sadat's experiment of *infitah* failed despite the support of the West because of a lack of capitalists and a lack of a legal framework that could regulate the market. Laws are often introduced by different ministries with conflicting interests and little input from the private sector. The low capacity of Egypt's court system also hinders investment. Nathan Brown notes how foreign businesses in Egypt sign arbitration clauses in all contracts to excuse them from having to settle business disputes in an Egyptian court: "The most obvious loser is domestic business. Less able in constructing private arbitration systems, but equally repelled by slow litigation procedures, owners of small businesses have few attractive options."[9]

All these factors have affected the process of privatization, which has been slow and selective. The state has been unwilling to cede control over certain sectors for fear of provoking worker unrest and of losing control of rents and labor. Egyptian business is simply too weak to bear the burden of development and absorb the labor force growing at 2.5 percent per year—half a million new entrants a year.[10] The privatization that has taken place has been in light industries, services, hotels, transportation, tourist facilities, and cement producers. Foreign investment does not threaten the state's sources of rents or patronage if directed into the energy sectors, telecommunications, transportation, or areas of infrastructure that the state does not want to finance. In some "sensitive" industries, the state has formed joint ventures with foreign capital, which allows the regime to maintain control of sectors that can now be privately financed. In doing this, as Nazih Ayubi has noted, the state is putting funds from divestiture back into the public sector—thus re-regulating, not de-regulating, the public sector—and not eliminating the state's role as a safety net as prescribed by the IFIs.[11] The World Bank in fact expressed concern that money earned from privatization ($3.3 billion by 1998) was being used for "recapitalization" of the public sector, "essentially repeating the cycle of squandering resources on more bad loans."[12]

Egyptian Business Federations

The weak organizational power of Egyptian business associations is crucial for understanding the slow pace of market reform. Business groups in Egypt do not have the autonomy and financial resources to engage in effective lobbying and remain dependent on the patronage of political leaders and thus, unlike Mexico, cannot enhance the state's developmental capabilities. The bourgeoisie that emerged after infitah remains divided, dependent on the state for opportunities and reluctant to make large investments. The most influential capitalists in Egypt, moguls such as Osman Ahmad Osman and Ahmad Bahgat, are cronies of Mubarak and receive protection, licenses, and access to credit in exchange for their political support. The Bahgat Group, which assembles electronic goods, successfully got Mubarak to insure that no competitor could enter their business. Likewise, when the Egyptian pound became overvalued in 1999 and imports increased, the automobile industry pressured the Ministry of Trade, through the president, to pass Decree 619, which prohibited the importing into Egypt of transshipped auto parts. The regime allows local capitalists with monopolies and oligopolies to operate in the protected domestic market. But unlike the East Asian developmental state, the Egyptian state does not push private enterprises to export to the international market but allows them to provide for the protected domestic markets.

In Egypt, as in Mexico, the regime either created certain business associations, like the Union of Chambers of Commerce, or commanded those from before 1952 such as the Federation of Egyptian Industries, but these groups rarely exerted any influence on the state. Business associations, the Federation of Egyptian Industries, and the American Chamber of Commerce are still governed by Law 32 of 1964 under which they were established, and the government selects their board members. After infitah, the Egyptian Businessmen's Association and the Egyptian-American Business Council were founded. These last two organizations are less docile and lobbied for protection and licenses. Today the Egyptian Businessmen's Association and the Federation of Egyptian Industries are stronger and more organized, but they are still not effective as instruments of state control.

Both the American-Egyptian Chamber of Commerce and the Egyptian Center for Economic Studies, which the United States helped establish, remain weak in terms of capital. The business federations are still led by elites close to the president, or his son Gamal Mubarak; and in parliament, business leaders are discouraged from voting for the opposition. Some businessmen are resisting reform, particularly small and medium-sized manufactures who fear competition, tariff reductions, higher taxes, and the little access to capital that they will have if the reform process continues.

Laissez Faire "Success Story"?

Toward the end of the 1990s, Egypt was being hailed as an IMF success story, and one IMF study celebrated the "remarkable turnaround in Egypt's macroeconomic fortunes."[13] The economy was growing at 5 percent per year, and the private sector was providing two-thirds of domestic investment. Tight monetary policy had reduced the government's budget deficit from 15 percent of GDP down to 3 percent. Were these achievements due to the operation of free markets and neoliberal policies or state intervention? Were Egypt's economic policies accurately understood and represented? As in Mexico, the hoopla over Egypt's economic growth downplayed or did not mention the sharp fall in living standards during the reform period. Real wages in the public sector dropped by 8 percent from 1990–91 to 1995–96. The proportion of people living below the poverty line increased from 40 percent in rural and urban areas to 45 percent in urban areas and 50 percent in rural areas.[14] More recently, following the currency depreciation in 2003, prices on basic foodstuffs rose by 40 percent, and according to government reports, 6.8 million government and public sector employees lost half their salaries.[15]

Interventions by the Egyptian government and by the United States aided the process of economic stabilization. The Egyptian state intervened to protect the local currency from the global foreign exchange market. As the value of nonoil exports fell from 1995 through 1997, Egypt became dependent on oil for 52 percent of its export earnings. The drop in oil prices in 1998 made the situation worse, such that Egypt at one point had to halt oil exports until the U.S. government, following negotiations with Saudi Arabia, Iran, and Venezuela, managed to have OPEC cut production and double the price of oil.[16] It was the American political intervention and not the free market that alleviated the crisis and spurred growth; the ensuing boomlet was a product of Egypt's relationship to the United States. Like Mexico, Egypt's economic reform process was aided by American largesse—subsidies in the form of loans and debt write-offs—but American subvention ultimately could not compensate for the Egyptian state's lack of institutional capacity and the private sector's weakness.

Government intervention was also evident in the financial sector, where the boundary between the public and private sector was also often blurred. Seventy-five percent of bank deposits continue to be held by state banks, and the remaining are held in twenty-three joint venture banks, which are at least partially owned by the big four public sector banks. Mahmud Abdel Aziz, chairman of the biggest public sector bank, the National Bank of Egypt, is also chairman of the biggest '"private" bank, the Commercial International Bank (CIB). In the mid-1990s, the state intervened on behalf of the banking sector, restructuring credit and raising interest rates initially as high as 14 percent above international market levels. Portfolio investment flocked into Egypt, but when the interest rates were brought down in 2000, the investment boom ended. Economic reform did not lead as intended to a rise in exports (in fruits and vegetables to Europe and the Gulf) but caused a real estate boom as the state emerged as an entrepreneur subsidizing urban property developers, selling public land at low prices, and constructing bridges and roads for real estate development. The conglomerates such as the Osman, Bahgat, and Seoudi groups received preferential treatment from banks in terms of access to loans. When the Middle East Refinery (Midor), initially envisioned as a joint venture between an Egyptian and Isreali industrialist to export petroleum products, failed to attract sufficient private investment, the state decided to increase its share of investment to 60 percent and to target the domestic market.[17]

Since the economic downtown triggered by the attacks of September 11, 2001, FDI had climbed back up to $3.9 billion by mid-2006 and Egypt's currency reserves had risen to $23 billion thanks to higher net capital inflows from tourism and Suez Canal revenues.[18] But the Egyptian state is still struggling to reverse capital flight and to gain business's full backing. Mubarak is consulting periodically with different private sector groups and trying to bring business into the NDP. This is a significant change of position for a regime that does not have a good record of dialogue with civil society. Sadat rarely sought the endorsement of business leaders or professional syndicates. He even clamped down on the Wafd Party, which historically represented business interests and was conceivably his natural ally in the infitah project. But Mubarak is trying to forge a new bargain with the private sector. If Mexico transformed state-society relations and allowed for capital accumulation through a bargain of "limited democracy," Egypt seems to be moving toward a more exclusionary system of "authoritarian accumulation" that would limit the economic demands of labor. If Mubarak's earlier attempt at political liberalization between 1987 and 1990 was complicated by a low voter turnout, populist and Islamist opposition to reform, and resistance to adjustment even from within the ruling party, by the mid 1990s, the Egyptian leader had abandoned political liberalization and seemed set on pushing the reform process even with a narrow and limited political base. Regime elites thus sought to build a new rural-urban support coalition.

Market Reform and Rural-Urban Divide

The Egyptian state controls the countryside better than urban areas. Scholars have long understood that the rural elite are a pillar of the regime, a social group that Cairo uses to rule the Egyptian hinterland. The rural middle class has long served as a counterweight to urban interests, particularly after 1967. Before the six-day war, the ASU did deliver an urban constituency for Nasser, but after 1967, as James Toth has argued, urban areas would once again be unrepresented and be seen as a source of threat. When Sadat came to power in 1971, faced with unruly urban groups, he sought to shore up the support of his rural allies by, among other things, changing the definition of "peasant" from someone who owned twenty-five feddan to someone who owned fifty feddan to allow small landowners to have positions in the parliament.[19] In the 1976 elections, Sadat further curried the favor of landed interests through a series of measures: ending a freeze on agricultural land rents in effect since 1952, eliminating a disputes committee used to arbitrate conflicts between landowners and tenants, and desequestering land taken from landowners after the revolution. Analysts have argued that when Sadat launched his Corrective Movement, purging the state and arresting adversaries in the bureaucracy, party, and military, he prevailed because of support from the armed forces and from rural elites in the National Assembly.

The NDP's primary objective in the late 1970s was to establish control over the bureaucracy and syndicates and broaden its urban base—a goal that the regime is still trying to achieve. In response to the student riots of 1968, Sadat broadened university enrollment by admitting nearly all high-school graduates. (Under Nasser, it was mostly middle class youth who went to university.) The infitah policies aimed to satisfy the middle class's demands for consumer goods. With Sadat's economic opening, rapprochement with Israel and turn toward the West was thus underpinned by a particular coalitional strategy and an attempt to successfully balance urban and rural interests. But the NDP's base of support was still in the rural areas. As Ansari observes, when the ASU was broken up into different political platforms, "the representative system remained heavily biased towards rural areas."[20] The NDP has, since its creation, received more votes and generated a higher voter turnout in the rural areas than in Cairo or other large cities.[21]

Like Sadat, Mubarak used the ruling party to mobilize rural support to counter urban political movements, in particular the Wafd and the Muslim Brotherhood. In 1984, fearing that people might vote for the Wafd, Mubarak appealed to rural landowners to turn out the peasant vote; in return, the government allowed rural interests to prepare a law for land reform and looked away when some landowners raised rents and evicted tenants.[22] As Minister of Agriculture Yusuf Wali stated in 1982, "The rural sector and the farmers in particular, will always remain the backbone of the political power supporting the philosophy of the NDP."[23] As minister and secretary-general of the NDP, Wali saw the rural vote as a priority and called on the regime to end government crop procurements as a way of gaining the support of rural voters. Wali's strategy would eventually succeed in gaining the backing of rural notables, whose support would prove crucial in liberalizing agriculture and reversing social policies protecting tenant farmers against eviction (policies that World Bank consultants said "were creating disincentives to more efficient use of land."[24])

In 1992, the NDP pushed through parliament Law 96, amending Law 18 of the 1952 land reform, and raised the maximum rent from seven to twenty-two times the land tax for a five-year transition period, giving landowners the unprecedented authority to raise rents sharply and evict tenant farmers. When the law went into effect in 1997, it led to a wave of protests[25] and affected approximately 905 thousand tenant farmers, almost half of whom became landless. Despite the lack of funds to compensate all farmers affected, the state forged ahead with the liberalization program, violently repressing protests and relying on rural elites to maintain social peace. Like workers affected by privatization, peasants did not have a corporatist channel for representation or mobilization. The regime used NDP-affiliated rural allies to contain peasant protest.

Despite the "success" of agricultural liberalization, the regime cannot effect similar policies in urban areas that would result in the layoff of hundreds of thousands of workers; state and party control exercised through rural elites is what allowed for such drastic measures and contained peasant protest. Urban popular discontent is stronger and more destabilizing than rural opposition. Sociologists have described how Cairo's areas of informal housing (*ashwa'iyat*), which are Islamist strongholds, are impervious to state control and surveillance; having arisen outside of state planning, these *ashwa'iyat* are not easily accessible via paved roads and are not connected to public transportation systems, which physically—and politically—isolates the populations of these areas from the state.[26] And since the state and party apparatus do not reach these areas, private companies have come in selling services, but it is mostly Islamist organizations who provide security and social services.[27] As Garreton has written of Pinochet's Chile, when a regime closes off regular party channels, other spaces emerge "by default" as sites of political contestation;[28] these "substitute" sites, as the case of Egypt shows, can often appeal to the mass public and develop substantial followings—and the authoritarian state may be unable to prevent or co-opt these "autonomous zones" from appearing and expanding.

Regarding the ruling party's thin urban support, Salama has argued that the NDP's social base in urban areas is bureaucrats and businessmen, who have little grassroots support.[29] In rural areas, the party relies on rural notables, even religious teachers, who see that the NDP is the best provider of patronage. The lack of intermediaries linking the state/party to the popular classes in urban areas explains the NDP's weakness in cities, especially in the capital Cairo. In the 1990 elections, Muhammad Shuman notes, as workers voted against the NDP and flocked to the opposition, the ruling party's "institutional fragility" and "lack of presence" became embarrassingly evident in the urban centers of Cairo, Alexandria, Port Said, and Suez. He underlines the "collective aversion" (*uzuf*) to the NDP in Cairo, even from urban constituencies whose interests should coincide with the ruling party's program, and this he attributes to a lack of civic training and ideological outreach by the party.[30]

The Egyptian state's limited control over urban areas was evident during the antiwar protests of spring 2003. On March 20 and 21, thousands of protestors broke through security cordons in downtown Cairo and tried to march on the American and British embassies. This demonstration defied a decades-old ban on street protests that had been in place since the "food riots" of January 1977 and drew a strong response from the police, who even arrested members of parliament in violation of their legal immunity. Fahmy Howeidy, a prominent Islamist commentator, noted that the Iraq War had prompted "the rise of the unorganized,"[31] which included scores of students and ordinary citizens eager to participate but with no political channels available and which exposed the institutional vacuum existing between the state and society, a vacuum that the Islamists were filling faster than the state. Critics warn that by not allowing for the legalization of Islamist parties and severely restricting the activities of secular parties, the regime allows no political outlet for Egypt's youth and Islamists, which could unleash new cycles for violence.

Egyptian state elites have long responded to urban unrest by shoring up rural support. Mubarak used agricultural liberalization to solidify his alliance with landowners and the rural middle class. Underlining the increased role of the rural notables in legislative elections, al-Khawagga believes that this could be an attempt by the regime to "recompose" the political class, adding that "the recourse to [rural] notables guarantees local control and is more of necessity than a deliberate attempt to 'retraditionalize' politics."[32] Alain Roussillon in turn thinks that that the regime's failed attempts to co-opt urban-based Islamists as new intermediaries have made rural elites even more indispensable. As he put it,

> The Egyptian state's recurrent problem as a central/centralized state is that of identifying the intermediaries through which it may preserve global control over these collectives, maintain public order and impose social items regarding which the regime refuses to negotiate. Under the old regime, the role of the intermediary between central power and the local level was played, in the countryside, by the owners of the latifundiae enjoying absolute authority over their villages and peasants, through an army of foremen, managers, lenders, right-hand men, and in the city, by the notability system and the futuwwa network. . . . Under Sadat, and more clearly still under Mubarak until the 1980s, the regime attempted to coopt the Islamist trend for this role; the failure of this attempt is what constitutes the framework of [today's] confrontation.[33]

Because of Nasser's distrust of parties, today the most influential movements in Egypt stand opposed to the state. The standoff between the regime and various urban-based groups—but particularly with the Muslim Brotherhood—is shaping the coalitional and adjustment strategy adopted by reformers. This state-society situation has also affected attempts to restructure the Egyptian bureaucracy and rebuild the ruling party.

Bureaucracy and Capacity Building

In Mexico, the PRI regularly mobilized the population for elections. Aside from some experimenting during the 1960s, Nasser never mobilized citizens into parties. With the employment drive of the 1960s, the regime canalized political participation into the state apparatus. Nasser's understanding of autonomy did not mean bureaucratic autonomy from societal interests but rather the executive's independence from the popular classes whose quiescence was purchased by welfare guarantees, including jobs in the bureaucracy and public sector. Without a party, the Egyptian state would become politicized and emerge as the sole target of societal demands. Schneider's description of Brazilian state corporatism, where in the absence of party and legislative politics "the military forced politics into the executive," captures the Egyptian case: "With other avenues blocked, bureaucratic appointments became the primary means for recruitment and elite representation. . . . As institutions recede, personalities grow in stature."[34] Vested bureaucratic interests would rise, jealously guarding their turf within the Egyptian bureaucracy, and, as Mustafa Kamal al-Sayyid argues, would undermine all efforts to create party organizations.

Scholars have long argued that Egypt's massive and politicized bureaucracy is a major obstacle to the country's economic development. The regime's institutional weakness and emphasis on control has resulted in low technical capacity, overstaffing, overlapping jurisdictions, constant reshuffling of administrators, lack of career incentives, "primitive record keeping," and conflicting rules and regulations, all of which contribute to the bureaucracy's inefficacy.[35] The large number of ministries (there are usually thirty-two ministries with two hundred agencies under their authority) with overlapping jurisdictions allows top decision makers to divide and rule different social groups.[36] Agencies are often created to appease a particular lobby or societal interest, and ministries are constantly being merged or reorganized so that policy is fragmented and incoherent.

El Shirbini demonstrates how the process of economic policy making is divided among four ministries—industry, economy, finance, and planning—with little interministerial coordination.[37] Since the era of ISI, there has been a struggle in the Egyptian bureaucracy between the Ministry of Planning, which designed the five-year plans, and the Ministry of Finance, which critics argued was better suited to design the strategy of industrialization. Various accounts have highlighted Egypt's "problem of planning," underlining the weakness and "ambiguous legal status" of the ministry of Planning in contrast to the ministries of finance, production, and industry and the absence of coordination between these entities. Moreover, the agencies that are often beholden to special business interests (i.e., investment, supply, construction, industry, transportation, energy, and agriculture) are often opposed by welfare ministries that distribute benefits to larger, poorer constituencies (i.e., social affairs and insurance, health, youth, manpower and technical training, and pious foundations).[38] Both neoliberal reformers and statists seek support for their policy positions by appealing to constituencies outside the state, be it from social groups or international financial institutions.

Bureaucratic reform and capacity building do not occur overnight, as shown by Mexico's decades-long process of administrative reform that concentrated power in the presidency, created a pilot agency, and allowed for the ascendancy of neoliberal technocrats. Although there have been efforts to streamline Egypt's policy environment, such attempts have not been as far-reaching, and the economy remains regulated by an estimated fifty-eight thousand laws and bylaws.[39] The bureaucratic reform necessary for structural adjustment has taken place in a limited fashion in Egypt. Jreisat's account of administrative reform and capacity building in

Egypt concludes that most attempts have failed for lack of political will, infighting, and overlapping jurisdictions, even in the process of bureaucratic reform. Three offices have clashed in implementing reform: the Central Agency for Organization and Administration, which produces studies describing the responsibilities of different positions and reorganizing different agencies; the National Institute for Administrative Development, which is responsible for training and leadership development; and the Ministry of Administrative Development, which hires foreign consultants and oversees changes in the information system.[40]

If the rise of the SPP and its role as a planning agency was crucial to reform in Mexico, the Ministry of Planning in Egypt remains a weak unit. The Public Enterprise Office (PEO) was set up in 1992 as part of the Public Sector Ministry to oversee the privatization process, but it has limited decision-making power; the PEO's twenty-five staff members will often negotiate agreements with donors or IFIs, only to be overruled by other ministers. But various institutional reforms have been introduced to facilitate privatization. In 1996, the High Ministerial Privatization Committee was established, including officials from the Ministry of Finance, the Prime Minister's Office, and the Public Sector Minister, intended to insulate officials in charge of divestiture from societal and bureaucratic pressures. Along these lines, Yusuf Boutros Ghali attempted a restructuring of the Ministry of Economy, which has not been streamlined since its founding in the 1950s. Boutros Ghali tried to expand the research and the financial institutions sector and added a fifth sector focusing on investment, overseeing the securities market, and helping small and medium enterprises.[41] In June 2006, a ministerial committee was created with the aim of adjudicating the disputes that often arose when the Ministry of Investment came up with an evaluation of an SOE slated for sale; comprising this committee are the ministers of investment, trade and industry, finance, planning, labor and manpower, and the governor of the Central Bank, who would approve final evaluations and all sales.

Despite the adjustment process, the Egyptian bureaucracy is still growing; between 1988 and 1998, the Egyptian state was still the employer of last resort; government employment grew 4.8 percent each year, making up for 42 percent of job creation in the 1990s.[42] This expansion of the bureaucracy serves to show that privatization is not necessarily shrinking the state, as neoliberalism would predict. Economist Samir Radwan has argued that privatization-related layoffs reduced employment in SOEs, but the civil service is expanding and continues to be one of the primary mechanisms of labor absorption: government employment in Egypt grew from 22.1 percent in 1990 to 27.7 percent in 2001, compared with a worldwide average of 11 percent.[43]

Political Elite and Bureaucratic Reform

A comparative study of economic liberalization in Egypt and Algeria shows that the state elites who ran the state-dominated economies in the 1970s were the same ones in charge of reforming the state and switching from ISI to export-led growth.[44] Mubarak benefited from Sadat's purging of the state, but despite frequent reshuffling, since 1981 there has been little genuine circulation among Egypt's bureaucratic elite. Since the reform process began, Egypt has had three different prime ministers—Atif Sidqi (1986–96), Ganzouri (1996–99), and Atif Ebeid (1999–2004)—but these men have been part of the ruling elite for decades and hardly represent change in the bureaucratic corps. Ganzouri and Ebeid both were ministers under Sidqi, then Ebeid was one of Ganzouri's ministers during the latter's premiership. Other ministers have remained in office since Mubarak's assuming office in 1981, including Yusuf Wali as minister of agriculture and deputy prime minister, Safwat Sharif as minister of information, Mohamed Tantawi as minister of defense, and Suleiman Metwalli as minister of transport and communications. Many of these so-called "old guard" are drawn from the Vanguard Organization (*Tanzim Tala'i*), the group of civilian apparatchiks Nasser brought into the ASU in the 1960s.

While the "political posts" concerned with political control and society have not seen much change, technocrats have taken over many of the key economic positions. Viewed by the international community as a credible reformer, Yusuf Boutros-Ghali has repeatedly declared his commitment to reforming the Egyptian state: "What we are trying to achieve is a change of governance. We must change the concept of the state from that of a predator to that of a mediator or a facilitator. People should react to market forces, not to administrative fear. . . . The regulatory system must work in a predictable way."[45] International observers were particularly pleased by the cabinet shuffle of July 2004, which brought businessmen to ministerial positions (described as a "critical mass of reformers"), though Egyptian critics saw this is as another case of the regime's crony capitalists gaining political power. Many of the ministers, commentators noted, are part of Gamal Mubarak's group based in the NDP's Policies Secretariat discussed below, including the McGill-educated Prime Minister Ahmed Nazif, Industry Minister Rashid Mohamed Rashid (CEO of the Unilever Egypt), Tourism Minister Ahmed El-Maghrabi (CEO of the French tourism group Accor), Youth Minister Anas al-Fiqqi, and economist Mahmoud Mohieddine who heads the newly established Investment Ministry. Political scientist Magdy Sobhy has underlined the new cabinet's strong ideological leaning toward monetarist supply-side economics and noted how the new government swiftly cut personal income and corporate taxes (capping the latter at 20 percent) and reduced custom duties by fifty percent.[46] (Observers are also wary of the new team's exclusionary approach to market reform; as Gamal Mubarak told the faculty of Cairo University, constitutional reform and ending twenty-three years of continuous emergency rule "are not among the priorities of the National Democratic party . . . it is not possible to follow the wishes of the man on the street on everything and make them a reason for effecting foundational changes.")

As in Mexico, the economic crisis and need to negotiate with IFIs has strengthened the technical capacity of Egypt's ministries of finance and panning. But the Egyptian bureaucracy simply lacks the flexibility and institutionalized personnel turnover of Mexico. In this regard, it is important to recall a key difference between Egypt and Mexico: the *sexenio*, which facilitated economic reform by allowing for an infusion of reform-minded technocrats into the state apparatus and for the co-optation of thousands of opponents and supporters into the state and party bureaucracy. The sexennial elections of Mexico and the subsequent turnover of elites not only allowed for co-opting labor but also for purging the state. And while the "economic" posts do see new blood, it is not clear that technocrats in Egypt have decision-making powers. The president along with the prime minister and his appointees prepare the public budget and development plan. Certain specific economic policy decisions are made by the council of ministers again under the president's aegis, but policy is ultimately decided by the Higher Policy Committee (HPC), a body of officials, mostly cabinet ministers and the head of the Central Bank, who decide pricing policies, control the public sector, and can overrule the decisions of ministers.

Like its Mexican counterpart, the Egyptian constitution grants the president tremendous policy-making power. The constitution reflects Sadat's obsession with autonomy and presidential power during his power struggle with Sabri in 1971. The Egyptian president can introduce bills to the parliament (which individual deputies can do in theory but rarely do), veto laws passed by the People's Assembly, and even dissolve the assembly. Articles 126 and 127 give the president the right to dismiss all ministers. During the Egyptian presidential elections—which take place every six years—the assembly selects the only presidential candidate who is then confirmed by a majority of two-thirds in the assembly. The constitution allows for the reelection of the incumbent president or (as in Mexico pre-1994) for his selection of a successor.[47] But while power may be centralized in the presidency, the Egyptian executive lacks the institutional reach that de la Madrid and Salinas had. Moore and Springborg assert that with the creation of a command economy, the executive became the Arab state's tool for achieving two objectives—control/surveillance of the population and the cultivation of support through the distribution of patronage.

Institutions for the formulation and implementation of policy were never fully developed or granted the necessary autonomy.

Privatization and Political Control

Despite the battles over reform within the Egyptian state, the depiction of Egyptian reformers as embattled neoliberals obstructed from "shrinking the state" by entrenched bureaucratic interests neglects the fact that the state has not entirely relinquished control of the restructured or privatized SOEs and that, through joint ventures, the regime in effect has outsourced its management to corporate allies. This new method of control can be seen in Law 203 of 1991, which created holding companies to prepare SOEs slated for privatization with the aim of delinking the SOEs from the five aforementioned ministries that were controlling them; but implementing such "delinking" would imply loss of control and patronage, so the state has preferred public-private arrangements. Thus state-holding companies have set up private sector subsidiaries such as Al-Ahram Cement; and the Ministry of Information, with financing from public sector banks, has established the ostensibly private Media Production City, touted as "the largest media production company in the Arab region" and traded on the Cairo and Alexandria Stock Exchange.

Commenting on the how the Egyptian state is encouraging private investment in electricity, petrochemicals, waste management, and insurance, sociologist Eric Denis writes, "The state has privatized the building of parking garages, the subway system, roads and tunnels through 'build, operate and transfer' contracts (where private transnational companies, usually based in Europe or the United States, build infrastructure, profit from it by toll or fee collection, then much later transfer it to the Egyptian state and public)."[48] Plans to outsource and lease state infrastructure to big business have drawn protests from a variety of quarters. Popular groups and consumer protection organizations have arisen—again outside the corporatist and party system—to resist the privatization of public services, the high service fees, and impending layoffs; among these groups are the Popular Association for the Protection of the Citizen from Taxes and Corruption, and the Citizens' Rights Committee headed by journalists Farida al-Shubashi and Ahmad Taha. But even the Wafd Party—historically a bastion of economic liberalism—released a statement declaring that "major projects of a national nature and strategic importance must remain in public hands." And when the People's Assembly passed a law in August 2006 allowing the state to privatize the Egyptian Railway Authority, NDP members of parliament denounced the impending selloff; NDP spokesman Abdel-Ahad Gamaleddin said the law is very serious "because the privatization of the railway services could be very bad for poor and limited-income people."[49]

Hardcore statists still exist in the upper echelons of the state, and bureaucratic interests have on occasion blocked attempts at divestiture—such as when bureaucratic resistance led to the canceling of a deal with General Motors on automobile production and the sale of the state-owned Meridian Hotel in Cairo. But these instances occurred often when state officials felt that the state was losing control or being short-changed in the proposed venture. Tensions arise when the proposed joint venture appears to be leading to foreign domination, as when the Italian company Italcementi raised its stake in Egypt's largest cement producer to 70 percent.[50] But overall the rift in the state bureaucracy between reformers and étatistes has softened, for the reason that public-private ventures and ambiguous public-private boundaries allow statist factions to maintain patronage and control over "privatized" SOEs. Investment Minister Mahmoud Mohieddin's declaration that there is no such thing as a "strategic commodity or strategic sector" masks the fact that most of these strategic SOEs were leased to private actors but were ultimately still under state control.[51] The reforms triggered by Law 203 are thus not depoliticizing economic decisions and rationalizing industrial production. The state is still exercising control albeit through new state agencies and via new private sector allies. One study observes that the holding company's "responsibility for portfolio management led to an interest in building a strong and mutually supportive conglomerate of affiliated firms rather than dismantling it by privatization."[52] Dillman similarly expresses skepticism about public holding companies being a purported step to privatization: "Granted the same legal status as private companies, they are still subject to government interference. Many joint ventures with multinationals provide holding companies with new technology, capital, and access to foreign markets. The process does not get rid of state ownership, but continually shifts and redefines the boundaries between public and private."[53] Institutional measures like Law 203 allow the state to draw foreign capital and collaborate with big business, which can eliminate commitments to labor, even lay off workers, while the regime maintains control over economic decisions.

The NDP and Coalition Building

Economic liberalization has caused the old populist coalition to unravel. The historical beneficiaries of state largesse have experienced material losses as public expenditure is cut; medical care, education benefits, and housing programs are reduced; and civil service jobs diminish for university graduates. With the budget cuts, the state's control in urban areas has been further compromised and challenged by the Islamist opposition. The regime is now trying to build a pro-reform coalition using the ruling party. But despite the opposition's calls for political liberalization—the Wafdist leadership has repeatedly called on the state to engage the private sector, saying that "economic prosperity depends on political stability, which in turn is based on democracy"[54]—the regime has opted for an exclusionary strategy because of its lack of support in urban areas and the party and corporatist system's inability to mobilize voters.

The NDP's electoral mechanism and patronage machine is now being used to marginalize large sections of the population, particularly the lower classes, and to include the propertied classes. The Egyptian regime is in a difficult position, losing the trust of old populist allies and being outflanked by Islamist groups in urban areas. Mubarak is trying to draw capital's support and retain workers' political support, while excluding them economically. He is also, by some accounts, trying to develop a working relationship with the Muslim Brotherhood while isolating the more anti-reform and militant Islamists groups. The Egyptian regime's coalition-building efforts are most visible in the electoral arena. The rebuilding of the ruling party is reflecting a contradictory mix of political imperatives, as can be seen in recent policy decisions; the NDP is trying to adopt a market-driven and pro-business direction, but popular protest keeps forcing party leaders to maintain a pro-welfare appeal.

The NDP's ideology has evolved and grown more nuanced. The 2002 party congress described the new NDP as a "party for all Egyptians" and described the party's "active centrism" as reflecting the "moderation of the majority of Egyptians" and underlined the NDP's support for the free market and export-led growth, but like the rector state (*Estado rector*) Salinas had called for, the NDP leadership recognizes the state's role in insuring equality.[55] The NDP's position on economic reform at the 2002 congress marked a significant change from its position in July 1998, when party leaders had stated their adherence to the July 23 Revolution and emphasized the role of the state in protecting citizens from the vagaries of the market. Regarding privatization, in 1994, the NDP Economic Committee had called for legislation to facilitate divestiture—Unified Labor Law, Unified Investment Law, Housing Law, and Traffic Law.[56] But in 2002, the NDP declared its belief in market solutions and called for the privatization of key sectors including health care. One policy paper stated that the socialist principle of providing free public services, especially in the state-controlled sectors of health and education, should be ended: "The NDP believes that opening the door for the private sector in private services will lead to streamlining the administrative systems of these services and an improvement in quality. This is because the NDP believes that a competitive market economy is the best way to achieve greater efficiency in the use of natural and human resources."[57]

The party is being restructured and steered toward the right to include and reflect corporate interests. Before the elections of February 2000, the president shook up the NDP's Political Bureau, dropping former prime minister Atef Sidqi and bringing in Atef Ebeid. Mubarak also shuffled the party's General Secretariat, bringing in Yousef Boutros-Ghali as minister of economy, Nadia Makram Ebeid as minister of environment, and Alayeddin Hilal Dessouki as minister of youth, and three prominent business leaders, Ibrahim Kamel of Kato Investments, Ahmad Ezz of Ezz Steel, and the president's younger son, Gamal Mubarak. (The induction of the latter three into the NDP's upper echelons put to rest rumors that Mubarak's son was going to build a business party called al-Mustaqbal; the NDP, it appears, is the business party). Mubarak has sought to make the private sector a key NDP constituency, and in the last decade business groups have clearly gained a voice in the party via the Public Business Secretariat and the NDP's Economic Committee, which has basically become a lobby instrument for business. The elections of 1995 and 2000 also saw a sharp increase in the number of businessmen joining the NDP; businessmen would represent just over 14 percent of all deputies. The rivalry between the NDP and other political groups for the loyalty of urban constituencies is seen clearly in parliamentary and municipal elections.

Political Stalemate: NDP versus Muslim Brotherhood

Egypt's parliamentary, municipial, and professional union elections—and particularly the squabbling over the interpretation of Law 73 of 1956 stipulating judicial supervision over elections—revealed the rifts between the judiciary (the Supreme Judicial Council) and the executive and between the regime and the Islamist counter-elite and illustrate the Egyptian regime's ongoing evolution.[58] Electorally, the NDP is attempting to gain the support of business, the middle classes, and the labor elite, while trying to demote the rank and file who could potentially obstruct economic reform. Observers note that the 2000 elections saw the largest turnout in a decade in part because the judiciary supervised the subsidiary polling stations. The Supreme Constitutional Court was called to monitor the elections of 2000 after its judges passed a ruling invalidating the 1995 elections. The elections to the People's Assembly in 2000 reduced the NDP's majority from 94 percent to 87 percent of the seats, its worst performance since its creation in 1978, a decline partly due to the supervision of the elections by the judiciary but also due to the NDP's unpopularity and low capacity. The NDP won a precarious majority (388 seats), but only 237 seats went to candidates officially chosen and endorsed by the party.[59]

Analysts termed 2005 Egypt's "year of elections" because of the May 25 referendum on amending Article 76 of the 1971 constitution to allow for direct, multicandidate presidential elections, presidential elections on September 7, and the November-December parliamentary elections. The amendment placed tight restrictions on who could run for the presidency and made it even more difficult for candidates from small "legal" opposition parties to get the necessary number of endorsements from elected officials. The subsequent legislative elections were also a debacle because although the NDP kept its majority—316 seats, 73 percent of the total— more than half of its candidates were defeated. Technically, since only 149 out of its 444 candidates actually won, NDP candidates obtained only 38 percent of the seats. Official NDP candidates won no seats in three governorates (Suez, Ismailiyya, and Matruh). The remaining 167 seats were taken by NDP candidates, who were not selected as official candidates but ran as "independents." This was ironic given that Gamal Mubarak, in restructuring the party, had said the NDP would no longer tolerate "rebels" challenging its favored candidates but would field experienced party cadres.[60] Yet Gamal Mubarak's preference was overruled by party elders, like Secretary-General Safwat al-Sharif, who led the effort to allow the independents to join the NDP.

The 2005 election was ultimately a fiasco for the ruling party, which was able to maintain a majority only by readmitting the "rejected" independent candidates and using the state apparatus to promote the party. "The NDP," as one observer wrote shortly after the 2005 elections, "remains mostly a party of opportunists who join it for access to state resources and regime networks. Gamal Mubarak's purported efforts at 'party building,' hailed in the past three annual conferences and in the aftermath of the presidential election, have been revealed as hollow."[61] Analysts argue that Gamal Mubarak's prominent role hurts the party, highlighting its proximity to the presidency and regime; and critics often refer to the ruling party "as a vehicle for presidential succession." The NDP's closeness to the regime became even more of a liability with the outbreak of the Iraq War. The party was heavily criticized for adopting a position widely seen as pro-American, and on the second day of the war the party's downtown headquarters were almost vandalized by crowds carrying large posters of Nasser and Palestinian leader Marwan al-Barghouthi. Provincial secretaries and newly formed councils had been given orders to not describe the war as a new crusade or war against Islam, but in face of public outrage and seeing themselves outflanked by the opposition, party leaders soon changed their tune, with NDP Secretary-General Safwat El-Sherif saying that "volunteering to fight for Iraq is a guaranteed right for all Egyptians." This about-face though did not reverse the party's electoral fortunes.

In the 2005 elections, the Muslim Brotherhood obtained a total of eighty-eight parliamentary seats, the strongest performance by an Egyptian opposition party since 1952, and increased their number of seats sixfold from 2000. Almost 70 percent of the NDP candidates who ran against Muslim Brotherhood candidates lost. Egyptian political parties with their weak institutional capabilities proved no match for the Islamist organization.[62] The results lent credence to Saad Eddin Ibrahim's observation that the Muslim Brotherhood is Egypt's only real political party.[63] Following the 2000 debacle, the annual Arab Strategic Report devoted five chapters to the "bankruptcy of (Egyptian) political parties," stressing how the Muslim Brotherhood "was in direct contact with the people through social, cultural, and economic activities," while the NDP was out of touch and unable to even gain the votes of its own parliamentary members.[64] The Muslim Brotherhood's unprecedented performance showed how far the group had moved toward active political participation and evolved from "a highly secretive, hierarchical antidemocratic organization . . . into a modern multivocal political association," responding to the institutional rules of participation set by the state. The movement's philosophy has evolved as well, as its leaders have called for party pluralism moving away from Sayyid Qutb's famous denunciation of parties as "partisanship" (hizbiyya) and toward moderate Islamist conceptions of democracy, women's rights, religious and political pluralism, and a rejection of political violence.[65] As the Muslim Brotherhood won more seats, the organization's leadership stated—to reassure different groups—that the organization was committed to the democratic process and would focus on reform rather than the Islamization of Egyptian society.

But the Muslim Brotherhood is still not recognized as a political party, because the constitution bans the establishment of political parties on religious bases. Between 1984 and 1991, the government tolerated the Muslim Brotherhood, allowing members to form an alliance with the Wafd in 1984 and with the Labor and Liberal Parties in 1987, when the triple alliance won sixty seats, the largest number ever won by the opposition. The regime, however, restricted the Muslim Brotherhood's activities after the outbreak of violence in 1992; the group then proceeded to win landslide victories in professional syndicate elections. The Muslim Brotherhood currently controls several student unions and professional syndicates, including the Bar Association and the Doctors' Syndicate. And since assuming office in 2006, the Muslim Brotherhood's parliamentary bloc has been acting like a real political party and reinvigorating parliamentary life, working across ideological lines to serve constituents and drawing attention to a range of issues.

State officials and NDP elites are pondering how to deal with the Muslim Brotherhood, whether to grant them legal status as a party or as an association. Those in favor of legalization hold that as long as Islamists are not allowed to form their own party, they will penetrate other parties, state institutions, and civic associations. They also argue that legalizing the Muslim Brotherhood would "revitalize" the NDP by forcing the ruling party to compete for votes with an organization that has a large following; legalizing smaller parties would not reinvigorate politics, because they do not pose a challenge to the ruling party. Others warn that legalizing the Muslim Brotherhood immediately would lead the group to dominate the political arena, since other parties—including the NDP—would be overwhelmed, and could destabilize the state as in Algeria, where the legalization of the Islamic Salvation Front led the party to monopolize the representation of Islamists and the urban poor (though critics retort that the FIS was about to form a majority in the Algerian parliament, while the Muslim Brotherhood will only form a minority.)[66] But political analysts across the political spectrum contend that the regime should try to level the political playing field in favor of other parties. As long as the regime—through the PPC and other legal mechanisms—prevents opposition parties from challenging the ruling party, opposition will emerge outside the party system.

The Muslim Brotherhood has been the regime's bête noire since 1952 and has shaped the coalitional strategies of successive strategies, but it is also affecting the political calculations of other political players. Leaders of the Tagammu and the Wafd are considering whether to form an alliance with the Islamist organization. Even Ayman Nour, the incarcerated leader of the recently formed Al-Ghad Party who was expelled from the Wafd after falling out of favor with party elder No'man Goma'a (though some analysts have held that the regime pressured Goma'a to expel Nour),[67] has sought the support of the Muslim Brotherhood. In August 2005, the Wafd leader No'man Goma'a met with General Guide Mohamed Mahdy Akef, who declared that there were deep historic ties between the Muslim Brothers and the Wafd.[68] There was speculation in Egyptian newspapers that the Muslim Brotherhood might renew its political alliance with the Wafd, which had existed in the 1980s.

A Wafd-Brotherhood alliance has not arisen, but the three main opposition parties—the Wafd, Tagammu, and the liberal Al-Ghad Party—have all called for the empowerment of parliament and detailed specific reforms to break through the current NDP-Brotherhood stalemate (including the elimination of the Political Parties Committee, which constrains the rights of opposition parties, a revision of the law to allow NGOs to forge links with political parties and a reform of the system of local elections so as to end the NDP's dominance of local government). The institutional rules at the local level also help insure NDP dominance. As Mustafa Kamel writes, "The judiciary is prevented from monitoring local elections as required by the constitution, because regime officials hold that local councils are part of the executive rather than legislative branch of the state, so that the constitutional provision requiring judicial supervision over legislative bodies does not apply."[69] The polarized political landscape—the standoff between the NDP and the Muslim Brotherhood, the Islamists' impressive electoral show, and the ruling party's poor handling of the election—has left many political actors feeling disgruntled. Abdel Moneim Said has argued that Egypt needs a new political party to occupy the space between the NDP and the Muslim Brotherhood in order to mobilize the "silent majority" that is drawn to neither alternative and to depolarize the political arena.

The Muslim Brotherhood, many of whose leaders are members of the "infitah class" produced by Sadat's economic liberalization, supports market reforms and as such poses a different challenge to the regime than the militant Islamic Groups. When Sadat began his "de-Nasserization" program, and even more recently during the debate on land reform, the Muslim Brotherhood sided with the large landowners against the smaller farmer.[70] By tolerating the Muslim Brotherhood in elections, the regime seems to be trying to achieve a new modus vivendi with the pro-reform propertied Islamist opposition who are gaining a following among small businessmen. In June 2005, following a meeting between two independent MPs belonging to the Muslim Brotherhood and Zakaria Azmy, a close associate of Mubarak, there was speculation that the group would receive some kind of legal status. The legalization has not occurred, but analysts have pondered if the behind-the-scenes meetings are a sign that the Egyptian state may be considering a rapprochement with private sector Islamists to counter challenges from leftist groups, and that the regime is trying to "depolarize" mass politics and recast society's "cleavage structures" by engaging the Muslim Brotherhood, accommodating business groups, and excluding anti-reform populist groups and more militant Islamic Groups.[71]

Others point to Recep Erdogan's Justice and Devlopment Party in Turkey, which is clashing with labor unions in its efforts to sell off SOEs, and argue that through a cautious accommodation the Egyptian regime may be able to enlist the support of the Muslim Brotherhood in the push for privatization. After all, most analyses of the Muslim Brotherhood's economic philosophy underline the group's calls for a "shrinking of the government bureaucracy and having the private sector as the backbone of the economy.[72] But it seems more likely that the regime will opt for further exclusion and repression. Fears that the Muslim Brotherhood bloc could undermine the NDP's majority or embolden the legislature against the executive or block privatization have already led to warnings that MPs attached to the Muslim Brotherhood may not be allowed to hold office. State officials have intimated that a new electoral law would be introduced to prevent "banned organizations" from entering parliament. Prime Minister Ahmad Nazif put it candidly: "Islamists who say they belong to an illegal organization have been able to go into Parliament and act in a format that would make them seem like a political party . . . We need to think clearly about how to prevent this from happening."[73]

Incorporating Islamist Associations

The year 1992, which saw armed confrontations between Islamists and the police in Imbaba and Asyut, was a turning point in the state's dealing with the Islamist opposition, as state elites began opting for exclusion as the most effective way to neutralize their challenge—and to push through neoliberal measures. The regime had previously attempted to appease and co-opt the Islamists, even allowing them to launch highly publicized court cases against authors deemed anti-Islamic, such as Naguib Mahfouz, but with the escalation of violence, the regime resorted to repression. The first significant military assault on the Islamists took place in December 1992 when Mubarak sent five thousand troops to the popular district of Imbaba in Cairo after the local Islamist leaders declared the area the "Islamic Republic" of Imbaba.

While the regime has unilaterally defeated the Islamist Groups (Gama'at) and rural notables have been able to maintain social peace in rural areas, the state still does not control urban areas or large parts of the hinterland.[74] And in many cases where the regime did co-opt or gain control over Islamist charities or mosques, the state would shut down these institutions but not deliver services of its own, thus recreating the vacuum that had led to the initial rise of these Islamist associations. While employing violence against militant groups, the regime has attempted to co-opt different Islamist associations, to incorporate their constituencies thereby expanding the state's social base. But the state lacks the capacity and legitimacy to incorporate large segments of the mass public—or even specific political actors such as the Islamist counter-elite and their "alternative social infrastructure."

Different analysts have noted that with its withdrawal from the provision of welfare and services, the Egyptian state lost control over parts of the country—particularly Upper and Central Egypt—to organized Islamist groups. The state is conspicuously absent in these regions. The

Egyptian state has never successfully penetrated Upper Egypt, which includes the country's eight southern governorates, a region that, historians point out, neither Napoleon nor the British could subdue and that has long been ruled through the state's alliances with rural notables, the so-called *arab* and *ashraf* families.[75] Mamoun Fandy has noted that the central government in Cairo has "depended on the local notables [of the Sa'id] and their traditional authority to ensure order. . . . In fact, southern villagers consider it shameful to involve the courts or police in their disputes." Immigration to Saudi Arabia and Kuwait further strengthened the Islamist movement, as migrants returned to building mosques, community centers, and clinics and challenging the *umdas* power to mediate disputes. The return of Egyptian migrants from the gulf during the Gulf War of 1991 and the passage of the 1992 Tenancy Law would infuriate these groups, which eventually turned to violence.[76]

The political violence would prompt the regime to announce an initiative to incorporate thousands of mosques that had proliferated outside the state's control and to annually bring ten thousand of these institutions under the control of the Ministry of Religious Endowment. Law 175 of 1960 gave the ministry the authority to incorporate these mosques, but the state simply lacked the funds and manpower to do so. In addition to a shortage of state-trained imams, each mosque cost an annual six thousand Egyptian pounds to maintain. By the late 1990s, an estimated 45 percent of the mosques and *zawiyas* were under government control, but as Muhamad Ali Mahgub, the minister of religious endowments acknowledged, thirty thousand mosques remained outside state control. And the number of mosques has continued to grow rapidly. According to government statistics, in 1986, there was one mosque for every 6,031 Egyptians; by 2005, there was one mosque for every 745 people, and the country's population had doubled to seventy million.[77] And as Carrie Wickham has demonstrated, many of these mosques have learned how to escape the central state's reach by "develop[ing] ties with members of municipal councils which allow them to avoid government annexation efforts by shifting their activities to smaller, less visible outlets, such as basement zawiyas, obtaining licenses from local town council, without informing the ministry of religious endowments."[78] The state has tried to counter the mobilization efforts of the Islamists by offering services and in some cases cash payments. In the 1990s, the government began to fund non-Islamist groups in university campuses, and, by one account, administrators at a campus in Upper Egypt began to hand out monthly cash allowances to needy students to keep them away from Islamist groups.[79]

Party Building and Institutional Reform

Despite the NDP's electoral travails, reformers see the ruling party as a tool to incorporate groups and enhance the state's reach and are rebuilding the party to both extend and bypass the state bureaucracy. The newly created NDP's Policies Secretariat—a 123-member group of young economists, academics, and businessmen, which has grown rapidly in influence under the leadership of Gamal Mubarak (some have described it as a "shadow government" that allegedly circumvents the cabinet)—is an example of the institutional building underway. The role of the Policies Secretariat is to manage the transformation of the NDP from a state patronage machine led by old-guard party bosses to a modern majority party streered by technocrats. But the ruling party's factionalism and the country's participation crisis have complicated the technocrats' efforts. Analysts point to the NDP split between the old guard led by Kamaal Al-Chazli and Youssef Wali and the Young Turks led by Gamal Mubarak. Others see the party fragmented into three camps: the former ASU apparatchiks who make up the old guard and the left wing of the party, the Sadatist cadres appointed by the late president, and the reformist camp made up of Gamal Mubarak, Minister of Education Hussein Kamel Bahaeddine, Director of the Presidential Cabinet Zakariya, and other pro-reform business leaders.[80] Others point to yet a fourth camp within the NDP—the Islamist camp that brought the court case against author Naṣr Abu Zeid. These schisms surface during the electoral period. After bitter infighting during the 2000 elections, Gamal Mubarak's committee for party reform introduced changes to make the NDP more responsive to the base: Candidates for elections would no longer be selected by the secretary general but would henceforth be chosen by the "base." In every governorate, an electoral college was formed to elect candidates.[81]

The weakness of the Egyptian party system is related to the country's crisis of participation, and both undermine the state's capacity. According to a 1995 poll conducted by *Al-Ahram Weekly*, 40 percent claimed that no political party in the country represented them.[82] A more recent study showed that only 4.1 percent of Egyptians between the ages of eighteen and twenty-five are members of political parties, compared to a national average of 8.4 percent.[83] A study released on the eve of the March 2007 referendum on constitutional amendments noted that "less than 5 percent of Egyptian citizens are organized in political parties."[84]

Party weakness is both a cause and effect of the country's widespread "political abstinence." By one account, voter turnout during the presidential election was 23 percent, while only 15 to 20 percent showed up at the polls for the first and second rounds of the 2005 parliamentary elections.[85]

Diya Rashwan of the Ahram Center for Political and Strategic Studies has noted how the degree of public alienation from political life and "the lack of political demand" contributes to party weakness and to the isolation of the political elite: "The problem is much deeper than the weakness of the parties . . . We do not have a real political demand in the country. For the Egyptian masses, the real demands are socio-economic. Where the masses are concerned, we don't find big numbers demanding political rights . . . Only external affairs issues—Palestine, Iraq—get the people onto the streets."[86]

Unlike the PRI, which is almost a century old, the NDP was founded in 1978, and the party structure is still being developed. The NDP's current three million membership outstrips the party's financial and infrastructural capacities, as becomes evident during election time when the NDP has trouble turning out voters and must rely on family ties and nepotism. In contrast to the opposition parties, the NDP also suffers from more centralization of power and decision making. As with the trade union confederation, critics point to the practice of *jam'* where government ministers hold most of the top leadership positions (as heads of committees and so forth) in the party.[87] The NDP's institutional weakness and lack of "ideological direction"—its attempts to preempt challenges from the opposition by trying to represent all constituencies, populist, business, and even Islamist interests—lead to programmatic incoherence and lack of appeal. An effective ideology of development—that recognizes past errors and promotes dialogue about developmental objectives—can broaden the social base of support to sustain reforms. But in the Egyptian case, Ansari's observation two decades ago that containment does not make for good ideology still holds true: "Ideology is the handmaiden of mobilization and containment is necessarily an ideology that lacks coherence and its impact on the masses is confusing."[88]

The ideology of the Egyptian regime is currently a mix of populism, neoliberalism, and Islam. Recent constitutional amendments did away with references to socialism, the "alliance of working forces," and the leading role of the public sector, but, as I have argued, the public sector continues to play a central role, albeit often in conjunction with private actors. While amendments promise greater opportunities for political parties and aim to increase voter turnout, Article 5 proscribes forming parties with a "religious frame of reference," a clause that will be used to impede the Muslim Brotherhood and possibly even other parties, since today the NPUP is the only opposition party that is staunchly secular. Mubarak has spoken of the "grave legacies of the past," but as yet no ideological campaign has been undertaken to prepare the public for economic reform. The NDP is moving in a neoliberal direction while adopting stop-gap populist measures to appease social discontent. The stated desire to mobilize popular support has not generated institutions to reach the popular classes.

Toward Bureaucratic Authoritarianism?

While rebuilding the NDP, the state is moving toward exclusion: the lower classes—all potential opponents of economic reform—are being marginalized from the electoral and corporatist system, while the propertied classes are being brought in. This raises the question of whether the Egyptian regime is moving toward bureaucratic authoritarianism, an issue that has long concerned scholars. Waterbury has written that Nasser's regime, starting in 1952, ended the easy phase of ISI (of textiles and processed foods) and moved on to a state-led ISI that produced intermediate and capital goods. In this view, Nasser's regime was "bureaucratic authoritarian," and the economic policy after 1952 reflected a type of "deepening." But this argument is problematic because, unlike bureaucratic authoritarian regimes in Latin America, the Egyptian regime was never allied with the private sector; in fact, it appropriated private property and seriously weakened and alienated the bourgeoisie. Moreover, since 1952, the regime has remained populist distributive. Ayubi, on the other hand, contends that Egypt never moved toward bureaucratic authoritarianism because of the weakening of the Egyptian state after the 1967 defeat and the availability of rents following the 1973 war, which allowed the state to continue its populist policies.

Given the Egyptian state's limited control over the labor movement, a shift to exclusionary corporatism or a bureaucratic authoritarian regime will require high levels of coercion and repression, as in Chile or Brazil, and will not be as swift as Mexico's economic-political transformation. Thus the Egyptian regime will probably not opt for total exclusion, though inclusion as in Mexico will be difficult to maintain. In addition to the regime's low institutional capacity, the polarized nature of state-society relations in Egypt along with the protracted ideological and, on occasion, military confrontation between the regime and Islamist opponents have made a coalitional strategy based on incorporation or some type of accommodation difficult to achieve. As Stepan observed of Chile, the high level of polarization meant that leaders had "virtually no chance of creating a hegemonic inclusionary corporatist system." The Egyptian regime has tried unsuccessfully to co-opt Islamists as intermediaries to enhance its rule. As long as the NDP and the corporatist system are functioning, albeit poorly, Egypt will not move to a full-blown bureaucratic-authoritarian regime where parties and unions are banned; state elites will limit participation in a less drastic fashion.

The Egyptian leadership is making up for a loss of control as the populist coalition unravels by imposing further restrictions on participation and individual liberties. In 1994 the state of emergency was renewed for three years and then again in 1997 and in 2000. In 1992, Law 97 was passed, amending the legislation governing the state and supreme state security courts of 1980 and introducing the concept of terrorism (*irhab*), which could lead to the arrest of anyone using force or the threat of force to violate the "public order." The revocation of law 105/1980, which introduced the state security courts, was celebrated by state officials as a step toward democratization, when in reality the Emergency Law (in effect since 1981) provides for emergency state security courts, which play a similar role. To keep Islamists and not so compliant bureaucrats from establishing a presence in state institutions, the regime began to appoint deans of faculties and universities and *umdahs* and officials in professional associations—positions previously open to election. Law 20 of 1998 increased the power of the minister of interior to appoint high ranking officials and police officers.

The irony, however, is that the more the Egyptian regime excludes, the weaker and less capacious it becomes; the more channels of participation are closed off, the more the state loses the ability to control labor and the lower classes who join alternative organizations. The state's pro-reform coalition is limited, and exclusionary tactics further narrow the regime's social base. An indication of this weakness is that laws regarding economic liberalization cannot muster a majority to pass in parliament. By law, amendments to the Egyptian constitution and election of the president require a two-thirds majority, but laws concerning the economy just need a majority to pass. In 1993 and 1994, the regime twice failed to find the necessary majority for passing tax legislation recommended by the IMF. This precarious coalition and narrow base of support has not prevented the regime from pursuing a particular strategy of reform; the increased political closure is solidifying the alliance between state officials and crony capitalists, introducing a new form of state control through joint ventures between the state and private actors, and as in Mexico, producing a group of super-rich state-allied businessmen.

Rents and Representation

Proponents of the rentier state and "soft constraints" argument claim that the Arab state became the recipient of external revenues from oil and aid, which hindered domestic productive activity and attenuated demands for participation. This thesis holds that welfare politics stunted the development of class politics and "interest-based associational life" and instead promoted an identity politics, as seen in the rise of Islamism.[89] But, as I have argued, there was class politics in rent-reliant post-revolutionary Egypt, though the most powerful classes—the private sector and landed elite—were weakened by Nasser, and the left was suppressed by Sadat's clampdown in the 1970s; business and labor may be weak, but there is hardly a "class vacuum" in Egypt as rentier theorists would predict. Interest-based associational life does exist, within the corporatist framework and often beyond the state's control: civic and interest groups have mobilized calling for democracy, protesting the regime's foreign policy decisions, and workers' groups have repeatedly blocked privatization. The rise of Islamism is certainly related to the "rentier effect" and the post–Camp David Saudi-Egyptian alliance since Saudi Arabia, which provides aid and work for Egyptian migrants, promotes Wahhabism. But political parties are weak in Egypt, and participation is low, not because of an external dependency on external rents but because of a political decision to disband parties and check participation during the period of state building after 1952—long before foreign aid from the United States and Saudi Arabia began flowing in 1979—a decision that has had grave consequences for Egypt's development. (As Issam Elerian of the Muslim Brotherhood recently put it, "The political system over the last century has killed the political capacities of all the people.") Egyptian policy immobilism and the current political stagnation are better understood by looking at the origins of the postcolonial state rather than simply at the flow of rents.

One often also hears the claim that Arab states lack participatory politics because of low taxation politics. As various scholars have shown, the Middle East is not undertaxed; moreover, the relationship between rents, taxation, and representation, like the relationship between rents and economic reform, is not clear. Taxation could lead to calls for redistribution and new welfare commitments (subsidies, low prices, etc.) rather than political representation. The Arab states of the Middle East, which are heavily taxed, thus pose an empirical challenge to the proposition that taxation leads to representation. Countries with much lower taxation rates in sub-Saharan Africa and South Asia have developed representative political systems. Mexico, which has lower taxation rates than Egypt, has had participatory politics and institutions (as have some sub-Saharan African states, such as Senegal and Mali, which have among the lowest taxation rates in the world). As Michael Ross has argued, oil has had a "harmful influence" on the Middle East and made democratization harder in Indonesia, Malaysia, Mexico, and Nigeria, but "there is nothing inevitable about the resource curse: states like Malaysia, Chile and Botswana have done relatively well despite their oil and mineral wealth."[90] Moreover, the rentier thesis is at a loss to explain the flurry of institution building that has taken place over the past fifteen years: why would state officials expend resources in building and expanding the ruling party, trying to incorporate different constituencies, in face of repeated humiliations at the ballot box, if American aid "disincentivizes" reform?

The Egyptian state never developed the capacity to adequately manage and reconcile the competing claims of distribution and accumulation. State officials are trying to build those capabilities today as they struggle to reshape the Egyptian social-political environment. State-society relations are being fundamentally altered as the regime reaches out to business and attempts to politically exclude workers, abrogating a fifty-year long pact. Egypt's current reform policies and coalitional strategies have been shaped by institutional legacies and the ever-present Islamist challenge. The Muslim Brotherhood—and more broadly, the untried Islamist alternative—has profoundly shaped every Egyptian leader's strategy of reform. The state's objective of controlling urban discontent and preempting the Islamists from mobilizing the urban masses is also shaping the direction of the reform process today. The fiscal crisis has led the Egyptian state to try new modes of co-optation and exclusion, but limited institutional capacity has led regime officials to political deliberalization, which will lead to more polarization and possibly political violence.

9

Privatization and Exclusion

"The truth is that we have simultaneously too much state and too little state," writes Brazilian political theorist Joao Guilherme Merquior in describing his homeland but capturing the dilemma facing reformers in many developing countries.[1] As the Egyptian and Mexican cases show, state withdrawal requires state intervention. While withdrawing the state from some activities, reformers must redeploy other state institutions to enlist the private sector's backing and cushion the popular classes, a daunting challenge that requires strong interventionist capabilities and windfalls of revenue, both of which are increasingly scarce in a world economy where development aid is declining and the reigning discourse of neoliberalism is patently anti-statist.

Mexican reformers accomplished this task, overseeing one of the most far-reaching economic restructuring programs ever. De la Madrid and Salinas carried out extensive reforms, liberalizing trade, selling off much of the public sector, fundamentally changing property rights in rural areas, altering church-state relations, and liberalizing the financial sector, but, to insure the support of business and the popular classes for these measures, they introduced political reforms and created institutions that provided business with rents and subsidies and labor with more benefits, candidacies, and channels for demand making. Egypt won praise in the late 1990s for its privatization program, but labor opposition eventually brought the process to a halt. The question I have addressed is, Why were Mexican leaders able to overcome the opposition of a labor movement that was larger and more organized and whose electoral support was crucial to regime stability, while their Egyptian homologues were unable to override the opposition of a smaller, less militant, historically docile labor movement?

I have argued that the Mexican state enjoys a higher administrative and political capacity. Since incorporation, the Mexican state was a mediated state, controlling the popular classes through PRI-affiliated rural and labor elites. In Egypt, the regime also used the rural middle class to rule the hinterland, but in urban areas the regime has historically lacked control, preferring the departicipation of urban masses and relying on the cooperation of labor bosses to deliver benefits and insure the docility. Since incorporation, the bargain struck between the Mexican state and the popular classes—electoral support in exchange for benefits, representation, and the right to strike—was fundamentally different from the Nasserist bargain, which did not grant the right to strike and extended benefits in exchange for social peace. These differing bargains produced different state structures.

Moreover, labor in Mexico was mobilized and incorporated into the ruling party, and the PRI was a crucial institution for distributing patronage, representing interests, and co-opting opposition. The Egyptian regime, on the other hand, from its founding moment, used the state bureaucracy (and later the public sector) for political control. The brief flirtation with "popular participation" in the Liberal Age (1930s–'40s), was seen as a cause of the ancien régime's corruption and the failure to liberate Palestine in 1948. Nasser banned political parties and cut off all ties between labor and the Wafd, Muslim Brotherhood, and Communist Party, which had considerable support in poor working class areas. The Free Officers proceeded to follow a strategy of departicipation for the popular classes; the aim was to demobilize and depoliticize the lower classes, particularly in urban areas, so as to prevent their capture by the Communist Party or the more threatening Muslim Brotherhood movement, which had posed the greatest threat to the Free Officers. The state would thus develop few institutional linkages with organized labor other than the Labor Ministry, which delivered benefits and oversaw trade union elections, and a crop of elite unionists, whose duty was to control (not represent) the rank and file. Nasser would set up a series of single parties but would eventually dismantle them. Sadat would build the National Democratic Party but, fearing labor's mobilization, would cut off all ties between the ruling party and the labor confederation.

When the adjustment process began, Mexican state elites would use their numerous levers of control over labor—through the PRI and state bureaucracy—to gain workers' support for privatization. State elites initially relied on their traditional intermediaries and power brokers in the labor movement and rural areas (*charros* and *caciques*) to override labor resistance. But this strategy proved ineffective after the 1986 and 1988 elections when the PRI did very poorly in urban working class areas and rural areas. Realizing that top-down reform measures needed popular-level support, Mexican reformers went directly to the base, targeting lower-level unionists, the rank and file, and other unincorporated popular groups and enlisting new political intermediaries. The Egyptian state lacks the institutional ties to societal actors and control mechanisms of the Mexican regime. The Egyptian regime exemplifies the World Bank's "remote and imperious" low-capacity state that is unable to mobilize public resources and use them efficiently or effectively.[2] The ETUF elite have not been able to deliver labor's support or quiescence for privatization. The NDP lacks the reach and popularity to gain the backing of the lower classes, and the regime is facing a coalitional vacuum. The political apathy that Nasser aimed for has calcified, as the popular classes still believe that they should abstain from politics in exchange for welfare benefits. And if Mexican leaders could in crisis go directly to the base or work through pro-reform allies, the Egyptian state is not so able. Despite recent reforms, the NDP still lacks the PRI's reach, legitimacy, and institutional carrying capacity. No Egyptian ruling party has ever been able to reach all the way down to the lowest levels of the trade union hierarchy.

The Egyptian regime has historically relied on the rural middle class to deliver the rural vote, but in urban areas the regime's isolation was and still is striking. In moments of crisis, the Egyptian state revitalizes its alliance with the rural middle class and may extend some benefits to disgruntled urban groups, but this strategy has not succeeded because austerity measures have cut back welfare guarantees and fundamentally violated the Nasserist bargain. Lacking other intermediaries and with much of the population unincorporated, Mubarak is trying different support-mobilization strategies. Attempts to co opt Islamist notables, who provide public goods in popular areas, are failing. The current coalitional strategy appears to be using the ruling party to gain the support of the propertied classes—big business and landed elites—and slowly integrate pro-reform Islamist groups into the parliamentary system while excluding the more populist groups that could jeopardize the neoliberal project. As the NDP becomes more of a party for middle class and business interests, labor's importance will recede, and its veto power will be reduced. A strategy of exclusion however risks mass violence on the scale of the Chilean or Algerian experiences. The reformers who triggered the least violence in Latin America were those that rebuilt their party systems to include labor, at least partially through the granting of political voice and benefits.

Corroboration from Latin America

An examination of privatization in Latin America reveals that the states that have gone farthest in reforming their public sectors—Mexico, Venezuela, and Argentina—were all cases of party incorporation where reformers used long-standing party-labor links or restructured parties to solidify their urban base. For example, after 1989, Venezuela privatized extensively.[3] The Democratic Action Party (AD) had dominated the Confederation of Venezuelan Workers (CTV) since the 1940s, and, although in May 1989 during the privatization process the CTV joined other confederations in an anti-reform strike and came close to breaking their alliance with the governing party, the AD was ultimately able to retain the CTV's support passing a law enhancing worker rights and union privileges. The AD's institutional capacity—"organic ties to individual unionists"—and granting of candidacies to compliant labor leaders at all levels proved crucial in maintaining labor's support.[4] Argentina, like Mexico, was able to privatize broadly only after rebuilding the Peronist Justicialista Party, and developing a strong urban base of support. Like Nasser, Peron had banned political parties upon assuming power. The "poorly institutionalized nature of the party-union linkage," some have argued, allowed Argentine reformers to restructure the Peronist party, building territorial and urban-based networks that sidestepped unions and delivered patronage directly to urban working class and the unemployed underclass.[5]

Interestingly, the Latin American states that historically granted workers the right to strike were better able to "deliver" labor than those states that criminalized striking, such as Chile and Brazil. Chile, a case of state incorporation, privatized extensively but only by brutally repressing labor for two decades. Brazil, the other prominent case of state incorporation, is still struggling to reform the state and economy in face of labor opposition. Scholars have noted the similarities between Nasser's state and the Egyptian labor code and Vargas's Estado Novo and the Brazilian labor code, a code that was considered to be the "purest form of corporatism" and was imitated by Spain and Portugal, also countries that Nasser looked to during the state-building period. As in Brazil, where the state to this day is known as a *cabide de emprego* (source of jobs), successive Egyptian leaders would use the state bureaucracy to provide employment for every university graduate and as the main mechanism for support mobilization and control.

In Brazil, like Egypt, despite much rhetoric, privatization has gone forward haltingly, and various observers have attributed this to the country's weak parties and inchoate party system. Haggard and Kaufman have argued that countries with fragmented political systems—as opposed to an institutionalized two-party system or dominant-party system—have the most difficulty retaining labor's support during the adjustment process.[6] Since incorporation, Brazil has lacked a party to mediate state-society relations. Brazil's military regimes during the 1970s and 1980s failed to develop institutional mechanisms linking state to society, and in 1989 the country would emerge as a fledgling democracy with a fragmented party system, prompting some to describe Brazil as a "unique case of party underdevelopment."[7] Since the democratic transition, the Brazilian president's base has rested on a tenuous coalition of parties, some of which draw support from trade unions staunchly opposed to privatization and could bring the government down if the president attempts divestiture. Recently, Javier Corrales argued that it is Brazil's "state-without-party" condition that has prevented successive presidents—from José Sarney to Henrique Cardoso—from pursuing reform; Cardoso was forced to shelve plans to privatize the state-owned oil company because of lack of support from his ruling party and a strike by the leading labor union.[8]

Algeria

It has been argued that that the weakness of the Arab state is critical to understanding the lack of democracy in North Africa and the Middle East.[9] I believe that state weakness can also help explain the region's troubled experiences with economic restructuring. In North Africa and the wider Arab world, Algeria has gone furthest in implementing market reform, extensively restructuring the public sector and earning plaudits from IFIs for adjusting faster and further than Egypt and other regional pupils of the IMF. Because the Algerian story is also one of colonial legacies, state corporatism, and rentierism, it can serve as a useful foil for understanding the Egyptian case (and can offer a cautionary tale for Egyptian reformers about the perils of rapid reform or an alliance with neoliberal Islamists). The Algerian experience is worthy of note because the Algerian state was even more isolated than in Egypt and yet managed to radically transform state-society relations. Faced with resistance from the FLN, public sector managers, and labor, rather than reform the ruling party or try to gradually build pacted support, Algerian reformers rammed through with reforms eviscerating the public sector, building alliances with new political intermediaries, and shoring up the regime's capabilities and social base. To understand the origins of this reform strategy, it is necessary to examine the founding moment of the modern Algerian state.

Algeria's postcolonial regime came to power in July 1962 following a revolution, the eight-year war of independence against French rule. As in Egypt, despite the presence of a revolutionary party, the popular classes were incorporated into the party-state apparatus and granted myriad welfare benefits—free health care, education, public transportation, housing, subsidized foodstuffs, and even employment—so that many Algerians christened their government the "providential state." Labor and the peasantry were economically included but politically excluded; worker and peasant organizations had little say in policy making and were expected to offer quiescence and ideological backing—not electoral support. The General Union of Algerian Workers (UGTA) founded by the wartime FLN in 1956 would at independence be placed under the control of an institutionally undeveloped single party and expected to maintain docility and support the party line. At independence, the Algerian working class was very small, numbering 110 thousand urban industrial workers. (Some historians note that the 400 thousand Algerian migrant workers in Europe were better organized than their counterparts back home.) When Ahmed Ben Bella, the prestigious figurehead of the revolutionary regime (who played a similar role to General Naguib in Egypt), tried to encourage independent power centers and to bring the army under control, Colonel Haouri Boumedienne removed him from power.

When Boumedienne assumed power in 1965, he abolished the National Assembly, the Political Bureau, and the Central Committee of the FLN, establishing a highly centralized state apparatus ("bureaucratic dictatorship") and transforming "the single party into a powerless, parallel and inert administrative apparatus."[10] The FLN would emerge as a club of elites—military rulers and their clients—who would divvy up property confiscated from the departed French colons and land expropriated from landowners. Unlike Egypt, which had elections on and off with the Arab Socialist Union and tried to organize the lower classes, there was little electoral competition in Algeria, and the ruling party never developed the institutional capacity to mobilize workers and peasants for elections, channel participation, or manage inter-elite conflict. In 1967, Boumedienne dissolved the national secretariat of the trade union federation. He announced plans to develop political institutions—the FLN regularly proclaimed the "year of the party" and its own reorganization, but the party was never restructured, neither before nor after oil revenues began flowing, and Boumedienne died suddenly in 1978 before his revised blueprint for the FLN and various ancillary structures could be implemented. Despite the FLN's revolutionary aura and populist appeal, the party would remain an undeveloped shell of an institution.[11]

Although rentier theorists have argued that it was Algeria's access to oil rents that afforded the state such autonomy and allowed it to purchase popular acquiesce through a generous "preindustrial welfare state," recent scholarship shows that the postrevolutionary state's institutional weakness and isolation—a lack of intermediaries, which became starkly evident when the regime tried to reform the economy in the late 1980s—can be better understood by examining the disruptive effects of French colonialism. By this account, it was not oil revenue that stunted Algeria's institutional capacity but French colonialism, which thwarted the emergence of any viable Algerian intermediaries and the subsequent struggle for independence, which further decimated Algeria's intellectual and propertied elites. At independence, Algerian elites were largely exiled or discredited by association with the colonial power, and there were few power centers in civil society or leaders with mass following that the new regime could work with. As Clement Henry writes, "Algeria's institutional weakness was born in 1962, before the oil from Hassi Messaoud started to flow in significant quantities . . . The original sin then was not the 1956 discovery of oil, but the 1830–31 French invasion of Algeria and the subsequent destruction of the Ottoman governing infrastructure." Noting that "rentier theory, fixated on extraction capabilities and volatile petroleum revenues, cannot explain the pathology of bunker states [like Algeria]," Henry argues that such an approach "tells us little about rent-seekers or about institutional development and decay." Moreover, underlining the importance of disaggregating different state capabilities, Henry notes that Algeria in fact imposed high taxes in the 1960s and 1970s, and, "even if the assumption is correct that oil riches diminish a state's ability or willingness to tax, it is not clear if or how overall institutional capacity decays without an impetus for extraction."[12]

The lack of mediating institutions or social groups meant that the collapse of oil prices in 1986 had a devastating impact on the lower and middle classes. This fiscal crisis would lead to economic belt-tightening and a retrenchment of social services and would unleash urban riots in 1988 and prompt attempts at simultaneous economic and political reform. Earlier proposals to "decentralize" the public sector had been torpedoed by state elites, including members of the Securité Militaire, whose networks dominated the state monopolies. In 1989, Prime Minister Mouloud Hamrouche's reform team put forth an economic reform package that would eliminate monopolies, liberalize prices, and establish a framework for each public enterprise, including the banks, to operate as an independent enterprise responsive to market forces. As with Egypt's Law 203, which set up holding companies, in Algeria a similar system of state-holding companies was introduced in 1988 to replace the supervision of public sector enterprises by parent ministries. Each enterprise was to be released from its parent ministry and given the freedom to operate in partially deregulated markets. The state, however, lacked the administrative capacity to supervise the holding companies, and these reformist technocrats did not have broad societal support. Despite pro-reform legislation from the newly elected parliament, privatization was actively opposed by party officials, public sector managers, and labor, but the reformers enjoyed the backing of the president, Chadli Benjedid.

The reformers within the regime also had the tacit support of the Islamic Front of Salvation (FIS), which, like the Egyptian Brotherhood, controlled nine thousand mosques and a vast network of welfare, recreational, and educational associations and had repeatedly called for economic liberalization. The FIS leadership saw Algeria's economic predicament as part of the country's overall moral crisis, and the movement's "economic doctrine" had strongly attacked Algeria's centralized state economy as "discouraging the spirit of initiative . . . in favor of mediocrity and incompetence . . . [and] penalizing small enterprises." The FIS's economic program called for limiting state intervention in the industrial sector and protecting private property but also "watching that the latter not be transformed into a monopoly infringing on the public interest, for this would be an open door for economic, political and social parasitism."[13] Regime reformers and the FIS began to discretely and strategically work with each other. By pursuing political liberalization, the reformers allowed the FIS to formally enter the political arena, and, by vanquishing the FLN in the municipal elections of June 1990, the FIS discredited the regime's anti-reform hardliners and strengthened the reformers' hold over the FLN-dominated parliament.

But this curious collaboration between "moralizers" and "globalizers" would not last long. The alliance between regime reformers and the FIS and the attempt at simultaneous political and economic liberalization threatened to tear the regime apart. FIS leader Abbas Madani's call for a general strike in 1991 prompted military leaders, threatened by economic reform, to force President Chadli Benjedid to declare a military emergency, even as the strike was fizzling out. The reform government subsequently resigned, and, when the Islamist opposition resorted to violence, the junta behind Chadli adopted repressive counter-insurgency tactics and used the pretext of maintaining security to gain a free hand politically and economically. The fiscal crisis had severely constrained the regime's capacity to quell urban unrest; the attempted political opening was after all a way to appease disgruntled social groups and broaden the regime's support base. As the political violence escalated, many observers thought the Algerian regime was on the verge of collapse, and some have since argued that it was access to external rents that saved the state. A sharp dip in oil prices and a looming balance of payments crisis led the regime to sign an agreement with the IMF in 1993, which brought debt relief and by 1995 delivered the funds necessary to redouble the military's counterinsurgency efforts and roll back the Islamist guerillas.[14]

With the outbreak of the civil war, structural adjustment proceeded rapidly. The IMF reported that Algeria "adjusted faster" than other Arab states—Egypt, Jordan, Morocco, and Tunisia—that had embarked on reform earlier, and its macroeconomic performance had "equaled or even surpassed" them by the end of 1996.[15] Privatization also proceeded swiftly. As in Egypt, more public-private ventures appeared. If the 1992 investment law had permitted majority foreign investment in the non-hydrocarbon sector, the privatization and investment code of 2001 did away with the old distinction between foreign and Algerian investment and allowed foreign majority holding in the hydrocarbon sector as well. After the IMF agreement of 1994, SOEs were subjected to more stringent budgetary constraints. The subsequent restructuring eliminated hundreds of SOEs—by April 1998, some eight hundred had been privatized or dissolved—and threw an estimated 450 thousand workers out of work. In the construction sector alone, 93 thousand workers were laid off between 1995 and 1997. Another scholar estimates that privatization reduced the public sector labor force in the nonoil sector by half.[16] Organized labor simply could not block the divestitures. The UGTA organized waves of strikes against privatization and loudly opposed new legislation meant to facilitate public sector reform but ultimately to no avail; at the height of the civil war, the regime forged ahead prevailing over all opposition. As one analyst wryly noted, "With hundreds of enterprises closed down, the unions cannot be said to have been particularly powerful."[17]

The restructuring undertaken by the military junta dissolved hundreds of SOEs but also created scores of joint ventures—introducing a new mixed economy and concentrating wealth in the hands of state elites and their new clients. Some analysts think that public-private arrangements may have become the norm, the preferred property regime and method of control for the Algerian state: in 2000, a World Bank report noted that "after a decade of restructuring public enterprises, at an estimated cumulative cost of some DA840 billion (US$21 billion equivalent) and some 450,000 jobs, Algeria's privatization program has not yet resulted in a single sale of corporatized public enterprises to outside private interests."[18] By the late 1990s, writes Dillman, Algeria boasted "a liberalized economy operating through a circulation of rent between the military, a deficient public sector and a largely commercial private sector."[19] The privatization process in Algeria was also singularly "opaque," benefiting businessmen tied to the military, and would eventually engender a new class of economic actors and societal power brokers that would serve as the regime's new intermediaries. Privatization strengthened not only a coterie of state officials—and capitalists tied to the military—but also local notables ("emirs") who were able to exploit newly privatized sectors (shipping, *trabendo*) and expand their local authority. The state began to outsource its own fighting of the war to these local notables and their proxy forces; preferring to keep the Algerian army small, possibly to prevent Islamist infiltration, regime officials outsourced counterinsurgency to village defense forces and after 1997 to Islamist militias.[20] These new allies and proxy forces benefited from the adjustment process; various analysts have noted that all the groups involved in the Algerian civil war had a keen interest in the fate of the public sector.[21] One analyst observes that the more political violence intensified, the faster privatization occurred, noting that the Armed Islamic Group (GIA) frequently targeted unprofitable state-owned enterprises, and the most "exposed" state companies (e.g., transport) were often privatized following GIA attacks—suggesting that Islamist power brokers had an interest in privatization and were working with elements in the Algerian state.[22]

The Algerian experience shows that even reformers within a "bunker state" need allies. The adjustment process in Algeria, carried out with brute violence, restructured the economy and allowed the state to in effect create new social groups—local rural elites and urban capitalists—who benefited from the new market opportunities and have emerged as the regime's middlemen. The Algerian state has emerged—post-adjustment and civil war—as less isolated than it was before, and even the FLN has gained popularity, with many voters thinking it can govern better than the Islamists. Under the leadership of Prime Minister Ali Benflis, the FLN has moved away from its old ideology of populism and third worldism, now emphasizing economic development and winning 199 seats in the May 2002 parliamentary elections and performing impressively in local elections the following October.[23] But the adjustment process inflicted massive suffering and violence on the Algerian people. In addition to the one hundred thousand victims of the civil war, wages and living standards fell sharply. One study reported that 35 percent of the Algerian population lives in poverty, and unemployment continues to hover at 30 percent.[24] Between 1990 and 1995, over four hundred thousand Algerians emigrated, including tens of thousands of professionals and managers.[25] Algerian expats now hold an estimated thirty-five billion dollars overseas.

The Algerian story offers several lessons for Egypt. First, the Algerian case demonstrates that rents do not necessarily prevent reform and do not automatically preserve the political and economic status quo; external revenue subvented a fundamental transformation of state-society relations in Algeria. More importantly, Algerian reformers were faced with an institutional setting shaped by the country's colonial and postcolonial struggle, and it was only through mass violence that they were able to overcome these historically constructed obstacles and entrenched interests. Egyptian commentators across the political spectrum point to Algeria's violence to emphasize the importance of gradualism, dialogue, and institution building, warning Egypt's more ardent reformers of the perils of "shock therapy," exclusion, and repression. Better to peacefully integrate the Islamist opposition as in Turkey than attempt a rapid liberalization only to have to resort to drastic exclusion once the political opening fails. But analysts are also aware that the Egyptian state has more mechanisms and social actors to work with than its Algerian counterpart.[26] Unlike their Nasserist predecessors, Egyptan state elites today are aware of the importance of participation—that, as Amartya Sen says, "the need for popular participation is not just sanctimonious rubbish" but is crucial to successful development. The challenge is how to incorporate broad sectors of society, when the regime is lacking participatory institutions and when the lower classes are mobilized by a formidable Islamist counter-elite, which could block neoliberal reform.

The "rediscovery of the market" seems to have led to a "rediscovery of the state." Political economists now acknowledge that the Washington Consensus's desire to reduce state activity often led to the cutting back of state capacity across the board, and many now recognize the need to unpack the different dimensions of "stateness" and to show how they relate to economic development.[27] By the end of the 1990s, scholars were also aware that external IFI conditionalities and adjustment programs can erode a state's capabilities, allowing a leader to cut back on the provision of welfare (in the name of reform) while expanding the scope of the neo-patrimonial state by reconfiguring patronage and rent-seeking networks[28] and reconstituting the state according to a new political calculus. Markets cannot function well without a state that can formulate and implement the required policies, administer services, and respond to the demands of the citizenry.

Over five decades ago, in *The Great Transformation*, Karl Polanyi warned of the importance of "embeddedness" and social mediation in the transition to a market economy and cautioned how socially unmediated transitions where the individual is not protected from the vagaries of the market produced deep crises and led to the rise of extremist movements in Europe. Egyptian reformers seem aware of the importance of state intervention; they are pursuing a party-mediated economic restructuring and courting the support of influential social actors in economic transformation. But a key difference between the Mexican and Egyptian experiences was that market reform in Mexico was accompanied by the extension of rights and benefits to select groups in the lower classes, while in Egypt divestiture has entailed the withdrawal of rights and benefits to groups most impacted by market reform. To peacefully shift to a market economy as in Mexico, the Egyptian state needs to put in place a more inclusive pact, a new class compromise that will give voice and rights to the lower classes. Given the polarization between the Egyptian state and Islamist opposition, it is not clear if a coalitional strategy that excludes the lower classes will lead to peaceful reform and depolarization, or more repression, further polarization, and a resurgence of political violence.

Notes

Chapter 1

1. A series of seminars involving Egyptian and Mexican scholars produced the volume (Dan Tschirgi, ed., *Development in the Age of Liberalization: Egypt and Mexico* [Cairo: American University of Cairo Press, 1996]). See also papers from conference organized by the Arab Reform Initiative, La Fundación para las Relaciones Internacionales y el Diálogo Exterior (FRIDE), and the Club de Madrid ("Democratic Transitions in Europe and Latin America: Lessons for the Arab World?" Madrid, March 24–25, 2006).

2. *Mexico NewsPak, Human Rights Documentation Exchange* 1, no. 20 (1993); Maye Kassem, "Information and Production of Knowledge or Lobbying? Businessmen's Association, Federation of Labor Unions, and the Ministry of Manpower," in *Institutional Reform & Economic Development in Egypt*, ed. Noha El-Mikkawy and Heba Hendoussa (American University of Cairo Press, 2002), 62. In Mexico, an additional one million jobs were lost in the six months following the devaluation of 1994.

3. Mario Alejandro Carrillo, ed., *Neoliberalismo y Transformaciones del Estado Contemporáneo* (Mexico City: Universidad Autonoma Metropolitana, 1995), 56.

4. *Al-Ahram Weekly*, March 17–23, 2005.

5. See Alan Richards and John Waterbury's textbook, *A Political Economy of the Middle East* (Boulder, CO: Westview, 1996).

6. World Bank, *Global Development Finance 2000* (Global Development), vol. 1, CD-ROM.

7. "Egypt Survey: The IMF's Model Pupil," *Economist*, March 21, 1999.

8. Dieter Weiss and Ulrich Wurzel, *The Economics and Politics of Transition to an Open Market Economy: Egypt* (Paris, France: OECD Development Center, 1998), 55.

9. *Égypte/Monde Arabe* 23 (1995): 3.

10. Social Fund for Development, Annual Report 1996, Cairo, p.36. http://www.sfdegypt.org/index_e.asp

11. On the erosion of the Egyptian moral economy, see Marsha Pripstein Posusney, "Egyptian Labor Struggles in the Era of Privatization: The Moral Economy Thesis Revisited," in *Privatization and Labor*, ed. Marshe Pripstein Posusney and Linda J. Cook (Gloucestershire, England: Edward Elgar, 2001).

12. Agnieszka Paczynska, "Confronting change: Labor, state and privatization," *Review of International Political Economy* 14, no. 2 (May 2007): 333–56.

13. *Al-Ahram Weekly*, February 11–18, 1999.

14. A recent Carnegie study argues that "[Arab] states and institutions lack the capacity to design, implement, and manage reform programs," adding that "reliance on external rents—oil revenue in the case of oil-exporting countries, and remittances from abroad, strategic aid, and loans in the case of non-oil-exporting countries—is the core of the problem" (Sufian Alissa, "The Challenge of Economic reform in the Arab World: Towards More Productive Economies," *Carnegie Endowment*, May 2007).

15. See Ilya Harik, *Economic Policy Reform in Egypt* (Gainesville: University of Florida Press), 1997.

16. Stephen D. Morris, *Political Reformism in Mexico: An Overview of Contemporary Mexican Politics* (Boulder, CO: Lynne Rienner, 1995), 211.

17. Eva Bellin, "The Robustness of Authoritarianism in the Middle East: Exceptionalism in Comparative Perspective," *Comparative Politics* 36, no. 2 (January 2004), 139–57.

18. David Welch, "America Policy in the Middle East," speech for the English Public Lecture Series, Ewert Hall, American University of Cairo, January 28, 2002.

19. *Al Ahram Weekly*, June 10–16, 2004.

20. David Harvey, *A Brief History of Neoliberalism* (New York: Oxford University Press, 2005).

21. Kurt Weyland has described how a policy change in one country can turn into a "model" emulated—and misrepresented—by other states. See Kurt Weyland, ed., *Learning from Foreign Models in Latin American Policy Reform* (Baltimore, MD: Johns Hopkins University Press, 2004).

22. See Mauricio A. Gonzalez Gomez, "Crisis and Economic Change in Mexico," in *Mexico under Zedillo*, ed. Susan Kaufman Purcell and Luis Rubio (Boulder, CO: Lynne Rienner, 1998), 52.

23. One report released by the Carnegie Endowment observes that "despite the divergence between policy actions and economic results, the Mexican reforms were consistently praised by the media, financial experts, academics, and the multilaterals—including the World Bank and the IMF—as a major success. It is possible to argue that a Mexican 'miracle' was at least partially invented by these institutions." See Sebastian Edwards, "Bad Luck or Bad Policies? An Economic Analysis of the Crisis," in *Mexico 1994: Anatomy of an Emerging-Market Crash*, ed. Moisés Naím and Sebastian Edwards (Carnegie Endowment for International Peace, 1994).

24. Moisés Naim, "Washington Consensus or Washington Confusion," *Foreign Policy*, no. 118, Spring 2000, 87–103.

25. On the images versus practices of the state, see Joel Migdal, "Mental Maps and Virtual Checkpoints: Struggles to Construct and Maintain State and Social Boundaries," in *Boundaries and Belonging: States and Societies in the Struggle*

to Shape Identities and Local Practices, ed. Joel Migdal (New York: Cambridge University Press, 2004).

26. "Massive Potential, Minimal Dividends," *Al-Ahram Weekly*, no. 520, February 14, 2001.

27. David Stark, "Recombinant Property in East European Capitalism," in *The Laws of the Markets*, ed. Michael Callon (Malden, MA: Blackwell, 1998), 116–46.

28. For recent work that compares the Middle East with other regions, see Jason Brownlee's *Authoritarianism in an Age of Democratization* (Cambridge University Press, 2007), which examines attempts at democratization in Egypt, Malaysia, Iran, and the Philippines; Agnieszka Paczynska's *Confronting Change: Labor, State, and The Transition to a Market Economy* (Penn State University Press, 2008), which looks at state-labor relations in Egypt, Poland, Mexico, and the Czech Republic; and Eva Bellin's *Stalled Democracy: Capital, Labor, and the Paradox of State-Sponsored Development* (Cornell University Press, 2002), which analyzes democratization in Tunisia through a comparison with the cases of Mexico, Indonesia, South Korea, Turkey, and Egypt. See also Marsha Pripstein Posusney, "Middle East Lessons for Comparative Theory" *Comparative Politics* 36, no. 2 (January 2004).

29. On the Middle East's economic exceptionalism, see Adam Przeworski et al., *Democracy and Development: Political Institutions and Well-Being in the World, 1950–1990* (Cambridge: Cambridge University Press, 2000), 77. The authors exclude the oil-rich states of the Middle East from their study with no explanation other than their "ratio of fuel exports to total exports in 1984–86 exceeded fifty percent."

30. See Robert E. Blum, "The Weight of the Past," *Journal of Democracy* 8, no. 4 (1997).

31. See Michael Mann, *The Sources of Social Power, Vol I: A History of Power from the Beginning to AD 1760* (Cambridge: Cambridge University Press, 1986).

Chapter 2

1. See John Waterbury, *Exposed to Innumerable Delusions: Public Enterprise and State Power in Egypt, India, Mexico and Turkey* (New York: Cambridge University Press, 1993); Nazih Ayubi, *Over-stating the Arab State: Politics and Society in the Middle East* (New York: I. B. Tauris, 1995); Roger Owen, "Socio-Economic Change and Political Mobilization: The Case of Egypt," in *Democracy Without Democrats: The Renewal of Politics in the Muslim World*, ed. Ghassan Saleme (New York: I. B. Tauris, 1995); Dan Tschirgi, ed., *Development in the Age of Liberalization: Egypt and Mexico* (American University of Cairo, 1996); Jeffrey A. Nedoroscik et al., "Lessons in Violent Internal Conflict: Egypt and Mexico." *SYLFF Working Papers*, no. 8, March 1998; and Salama Ahmed Salama, "Egypt and Mexico: Similar, Yet Different," *Al-Ahram Weekly*, Issue 491, July 20, 2000.

2. See Mahmoud Mohieddin and Saher Nasr, "On Privatization in Egypt: With Reference to the Experience of the Czech Republic and Mexico," in *Privatization in Egypt: The Debate in the People's Assembly* (Cairo: Cairo University, 1996).

3. Maria Lorena and Graciela Bensusan, "Political Transition and Labor Revitalization," *Research in the Sociology of Work* 11 (2003): 229–67.

4. Ruth Berns Collier and David Collier, *Shaping the Political Arena: Critical Junctures, the Labor Movement, and Regime Dynamics in Latin America* (Princeton, NJ: Princeton University Press, 1991).

5. See Gosta Esping-Anderson, *The Three Worlds of Welfare Capitalism* (Princeton, NJ: Princeton University Press, 1991).

6. Migdal's conception of social control is akin to Mann's notion of infrastructural power: "State control involves the successful subordination of people's own inclinations of social behavior or behavior sought by other social organizations in favor of the behavior prescribed by state rules" (Joel S. Migdal, *Strong Societies and Weak States: State-Society Relations and State Capabilities in the Third World* [Princeton, NJ: Princeton University Press, 1988], 2). See Michael Mann, "The Autonomous Power of the State," in *States, War, and Capitalism* (New York: Blackwell, 1988), 22.

7. Jack Knight and Itai Sened, eds., *Explaining Social Institutions* (Ann Arbor: University of Michigan, 1995), 108.

8. Katrina Burgess, *Parties and Unions in the New Global Economy* (Pittsburgh: University of Pittsburgh Press, 2004).

9. See John G. Ikenberry, "The State and Strategies of International Adjustment," *World Politics* 39, no. 1 (October 1986), 53–77

10. Linda Weiss, *The Myth of the Powerless State: Governing the Economy in a Global Era* (Ithaca, NY: Cornell University Press, 1998), 14.

11. Merilee Grindle, *Challenging the State: Crisis and Innovation in Latin America and Africa* (Cambridge: Cambridge University Press, 1996), 44.

12. Migdal defines participation as the "repeated voluntary use of and action in state-run or state-authorized institutions." Joel S. Migdal, *Strong Societies and Weak States: State-Society Relations and State Capabilities in the Third World* (Princeton: Princeton University Press, 1988), 32.

13. See Niklas Luhmann, *Political Theory in the Welfare State* (New York: Walter de Gruyter, 1990).

14. See Joan M. Nelson. "Organized Labor, Politics, and Labor Market Flexibility in Developing Countries," *World Bank Research Observer* 6, no. 1 (January 1991): 37–56.

15. David Stark and Laslo Bruszt, *Postsocialist Pathways: Transforming Politics and Property in East Central Europe* (New York: Cambridge University Press, 1998), 130.

16. See Charles Tilly, "The Emergence of Citizenship in France and Elsewhere," in *Citizenship, Identity, and Social History*, ed. Charles Tilly (New York: University of Cambridge, 1996).

17. Max Weber, *Economy and Society*, ed. Guenther Roth and Claus Wittich (Berkeley: University of California Press, 1978), 1058.
18. Charles Tilly, "Why Worry About Citizenship?" in *Extending Citizenship, Reconfiguring States*, ed. Michael Hanagan and Charles Tilly (Lanham, MD: Rowman Littlefield, 1999), 254.
19. Jean Pierre Oliver de Sardan, "A propos de la privatisation des états," *Revue Tiers Monde* 41, no. 61 (January–March 2000): 217–21; Béatrice Hibou, "Retrait ou redéploiement de l'Etat?" *Critique Internationale*, no. 1, Autumn 1998, 151–68. Hibou borrows the concept "discharge" from Weber who held that such a mode of governance was preferred in "weakly bureaucratized contexts" and "an underdeveloped administrative apparatus." Béatrice Hibou, "From Privatizing the Economy to Privatizing the State: An Analysis of the Continual Formation of the State," in *Privatizing the State*, ed. Béatrice Hibou (New York: Columbia University Press, 2004), 15. This view of privatization as making way for a new form of indirect rule is associated with French political economists, who in the 1990s were suspicious of Washington Consensus thinking about how privatization would shrink the state and unleash the private sector.
20. Béatrice Hibou, "From Privatizing the Economy to Privatizing the State: An Analysis of the Continual Formation of the State," in *Privatizing the State*, ed. Béatrice Hibou (New York: Columbia University Press, 2004), 11–17.
21. Michael Walton, "Neoliberalism in Latin America: Good, Bad or Incomplete?" *Latin American Research Review* 39, no. 3 (2004), 165–83.
22. Joan Nelson and Samuel Huntington, eds., *No Easy Choice: Political Participation in Developing Countries* (Cambridge, MA: Harvard University Press, 1976), 14.
23. See David Waldner, *State-Building and Late Development* (Ithaca, NY: Cornell University Press, 1999).
24. Robert Bianchi, *Unruly Corporatism: Associational Life in Twentieth Century Egypt* (New York: Oxford University Press, 1989), 78.
25. Joan M. Nelson, "Organized Labor, Politics and Labor Market Flexibility in Developing Countries" *World Bank Research Observer* 6, no. 1 (January 1991): 42.
26. As Stark and Bruszt observe, "Evans ignores how political institutions that mediate state and society can be a fundamental source of policy coherence. ... [T]he mediating institutions of the political field practicing the politics of inclusion are a necessary source of state autonomy" (David Stark and Laszlo Burszt, *Postsocialist Pathways: Transforming Politics and Property in East Central Europe* [New York: Cambridge University Press, 1998], 127).
27. Samuel Valenzuela, "Labor Movements in Transitions to Democracy: A Framework for Analysis," *Comparative Politics* 21, no. 4 (July 1989): 445–47.
28. *Al-Ahram Weekly*, August 13, 1998.
29. Robert Wade, "East Asia's Economic Success: Conflicting Perspectives, Partial Insights, Shaky Evidence," *World Politics* 44 (1992): 270–320; Ziya Onis,

"Privatization and the Logic of Coalition-Building," *Comparative Political Studies* 24, no. 2 (1991): 231–53.

30. David Mares, "State Leadership in Economic Policy: A Collective Action Framework with a Colombian Case," *Comparative Politics* 25, no. 4 (July 1993): 455–73.

31. Karin Aziz Chaudhry, "Economic Liberalization and the Lineages of the Rentier State," *Comparative Politics* 27 (October 1994): 9.

32. Robert R. Kaufman, "Approaches to the Study of State Reform in Latin American and Postsocialist Countries," *Comparative Politics* 31, no. 3 (April 1999): 357–75.

33. Lisa Anderson, "The State in the Middle East and North Africa," *Comparative Politics* 20, no. 1 (October 1987): 1–18. Decades ago, S. N. Einstadt noted the political consequences of "precocious" bureaucratic expansion in developing countries: "The bureaucracy may tend to fulfill different types of political functions and, like parties, legislatures, and executives, become the center of different types of political activity" (*Political Systems of Empires* [New York: Free Press of Glencoe, 1963], 12).

34. Cited in Roger Owen, "Socio-Economic Change and Political Mobilization: The Case of Egypt," in *Democracy Without Democrats: The Renewal of Politics in the Muslim World*, ed. Ghassan Saleme (New York: I. B. Tauris, 1994), 195.

35. David Hirst, "Egypt Stands on Feet of Clay," *Le Monde Diplomatique*, October 1999.

36. Nathan J. Brown, Michele Dunne, and Amr Hamzawy, "Egypt's Controversial Constitutional Amendments," *Carnegie Endowment for International Peace*, March 23, 2007.

37. On polarization and exclusion, see Alfred Stepan, *The State and Society: Peru in Comparative Perspective* (Princeton, NJ: Princeton University Press, 1978).

38. John Waterbury, *Exposed to Innumerable Delusions: Public Enterprise and State Power in Egypt, India, Mexico, and Turkey* (New York: Cambridge University Press, 1993), 191.

39. See Kenneth S. Mericle, "Corporatist Control of the Working Class: Authoritarian Brazil since 1964," in *Authoritarianism and Corporatism in Latin America*, ed. James M. Malloy (Pittsburgh: University of Pittsburgh Press, 1977).

40. Miguel Angel Centeno, *Blood and Debt: War and the Nation-State in Latin America* (University Park, PA: Penn State University Press, 2002), 28.

41. John Waterbury, "From Social Contracts to Extraction Contracts: The Political Economy of Authoritarianism and Democracy," in *Islam, Democracy, and the State in North Africa*, ed. John P. Entelis (Bloomington: Indiana University Press, 1997). See also the World Bank's *World Development Indicators, 2001* (Washington, DC: Oxford University Press, 2001).

42. World Bank, *Lessons of Tax Reform*, Washington, DC, 1991.

43. World Bank, *World Development Indicators, 2001, Washington, DC.* See also World Bank *CD ROM*, 2000.

44. Carlos Bazresch and Santiago Levy, "Populism and Economic Policy in Mexico, 1970–1982," in *The Macroeconomics of Populism in Latin America*, ed.

Rudiger Dornbusch and Sebastian Edwards (Chicago: University of Chicago Press, 1991).

45. Linda Weiss, *The Myth of the Powerless State: Governing the Economy in a Global Era* (Ithaca: Cornell University Press, 1998), 7.

46. See Andrés Solimano, "The Chilean Economy in the 1990s: On a 'Golden Age' and Beyond," in *After Neoliberalism: What Next for Latin America*, ed. Lance Taylor (Ann Arbor: University of Michigan Press, 1999), 53–80.

47. Giacomo Luciani, "The Oil Rent, the Fiscal Crisis of the State, and Democratization," in *Democracy Without Democrats: The Renewal of Politics in the Muslim World*, ed. Ghassan Salamé (New York: I. B. Tauris, 1994), 130.

Chapter 3

1. Awad El-Morr is the former chief justice of the Supreme Constitutional Court. He is speaking on the fiftieth anniversary of the 1952 Revolution (cited in Maye Kassem, *Egyptian Politics: The Dynamics of Authoritarian Rule* [Boulder, CO: Lynne Riener, 2004], 1).

2. John Mason Hart, *Revolutionary Mexico: The Coming and Process of the Mexican Revolution* (Los Angeles: University of California Press, 1987), 132.

3. Rodney D. Anderson, *Outcasts in Their Own Land: Mexican Industrial Workers, 1906–1911* (DeKalb, IL: Northern Illinois University Press, 1976).

4. Gilbert M. Joseph, *Revolution from Without: Yucatan, Mexico, and the United States, 1880–1924* (Durham, NC: Duke University Press, 1988).

5. The context of the PNR's establishment is analyzed by Luis Javier Garrido, in *El partido de la revolución institucionalizada: La formación del nuevo estado en Mexico 1928–1945* (Mexico City: Siglo XXI, 1984). Garrido writes that in 1929 there existed at least 148 parties in twenty-eight states and refers to the PNR as a "confederation of cliques."

6. See the excellent essay by Wayne Correlius, "Nation-Building, Participation, and Distribution: The Politics of Social Reform under Cardenas," in *Crisis, Choice and Change: Historical Studies of Political Development*, ed. Gabriel Almond et al. (Boston: Little Brown, 1973).

7. Ruth Collier, *The Contradictory Alliance: State-Labor Relations and Regime Change in Mexico* (Berkeley: International and Area Studies, University of California, 1992), 26.

8. See Arnaldo Córdova, "En una época de crisis (1928–1934)," in *La clase obrera en la historia de México* (Mexico City, México: Siglo XXI, 1980), 48.

9. Nora Hamilton, *The Limits of State Autonomy: Post-Revolutionary Mexico* (Princeton, NJ: Princeton University Press, 1982), 273.

10. Ben Fallaw, *Cárdenas Compromised: The Failure of Reform in Postrevolutionary Yucatán* (Durham, NC: Duke University Press, 2001), 114–16.

11. See Pablo Gonzalez Casanova, *El estado y los partidos politicos en Mexico* (Mexico City: Ediciones Era, 1982).

12. Collier, *Contradictory Alliance*, 64.

13. Barry Carr, *El Movimiento Obrero y la politica en Mexico*, vol. 1 (Mexico City, Mexico: SepSetentas, 1976), 203.

14. See Joel Beinin and Zachary Lockman, *Workers on the Nile: Nationalism, Communism, Islam and the Egyptian Working Class, 1882–1954* (Princeton University Press, 1987).

15. See Maurice Deeb, "Labor and Politics in Egypt: 1919–1939," *International Journal of Middle Eastern Studies* 10 (1979): 187–203.

16. Joel Beinin, "The Communist Movement and Nationalist Political Discourse in Nasirist Egypt," *Middle East Journal* 41, no. 4 (Autumn 1987), 568–84.

17. P. J. Vatikiotis, "Egypt's Political Experience: The 1952 Revolution as an Expression of the Historical Heritage," in *Egypt from Monarchy to Republic: A Reassessment of Revolution and Change*, ed. Shimon Shamir (Boulder, CO: Westview, 1995), 120.

18. Patrick O'Brien, *The Revolution in Egypt's Economic System: From Private Enterprise to Socialism, 1952–1965* (New York: Oxford University Press, 1966), 72–73.

19. See James B. Mayfield, "Agricultural Cooperatives: Continuity and Change in Rural Egypt," in *Egypt from Monarchy to Republic.*

20. See Richard Adams, *Development and Social Change in Rural Egypt* (Syracuse, NY: Syracuse University Press, 1986), chap. 7.

21. Karima Korayen, "The Agricultural Output Pricing Policy and the Implicit Taxation of Agricultural Income," in *The Political Economy of Income Distribution in Egypt*, ed. Gouda Abdel Khalek and Robert Tignor (New York: Holmes & Meier, 1982), 165.

22. Howeida Adly, *al-Ummal wa al-Siyyasa* (Cairo: Al-Ahali, 1993).

23. This section draws on Joel Gordon's *Nasser's Blessed Movement: Egypt's Free Officers and the July Revolution* (New York: Oxford University Press, 1992), 80.

24. Abd al-Azim Ramadan, *Abdalnasser Wa Azmat Maris* 1954 (Cairo: Maktabat Ruz al-Yusuf, 1977), 142–44. See also Ramadan's *Al-Sira al-ijtima'i wa'l-siyasi fi misr mundhu thawrat 32 yulyu 1952 il nihayat azmat maris 1954* (Cairo: Maktabat Ruz al- Yusuf, 1975).

25. This section draws on a series of articles by Husayn Kamal al-Din, titled "Qissat Thuwwar Yulyu," in *al-Musawwar*, December 19, 1975, through January 25, 1976.

26. Nasser would later brag that the total cost of the demonstrations and the general strike of March 27–28 was no more than five thousand pounds, which he paid to al-Sawi (Hamrush, *Qissat Thawrat 32 Yulyu* 4: 159 Cairo: Dar al-Mawqif al-'Arabi, 1983). Ramadan contends that al-Sawi was paid ten thousand pounds in compensation for the material losses the workers might suffer as a result of the strike (118).

27. See also Ramadan's *al-Ikhwan al-Muslimin wa-al-Tanzim al-Sirri* (Cairo: Maktabat Ruz al- Yusuf, 1982), 139–42.

28. See Beinin and Lockman, *Workers on the Nile: Nationalism, Communism, Islam, and the Egyptian Working Class, 1882–1954* (Cairo, Egypt: The American University in Cairo Press, 1987), chap. 13.
29. O'Brien, *Revolution in Egypt's Economic System*, 68.
30. Robert Tignor, "Foreign Capital and Foreign Communities and the Egyptian Revolution of 1952," in *Egypt From Monarchy to Republic*.
31. *Al-Ahram*, August 31, 1954.
32. O'Brien, *Revolution in Egypt's Economic System*, 68.
33. See John Waterbury, *The Egypt of Nasser and Sadat: The Political Economy of Two Regimes* (Princeton, NJ: Princeton University Press, 1983).
34. Beinin and Lockman, *Workers on the Nile*.
35. See Dag Macleod, *Downsizing the State: Privatization and the Limits of Neo-Liberal Reform in Mexico* (University Park: Penn State University Press, 2004), 54–59.
36. Nora Hamilton, *The Limits of State Autonomy: Post Revolutionary Mexico* (Princeton, NJ: Princeton University Press, 1982), 71.
37. Raymond Baker, *Sadat and After: Struggles For Egypt's Political Soul* (Cambridge, MA: Harvard University Press, 1990), 84.
38. Nazih Ayubi, *Bureaucracy and Politics in Contemporary Egypt* (London: Ithaca, 1980).
39. Tareq al-Bishri, *Democracy and the July Revolution* (Beirut: Dar ash-Shuruq, 1986).
40. Joel Gordon, *Nasser's Blessed Movement: Egypt's Free Officers and the July Revolution* (New York: Oxford University Press 1992), 62.
41. Baker, *Sadat and Afte*, 121.
42. See Eric Davis, *Challenging Colonialism: Bank Misr and Egyptian Industrialization, 1920–1941* (Princeton, NJ: Princeton University Press, 1983).
43. Hamilton, *The Limits of State Autonomy*, 98, 177.
44. Ilkay Sunar, "The Politics of State Interventionism in 'Populist' Egypt and Turkey," in *Developmentalism and Beyond: Society and Politics in Egypt and Turkey*, ed. Saad Eddin Ibrahim et al. (Cairo: American University in Cairo Press, 1994), 110.
45. Manfred Halpern wrote that "for Egypt, certainly Yugoslavia has become the chief model of successful neutralism and rapid progress in internal reform" (Manfred Halpern, *Politics of Social Change in the Middle East and North Africa* [Princeton, NJ: Princeton University Press, 1963], 163).
46. Georges Vaucher, *Gamal Abdel Nasser et son équipe: Les années d'humiliation et la conquete du pouvoir* (Julliard, 1959).
47. See Ignacio Klich, "Towards an Arab-Latin American Bloc: The Genesis of Argentine-Middle East Relations: Jordan, 1945–54." *Middle Eastern Studies* 3, no. 31 (1995): 550–72.
48. See Juan Archibaldo Lanus, *De Chapultepec al Beagle: Politica exterior argentina, 1945–1980* (Buenos Aires: Emece Editores, 1984).

49. 'Abd al-Latif al-Boghdadi, *Muthakikirat*, vol. 1 (Cairo: al-Maktab al-Misri al-Hadith, 1977), 241–43.

50. Abdal Mughni Said, "Safahaat Majhula Min Tarikh al-Haraka al-Niqabiya," *al-'Amal* 236 (January 1983), cited in Robert Bianchi, *Unruly Corporatism: Association Life in Twentieth-Century Egypt* (New York: Oxford University Press, 1989), 37.

51. For a discussion about the RCC's interest in Peronism, see Kirk J. Beattie, *Egypt During the Nasser Years: Ideology, Politics, and Civil Society* (Boulder, CO: Westview, 1994): 122–25.

52. Christián Buchrucker, "Interpretations of Peronism: Old Frameworks and New Perspectives," in *Peronism and Argentina*, ed. James P. Brennan (Wilmington, Delaware: Scholarly Resources, 1998); Rogelio Garcia Lupo, "Generales Argentinos entre Francia y EE.UU, 1955–1965," *Clarin Suplemento*, April 22, 2001.

53. Edy Kaufman et al., *Israeli-Latin American Relations* (Edison, NJ: Transaction Publishers, 1979), 49.

54. See the U.S. Senate on Foreign Relations report, which refers to the "real specter of nascent Nasserism in Latin America" (*United States Military Policies and Programs in Latin America: Hearings before the Subcommittee* 1969), 36 Congressional hearing report (accessible via google books). For a discussion about "Latin American Nasserism," see chapter 8 of Edwin Lieuwen, *Generals vs. Presidents: Neo-militarism in Latin America* (New York: Frederick A. Praeger, 1964).

55. Mohamed Sid Ahmed, "The Future of Nasserism," *Al-Ahram Weekly*, no. 501, October 4, 2000.

56. Collier and Collier, *Shaping the Political Arena*, 186.

57. Philippe Schmitter, *Interest Conflict and Political Change in Brazil* (Stanford University Press, 1971).

58. Dietrich Rueschemeyer, Evelyne Huber Stephens, and John D. Stephens, *Capitalist Development and Democracy* (Chicago: University of Chicago Press, 1992), 193.

59. Waterbury, *Egypt of Nasser and Sadat*, 431.

60. Nathan J. Brown, "Nasserism's Legal Legacy: Successibility, Accountability and Authoritarianism," in *Rethinking Nasserism: Revolution and Historical Memory in Modern Egypt*, ed. Elie Podeh and Onn Winckler (Gainesville: University Press of Florida, 2004), 130. See also Misako Ikeda, "Toward the Democratization of Public Education: The Debate in Late Parliamentary Egypt, 1943–52," in *Re-Envisioning Egypt 1919–1952*, ed. Arthur Goldschmidt et al. (American University of Cairo Press, 2005).

61. Doreen Wariner, *Land Reform and Development in the Middle East: A Study of Egypt, Syria and Iraq*, 2nd ed. (London: Oxford University Press, 1962).

62. M. Riad El Ghonamy, *Affluence and Poverty in the Middle East* (London: Routledge, 1998), 160.

63. Samir Radwan, *Agrarian reform and Rural Poverty: Egypt, 1952–1975* (Geneva: International Labor Organization, 1977).

64. Robert Springborg, "Rolling Back Egypt's Agrarian Reform," *Middle East Report* 166 (September–October 1990), 28–30; Paul Rivlin, "Nasser's Egypt and Park's Korea: A Comparison of Their economic Achievements," in *Rethinking Nasserism: Revolution and Historical Memory in Modern Egypt,* ed. Elie Pdeh and Onn Winckler (Gainesville: University of Florida Press, 2004), 264–81.

65. Dani Rodrik, "Getting Interventions Right: How South Korea and Taiwan Grew Rich?" *Economic Policy* 10, no. 2 (April 2, 1995): 55–107.

66. Terry Lynn Karl, *The Paradox of Plenty: Oil Booms and Petro-States* (Berkeley: University of California Press, 1997).

67. Nathan Brown, "Nasserism's Legal Legacy," 130.

68. David W. Lesch, "Nasser and the United States: Enemy or Friend," in *Rethinking Nasserism: Revolution and Historical Memory in Modern Egypt,* ed. Elie Pdeh and Onn Winckler (Gainesville: University of Florida Press, 2004), 208.

69. Paul Rivlin, "Nasser's Egypt and Park's Korea: A Comparison of their Economic Achievements," in *Rethinking Nasserism: Revolution and Historical Memory in Modern Egypt,* ed. Elie Pdeh and Onn Winckler (Gainesville: University of Florida Press, 2004).

70. Kirk Beattie, *Egypt during the Nasser Years,* 193.

Chapter 4

1. See David Collier and Ruth Berins Collier, "Who Does What, to Whom, and How: Toward a Comparative Analysis of Latin American Corporatism," in *Authoritarianism and Corporatism in Latin America,* ed. James Malloy (Pittsburgh: University of Pittsburgh Press, 1977).

2. I am referring to Robert Michel's classic *Political Parties: A Sociological Study of the Oligarchical Tendencies of Modern Democracy* (New York: Dover, 1959).

3. This section draws on Jamal al-Banna's *al-Haraka al-Niqabiya al-Masriya: Tarikh wa Tandhim, 1895–1995* (Cairo: Dar al-Fikr al-Islami, 1995).

4. Ruth Berins Collier and David Collier, *Shaping the Political Arena* (Princeton, NJ: Princeton University Press, 1991), 185.

5. Howeida Adly, *al-Ummal wa al-Siyyasa* (Cairo: Ahali, 1993); Marsha Posusney, *Labor and the State in Egypt: Workers, Unions, and Economic Restructuring* (New York: Columbia University Press, 1997); Robert Bianchi, *Unruly Corporatism: Association Life in Twentieth-Century Egypt* (New York: Oxford University Press, 1989).

6. Howeida Adly Ruman, *Al-Dawr al-Siyyasi lil-Haraka al-Umaliya fi Misr, 1952–1961,* 136–49.

7. Marsha Posusney, *Labor and the State in Egypt,* 86.

8. Peter J. Williamson, *Corporatism in Perspective: An Introductory Guide to Corporatist Theory.* London: Sage, 1989), 39.

9. See Luis Javier Garrido, *El partido de la revolucion institucionalizada: La formación del nuevo estado en Mexico, 1928–1945* (Mexico City: Siglo XXI, 1984).

10. See Mark Thompson and Ian Roxborough, "Union Elections and Democracy in Mexico: A Comparative Perspective," *British Journal of Industrial Relations* 20, no. 2 (July): 201–17.

11. Collier and Collier, *Shaping the Political Arena*, 585.

12. Raúl Trejo Delarbre, "El movimiento obrero: Situación y perspectivas," in *Mexico, hoy*, ed. Gonzalez Casanova and Enrique Florescano (Mexico City: Siglo XXI, 1980), 130.

13. Roberto Newell and Luis Rubio, *Mexico's Dilemma: The Political Origins of Economic Crisis* (Westview, 1984), 121.

14. See Dale Story, *The Mexican Ruling Party, Stability and Authority* (New York: Praeger, 1986).

15. Miguel Angel Centeno, *Democracy Within Reason: Technocratic Revolution in Mexico* (University Park: Pennsylvania State University Press, 1997), 33.

16. Leonard Binder, *In a Moment of Enthusiasm: Political Power and the Second Stratum in Egypt* (Chicago: University of Chicago Press, 1978), 45.

17. Anouar Abdelmalek, *Egypt: Military Society* (New York: Random House, 1968), 149.

18. In October 1966, Sabri remarked, "Temporarily, until we have a peasantry sufficiently enlightened to take up a leading role, we will have to depend on the cultured elite of the villages, such as the physician, the agricultural supervisor, the school headmaster and the veterinarian" (James B. Mayfield, *Rural Politics in Nasser's Egypt* [Austin: University of Texas Press, 1971], 133).

19. See Rami Ginat, *Egypt's Incomplete Revolution: Lutfi al-Khuli and Nasser's Socialism in the 1960s* (London: Frank Cass, 1997).

20. Paul A. Cammack, "Strong States, Weak States, and Third World Development," *Manchester Papers in Politics* (Victoria University of Manchester, Department of Government, September 1992), 24.

21. Raymond Hinnebusch, "The Reemergence of the Wafd Party: Glimpses of the Liberal Opposition," *International Journal of Middle Eastern Studies* 1984: 99–121.

22. Bianchi, *Unruly Corporatism*, 144.

23. Bianchi, *Unruly Corporatism*, 85.

24. Ibid., 85.

25. Yahya Sadowski, *Political Vegetables? Businessman and Bureaucrat in the Development of Egyptian Agriculture* (Washington, DC: Brookings Institution, 1991), 31.

26. *Arab Strategic Report 1991,* Al-Ahram Center for Political and Strategic Studies (Cairo: Al-Ahram, 1992), 380–81.

Chapter 5

1. Kevin Middlebrooke and Eduardo Zapeda, eds., *Confronting Development: Assessing Mexico's Economic and Social Policy Challenges* (Palo Alto, CA: Stanford University Press, 2003), 15.

2. See Pascal Garcia Alba and Jaime Serra Puche, "Causas y efectos de la crisis economica en Mexico" *Jornadas 104*, El Colegio de Mexico, Mexico City, 1984.

3. Joseph Klesner, "Realignment or Dealignment? The Consequences of Economic Crisis and Restructuring for the Mexican Party System," in *The Politics of Economic Restructuring*, ed. Monica L. Cook et al. (La Jolla: Center for U.S.-Mexican Studies, University of California, San Diego, 1994), 159–91.

4. See Joe Foweraker, "Popular Movements and Political Change in Mexico," in *Popular Movements and Political Change in Mexico*, ed. Joe Foweraker and Anne Craig (Boulder, CO: Lynn Reiner, 1990).

5. Lorenzo Meyer, "El Corporativismo Mexicano en los Tiempos del Neoliberalismo," in *Estado y Sindicatos: Crisis de una relacion*, ed. Graciela Bensusan and Carlos Garcia (Mexico City, Mexico: Fundacion Friedrich Ebert-UAM, 1989).

6. Alejandro Alvarez-Bejar, "Economic Crisis and the Labor Movement in Mexico," in *Unions, Workers and the State in Mexico*, ed. Kevin Middlebrooke (San Diego: Center for U.S.-Mexican Studies, University of California, 1991), 48.

7. Juan Reyes Campillo, "El Movimiento Obrero en la Camara de Diputados," *Revista Mexicana de Sociologia* 3 (July–September 1990): 157.

8. *El Dia*, April 18, 1992.

9. Lorenzo Meyer, "El Corporativismo Mexicano."

10. Kevin J. Middlebrooke, *The Paradox of Revolution: Labor, the State, and Authoritarianism in Mexico* (Baltimore: Johns Hopkins University Press, 1995), 266.

11. See L. Manzetti and M. Dell'Aquila, "Economic Stabilization in Argentina: The Austral Plan," *Journal of Latin American Studies* 20, no. 1 (May 1988): 1–26.

12. Ruth Collier and James Samstad, "Mexican Labor and Structural Reform: New Unionism or Old Stalemate?" in *The Challenge of Institutional Reform in Mexico*, ed. Riordan Roett (Boulder, CO: Lynne Rienner, 1995), 9–37.

13. The Economic Stability Pact (PSE) was an agreement reached among the state, business leaders, and labor in December 1987, calling for combined efforts (i.e., Concertación) to limit price and wage increases in order to combat spiraling inflation. See Carol Wise and Manuel Pastor, "The Origins and Sustainability of Mexico's Free Trade Policy," *International Organization* 3 (1994): 459–89.

14. Collier and Samstad, "Mexican Labor and Structural Reform."

15. Gerardo Zamora, "La politica laboral del estado mexicano, 1982–1988" *Revista Mexicana de Sociologia*, March 1990, 131–32.

16. Ilan Bizberg, *Estado y Sindicatos en Mexico* (Mexico City: El Colegio de Mexico 1990), 123.

17. Dan La Botz, *Mask of Democracy: Labor Suppression in Mexico Today* (Boston: South End, 1992), 47.

18. Burgess, *Parties and Unions in the New Global Economy* (Pittsburgh: University of Pittsburgh Press, 2004), 67.

19. Burgess, *Parties and Unions*, 70.

20. Ilan Bizberg, "La Crisis del Corporativismo Mexicano," *Foro Internacionale* 30, no. 4 (April–June 1990): 695–735.

21. See Roderic Camp, *Politics in Mexico* (New York: Oxford University Press, 1993).

22. For a discussion of these proposals, see Judith Teichman, *Privatization and Political Change in Mexico (Pittsburgh*: University of Pittsburg Press, 1996), especially chap. 6.

23. Luis Mendez Berrueta and Jose Othon Quiroz Trejo, *Modernizacion Estatal y Respuesta Obrera, Historia de Una Derrota* (Azcapotzalco: Universidad Autónoma Metropolitana, 1994), 17.

24. Joseph Klesner, "An Electoral Route to Democracy? Mexico's Transition in Comparative Perspective," *Comparative Politics* 30, no. 4 (July 1998): 477–97.

25. Denise Dresser, "Salinistroika without Prisnost: Institutions, Coalition-Building, and Economic Reform in Mexico," Dissertation, Princeton University, Department of Politics, 31.

26. Denise Dresser, "Bringing the Poor Back In: National Solidarity as a Strategy of Regime Legitimation," in *Transforming State-Society Relations in Mexico: The National Solidarity Strategy*, ed. Wayne A. Cornelius, Ann. L. Craig, and Jonathan Fox (San Diego: Center for U.S.-Mexican Relations, 1994), 143–65.

27. *Latin American Weekly Report*, August 16, 1990, 6.

28. See Soledad Loaeza, "El Regrezo del Estado; por un nuevo intervencionismo," *Cuadernos de Nexos*, November 17, 1989.

29. See Jose Luis Pineyro and Gabriela Barajas, "Seguridad nacional y pobreza en Mexico: Notas sobre Pronasol," *El Cotidiano* 71 (September 1995): 78–87.

30. See Alejandro Moreno, "Agosto del 1991: Por que se voto por el PRI?" *Este Pais* 33 (December 1993).

31. See Carlos Salinas, "Production and Participation in Rural Areas: Some Political Considerations," in *The Political Economy of Income Distribution in Mexico*, ed. Pedro Aspe and Paul Sigmund (New York: Holmes & Meier, 1984).

32. Jonathan Fox, "Targeting the Poorest: The Role of the National Indigenous Institute in Mexico's Solidarity Program," in *Transforming State Societal Relations in Mexico*, ed. Wayne A. Cornelius, Ann L. Craig, and Jonathan Fox (La Jolla, CA: Center for U.S.-Mexican Studies, University of California, 1994), 267.

33. Judith A. Teichman, *Privatization and Political Change*, 175.

34. Stephen Morris, *Political Reformism in Mexico: An Overview of Contemporary Mexican Politics* (Boulder, CO: Lynne Rienner, 1995), 92

35. Alejandro Guevara Sanginés, "Poverty Alleviation in Mexico," in *Rebuilding the State: Mexico After Salinas*, ed. Monica Serrano and Victor Bulmer-Thomas (University of London, Center for Latin American Studies, 1996), 156.

36. Nikki Craske, "Dismantling or Retrenchment? Salinas and Corporatism," in *Dismantling the Mexican State*, ed. Rob Aitken et al. (New York: St. Martin's, 1996), 87.

37. Alan Knight, "Solidarity: Historical Continuities and Contemporary Implications," in *Transforming State-Society Relations in Mexico: The National Solidarity Strategy*, ed. Wayne Cornelius et al. (San Diego: University of California, 1994), 29.

38. Alan Knight, "Salinas and Social Liberalism in Context," in Rob Aitkin et al., *Dismantling the Mexican State?* 1996, 13.

39. See Anne Varley, "Delivering Goods: Solidarity, Land Regularizarion and Urban Services," in Rob Aitkin et al., *Dismantling the Mexican State?* 1996.

40. Julio Moguel, "Cinco criticas solidarias a un programa de gobierno," *El Cotidiano* 49 (1992): 41–48.

41. Global Exchange/Alianza Civica International Delegation. *Pre-electoral Conditions in Mexico, 2000* (San Francisco: Global Exchange, 2000).

42. John Bailey, "Centralism and Political Change in Mexico: The Case of National Solidarity," in Cornelius et al., *Transforming State Societal Relations in Mexico*, 109.

43. Alan Knight, "Salinas and Social Liberalism in Context," in Rob Aitkin et al., *Dismantling the Mexican State?*

44. Asa Christina Laurell, "The Transformation of Social Policy in Mexico," in *Confronting Development: Assessing Mexico's Economic and Social Policy Challenges*, ed. Kevin J. Middlebrooke and Eduardo Zepeda (San Diego: Stanford University Press, 2003), 320–49.

45. Diana Alarcon, "Income Distribution and Poverty Alleviation in Mexico: A Comparative Analysis," in *Confronting Development*, ed. Middlebrooke and Eduardo Zepeda, 446–85.

46. Gonzalez Gomez notes that in 1995, the Mexican economy shrank by 6.2 percent, the biggest decline since 1932. See Mauricio A. Gonzalez Gomez, "Crisis and Economic Change in Mexico," in *Mexico under Zedillo*, ed. Susan Kaufman Purcell and Luis Rubio (Boulder, CO: Lynne Rienner, 1998), 52.

47. "Iminente intervencion del gobierno para frenar las quiebras de los genios reprivatizados," *El Financiero*, December 4, 1992.

48. Carol Wise, "Mexico's Democratic Transition: The Search for New Reform Coalitions," in *Post-Stabilization Politics in Latin America: Competition, Transition and Collapse*, ed. Carol Wise and Riordan Roett (Washington, DC: Brookings Institution, 2003), 159–98.

49. See Judith A. Teichman's discussion in *The Politics of Freeing Markets in Latin America: Chile, Argentina and Mexico* (Chapel Hill: University of North Carolina Press, 2001), 77, especially footnote 28.

50. Monica Serrano, "Civil Violence in Chiapas: The Origins and Causes of the Revolt," in *Mexico: Assessing Neoliberal Reform*, ed. Monica Serrano (London: Institute of Latin American Studies, University of London, 1998).

51. Elizabeth Malkin, "Mexico's problems will expedite privatizations," *Privatisation International: The Monthly Intelligence Report on Privatisation and Private Infrastructure Worldwide*, no. 77 February 1, 1995.

52. On the sale of the Veracruz port, see *Business Mexico* 5, no. 9 (September 1995): 19. On the attempt to privatize fifty-eight airports, see *Traffic World* 243 (August 21, 1995): 18–19. See also the World Bank's positive appraisal of Mexico's privatized toll roads, *A Retrospective on the Mexican Toll Road Program (1989–1994)*, World Bank Group, 1997.

53. Pamela K. Starr, "Monetary Mismanagement and Inadvertent Democratization in Technocratic Mexico," *Studies in International Comparative Development* 33 (Winter 1999): 50.

54. *Latin American Weekly Report*, October 24, 1996, 487

55. Kenneth C. Shadlen, "Continuity amid Change: Democratization, Party Strategies and Economic Policymaking in Mexico," *Government and Opposition* 34 (1999): 418.

56. Judith A. Teichman, *The Politics of Freeing Markets: Chile, Argentina, and Mexico* (Chapel Hill: University of North Carolina Press, 2001), 168.

57. See Dag MacLeod, *Downsizing the State: Privatization and the Limits of Neoliberal Reform in Mexico* (University Park: Penn State University Press, 2004), 2.

Chapter 6

1. See Sylvia Maxfield, "The International Political Economy of Bank Nationalization: Mexico in Comparative Perspective," *Latin American Research Review* 27, no. 1 (1991): 75–103. By one estimate, by the mid-1980s, Mexico had accumulated a capital flight of over fifty billion dollars, representing nearly one-third of the GNP.

2. Roderic Camp, *Entrepreneurs and Politics in the Twentieth Century Mexico* (New York: Oxford University Press, 1989), 243.

3. Matilde Luna, "Hacia un corporativismo liberal? Los empresarios y el corporativismo," *Estudios Sociologicos* 5, no. 15 (1987): 445–76.

4. See Lawrence Whitehead, "Political Change and Economic Stabilization: The Economic Solidarity Pact," in *Mexico's Alternative Political Futures*, ed. Wayne Cornelius et al. (La Jolla: University of California, 1989).

5. Ben Ross Schneider, "Big Business and the Politics of Economic Reform: Confidence and Concentration in Brazil and Mexico," in *Business and the State in Developing Countries*, ed. Ben Ross Schneider and Sylvia Maxfield (Ithaca, NY: Cornell University Press, 1997), 200.

6. See Ken Shadlen, "Corporatism and the Associative Logics of Business: Small Industry and the State in Post-Revolutionary Mexico," PhD dissertation, University of California, Berkeley, 1997.

7. Robert Kaufman, Carlos Bazdresch, and Blanca Heredia, "Mexico: Radical Reform in a Dominant Party System," in *Voting for Reform: Democracy, Political Liberalization and Economic Adjustment*, ed. Stephan Haggard and Steven B. Webb (Oxford University Press, 1994), 360–411.

8. Ibid., 380.

9. As he told a national newspaper, "We gave the government a deadline to clean up its finances. It has met that goal. It has fulfilled the verbal promises it made to the business sector even earlier (which were not part of the Pact) such as the liquidation and dissolution of nationally important firms like AeroMexico and Cananea" (*Unomasuno*, May 19, 1988).

10. *La Jornada*, June 5, 1992.

11. *La Jornada*, November 2, 1991.

12. Francisco Valdes Ugalde, "From Bank Nationalization to State Reform: Business and the New Mexican Order," in *The Politics of Economic Restructuring: State-Society Relations and Regime Change in Mexico*, ed. Maria Lorena Cook et al. (Center for U.S.-Mexican Studies, University of California, 1994), 238.

13. Ibid., 280.

14. See Stephen Baker, "The Friends of Carlos Salinas," *Businessweek*, February 22, 1991.

15. Valdes Ugalde, "From Bank Nationalization to State Reform," 233.

16. See Guy Poitras and Raymond Robinson, "The Politics of NAFTA in Mexico," *Journal of Interamerican Studies and World Affairs* 36, no. 1 (1994): 1–35.

17. Blanca Heredia, "Making Economic Reform Politically Viable: The Mexican Experience," in *Democracy, Markets, and Structural Reform in Latin America: Argentina, Bolivia, Brazil, Chile, and Mexico*, ed., William C. Smith et al. (New Brunswick, NJ: Transaction Publishers, 1994), 276

18. Robert Kaufman, "How Societies Change Development Models Or Keep Them? Reflections on the Latin American Experience in the 1930s and the Postwar World," in *Manufactured Miracles: Paths of Industrialization in Latin America and East Asia*, ed. Gary Gereffi and Don Wyman (Princeton, NJ: Princeton University Press, 1990), 110–38.

19. On the emergence of Mexican presidentialism, see Jorge Carpizo, *El presidencialismo Mexicano* (Siglo Veintiuno Editores, 2002).

20. See Sylvia Maxfield, *Governing Capital: International Finance and Mexican Politics* (Ithaca, NY: Cornell University Press, 1990).

21. Alejandro Carrillo Castro, *La reforma administrativa en México: Evolución de la reforma administrativa en México (1971–1979)*, vol. 2 (Mexico City: Miguel Angel Porrúa, 1985), 221.

22. Centeno, *Democracy Within Reason*, 89.

23. Roderic Ai Camp, *Mexico's Mandarins: Crafting a Power Elite for the Twenty-First Century* (Los Angeles: University of California Press, 2002).

24. Susan Kaufman Purcell and John F. Purcell, "State and Society in Mexico: Must a Stable Society be Institutionalized?" *World Politics* 30, no. 2 (January 1980): 201.

25. Teichman, *Privatization and Political Change in Mexico*, 69.

26. Denise Dresser, "Salinistroika Without Prisnost: Institutions, Coalition-Building, and Economic Reform in Mexico," PhD dissertation, Princeton University, 1994, p. 100.

27. Macleod, *Downsizing the State*, 253.

28. Judith Teichman, *The Politics of Freeing Markets: Chile, Argentina and Mexico* (Chapel Hill: University of North Carolina Press, 2001), 147.

29. Delal M. Baer, "Electoral Trends," in *Prospects for Mexico*, ed. George W. Grayson (Washington, DC: Foreign Service Institute, United States Department of State, 1988), 35–62.

30. Stephen D. Morris, *Political Reformism in Mexico: An Overview of Contemporary Mexican Politics* (Boulder, CO: Lynne Rienner, 1995), 5.

31. Geraldine Lievesley, *Democracy in Latin America: Mobilization, Power and the Search for a New Politics* (Manchester University Press, 1999), 49.

32. Juan Reyes del Campillo, "Candidatos: Hacia una nueva Camara," *Nexos* 164, no. 8 (1991): 57.

33. *Latin American Weekly Report*, September 20, 1990.

34. José Ignacio Rodriguez Reyna, "Nuevo empresario: La politica como inversion," *Este Pais* 10 (January 1992): 2–8.

35. Ibid., 147.

36. Steven E. Sanderson, "Presidential Succession and Political Rationality in Mexico," *World Politics* 35, no. 3 (1989): 315–34.

37. Jonathan Heath, *Mexico and the Sexenio Curse: Presidential Successions and Economic Crises in Mexico* (Washington: Center for Strategic and International Studies, 1999), 10.

38. Peter Smith, *Labyrinths of Power: Political Recruitment in Twentieth Century Mexico* (Princeton University Press, 1979), 207.

39. David Arellano Gault and Juan Pablo Guerrero Amparane, "Stalled Administrative Reforms of the Mexican State," in *Reinventing Leviathan: The Politics of Administrative Reform in Developing Countries,* ed. Ben Ross Schneider and Blanca Heredia (North-South Center Press, University of Miami, 2003).

40. In an interview with *Proceso*, Vargas Llosa said, "The Mexican political system is not democratic—let's not kid ourselves. It is a unique system that has no equivalents in the world, that has managed to keep a party in power by adapting to circumstances with a versatility that no other authoritarian system has managed" (*Proceso*, no. 723, September 10, 1990, cited in Andrew Reding, "The Crumbling of a Perfect Dictatorship," *World Policy Journal* 8 [Spring 1991]: 257).

41. *Unomasuno*, February 21, 1991.

42. *Latin American Weekly Report*, May 12, 1991.

43. Teichman, *Privatization and Political Change in Mexico*, 146.

44. Vinod Aggarwal, *Debt Games: Strategic Interaction in International Debt Rescheduling* (Cambridge: Cambridge University Press, 1996), 47.

45. William R. Cline, *International Debt Re-examined* (Washington, DC: Institute for International Economics, 1995), 220.

46. Morris, *Political Reformism in Mexico*, 210–11.

47. Ibid., 314.

48. Philip L Russell, *Mexico Under Salinas* (Austin: Mexico Resource Center, 1994), 312.

49. Judith Teichman, *The Politics of Freeing Markets*, 61.

50. Ernest J. Oliveri, *Latin American Debt and the Politics of International Finance* (Westport, CT: Praeger, 1992), 77.

51. World Bank, *World Development Report 1997: The State in a Changing World* (New York: Oxford University Press for the World Bank, 1997), 25; Claudio Loser and Eliot Kalter, "Mexico: The Strategy to Achieve Sustained Economic Growth," *Occasional Papers*, 99 (Washington, DC: International Monetary Fund, 1992), 12.

52. Joseph Stiglitz would note that this post-1994 optimism was another case of "the IMF declaring victory prematurely: Mexico's crisis in 1995 was declared over as soon as the banks started to get repaid . . . the very fact that the IMF focuses on financial variables, not on measures of real employment, GDP or broader measures of welfare is itself telling" (Joseph Stiglitz, *Globalization and Its Discontents* [New York: Norton, 2002], 121). Similarly, Paul Krugman described the hoopla surrounding the Mexican model as being "a leap of faith, rather than a conclusion based on hard evidence" (Paul Krugman, "Dutch Tulips and Emerging Markets," *Foreign Affairs*, July/August 1995, 33).

53. John Sheahan, "Effects of Liberalization Programs on Poverty and Inequality: Chile, Mexico, and Peru," *Latin American Research Review* 32, no. 3 (1997): 24.

54. See Mauricio A. Gonzalez Gomez, "Crisis and Economic Change in Mexico," in *Mexico under Zedillo*, ed. Susan Kaufman Purcell and Luis Rubio (Boulder, CO: Lynne Rienner, 1998), 52.

55. Mehrene Larudee, "Integration and Income Distribution under the North American Free Trade Agreement: The Experience of Mexico," in *Globalization and Progressive Economic Policy*, ed. Dean Baker et al. (Cambridge University Press, 1999), 278.

56. Sarah Babb, *Managing Mexico: Economists from Nationalism to Neoliberalism* (Princeton University Press, 2001), 196.

57. Alexander Coleman, "O plomo o plata?" *New Criterion* 18, no. 4 (December 1999); Gerardo Otero, "Rural Mexico After the 'Perfect Dictatorship,'" *Latin American Studies Association Forum* 31, no. 3: 4–7.

58. Speech by President Miguel de la Madrid at Tuxla, Gutierrez, June 23, 1982, cited in Centeno, *Democracy Within Reason*, 195.

59. Speech by President Miguel de la Madrid, at Leon, Guanjuato, May 5, 1982, cited in Centeno, *Democracy Within Reason*, 197.

60. Hector Camin Aguilar and Lorenzo Meyer, *A la sombra de la Revolucion* (Mexico City: Cal y Arena, 1989).

61. Speech by President Carlos Salinas at the sixty-third anniversary of the PRI on March 4, 1992, cited in Merilee Grindle, *Challenging the State: Crisis and Innovation in Latin America and Africa* (Melbourne: Cambridge University Press, 1996), 117.

62. Richard Snyder, *Politics After Neoliberalism: Reregulation in Mexico* (Cambridge University Press, 2001), 15.

63. Jesus Guadalupe Aguilar Quintero, "Porque fracaso en Mexico la privatizacion de las carreteras de cuota?" in *El Neoliberalismo Mexicano*, ed. Hector Gaxiola Carrasco (Universidad Autonoma de Sinaloa, 2003), 150.

64. Diane E. David, "Law Enforcement in Mexico City," *NACLA*, September/October 2003; Marcos Pablo Moloeznik, "Public Security and Police Reform in Mexico," in *Public Security and Police Reform in Latin America*, ed. John Bailey and Lucia Dammert (University of Pittsburgh Press, 2006).

65. Nora Claudia Lustig and Jaime Ros, "Economic Reforms, Stabilization Policies, and the 'Mexican Disease,'" in *After Neoliberalism: What Next for Latin America?* (Ann Arbor: University of Michigan Press, 1999), 30.

66. See Timothy P. Kessler, *Global Capital and National Politics: Reforming Mexico's Financial System* (Westport: Praeger, 1999).

67. Kevin Middlebrooke and Eduardo Zapeda, eds., *Confronting Development: Assessing Mexico's Social and Economic Policy Challenges* (San Diego: University of California, 2003), 15.

68. See Hector E. Schamis, "Distributional Coalitions and the Politics of Economic Reform in Latin America," *World Politics* 51, no. 2 (1999): 236–68.

69. Jacques Rogozinski, *La privatización en México: Razones e impactos* (Mexico City: Trillas, 1997), cited in Dag Macleod, *Downsizing the State*, 99.

70. See Walter F. Weiker, *The Modernization of Turkey: From Ataturk to the Present Day* (New York: Holmes & Meier, 1981).

71. Thomas Skidmore, *Brazil: Five Centuries of Change* (New York: Oxford University Press, 1999), 100.

72. Maria del Pilar Tello, *Golpe O Revolucion? Hablan los Militares del 68* (Ediciones Sagsa, 1983), 324. See also Torcuato Salvador Di Tella, *History of Political Parties in Twentieth Century in Latin America* (New Brunswick: Transaction, 2005), 199.

73. Timothy Mitchell, "The Properties of Markets," *Working Paper No. 2*, Cultural Political Economy Research Group, University of Lancaster, 2004.

74. Kurt Gerhard Weyland, "Theories of Policy Diffusion: Lessons from Latin American Pension Reform," *World Politics* 57, no. 2 (January 2005): 262–95.

75. Barbara Stallings, "Capitalisms in Conflict? The United States, Europe and Japan in the Post–Cold War World," in *Global Change, Regional Response: The New International Context of Development,* ed. Barbara Stallings (Cambridge University Press, 1995).

76. David Harvey, *A Brief History of Neoliberalism* (New York: Oxford University Press, 2005), 7. On neoliberalism and the "El Salvador Option" being applied in Iraq, see also Greg Grandin, *Empire's Workshop: Latin America, the United States, and the Rise of the New Imperialism* (New York: Metropolitan Books, 2006). See also Omar G. Encarnación, "The Follies of Democratic Imperialism," *World Policy Journal* XXII, no. 1 (Spring 2005); Khaled Medani, "State Rebuilding in Reverse: The Neoliberal 'Reconstruction' of Iraq," *Middle East Report* 232 (Fall 2004).

77. "Seule la libéralisation peut garantir l'augmentation des exportations," *Ahram Hebdomadaire,* July 8, 1997; "L'Egypte doit se lancer dans l'economie mondiale," *Ahram Hebdomadaire,* June 6, 2001; "Les grands dossiers vus par Boutros-Ghali," *Ahram Hebdomadaire,* April 12, 2000.

78. On the Pronasol–Social Fund connection, see Alejankdro J. Grinspun, "Social Funds: Fertile Ground for South-South Cooperation," *Cooperation South Journal* (United Nations Development Programme) 1 (1995), http://tcdc1.undp.org/CoopSouth/1995_may/social_funds.asp

79. Weyland, "Theories of Policy Diffusion," 295.

80. Evelyne Huber and Fred Solt, "Successes and Failures of Neoliberalism," *Latin American Research Review* 39, no. 3 (2004): 150–64.

81. Centeno, *Democracy Within Reason*, 234.

82. See David Colander, ed., *Neoclassical Political Economy: The Analysis of Rent-Seeking and DUP Activities* (Cambridge, MA: Ballinger, 1984).

83. Joel Migdal, *State in Society: Studying How States and Societies Transform and Constitute One Another* (Cambridge University Press, 2001), 17. Foucault noted the difference between discourse and practice: "It is the tactics of the government which make possible the continual definition and redefinition of what is within the competence of the state and what is not, the public versus private, and so on: thus the state can only be understood in its survival and the limits on the basis of the general tactics of governmentality" (Graham Burchell, ed., *The Foucault Effect: Studies in Governmentality* [University of Chicago Press, 1991], 103).

84. Paul Streeten, "Markets and States: Against Minimalism," *World Development* 21, no. 8 (1993): 1281–98.

Chapter 7

1. Sherine Nasr, "Pushing ahead with Reform," *Al-Ahram Weekly*, June 6–12, 2002.

2. Moheb Zaki, *Egyptian Business Elites: Their Vision and Investment Behavior* (Cairo: Arab Center for Development and Future Research, 1999), 226.

3. Edward Gibson, "The Populist Road to Market Reform: Policy and Electoral Coalitions in Mexico and Argentina," *World Politics* 49, no. 2 (April 1997) 339–70.

4. See Robert Mabro, *The Egyptian Economy 1952–1972* (Oxford: Clarendon Press, 1974), 154–60.

5. Saad Eddin Ibrahim and Hans Lofgren, "Successful Adjustment and Declining Governance? The Case of Egypt," in *Governance, Leadership, and Communication: Building Constituencies for Economic Reform*, ed. Leila Frischak and Izak Atiyas (Washington, DC: World Bank, 1996), 162.

6. Ibid.

7. Howard Handy et al. *Egypt: Beyond Stabilization, Toward a Dynamic Market Economy* (International Monetary Fund Occasional Paper no. 163, Washington, DC, 1998).

8. "The IMF's Model Pupil," *Economist*, March 21, 1999. See Simon Bromley and Ray Bush, "Adjustment in Egypt? The Political Economy of Reform," *Review of African Political Economy* 60 (1994): 201–13. The authors open their article with the following statement: "Egypt is currently being hailed as an economic success story. Structural adjustment is working," 201.

9. Pratt, Nicola "Maintaining the Moral Economy: Egyptian State-Labor Relations in an Era of Economic Liberalization." *Arab Studies Journal*, Fall 2000/Spring 2001, 111–29.

10. World Bank, *Global Development Finance 2000* (CD-ROM version, vol. 1).

11. *Al-Ahram Weekly*, January 1–7, 1999

12. "Slow Pace of Egypt Privatization Draws Criticism," *Middle East Economic Survey* XLV, no. 11 (March 18, 2002).

13. *Al-Ahram Weekly*, March 10–16, 2005.

14. *Business Today Egypt*, August 1996.

15. *Al-Ahram Weekly*, May 19, 1999.

16. See Huwayda 'Adli Rouman, *Al-haraka al-'ummaliyya wa aliyat muqawamat al-ifqar, 1987–1993* (Cairo: Al-Ahali, 1997), 5.

17. Francoise Clémente, "Libéralisme, restructuration du secteur public et réforme du code du travail," in *Age libéral et néo-liberalisme: VIs recontres franco-égyptiennes de science politiques*, Dossiers du Cedej, 241–46 (Cairo: CEDEJ, 1996).

18. *Middle East International*, March 29, 1999.

19. Land Center for Human Rights Report, December 1998, July 1999, and April 2000, *Economic and Social Rights Series*, http://www.lchr.org.

20. *Cairo Times*, April 4, 2000.

21. Sherine Abdel-Razek, "Much ado about Kima," *Al-Ahram Weekly*, October 17–23, 2002.

22. *Al-Ahram Weekly*, June 1–7, 2006.

23. *Al-Ahram Weekly*, March 17–23, 2005.

24. *Al-Ahram Weekly*, February 5–11, 2004.

25. "Egypt: Flawed Elections, But . . ." *Democracy Digest* 2, no. 9 (September 13, 2005).

26. A renewed offer from the French company promised to not undertake mass layoffs for at least three years and promised two bonuses of six months pay if a successful deal was reached. Al-*Ahram Weekly*, March 10–16, 2005.

27. Joel Beinin and Hossam el-Hamalawy, "Egyptian Textile Workers Confront the New Economic Order," *Middle East Report*, March 25, 2007.

28. See Agnieszka Paczynska, "Globalization, Structural Adjustment and Pressure to Conform: Contesting Labor Law reform in Egypt," *New Political Science* 28, no. 1 (March 2006): 60.

29. *Cairo Times*, March 17, 1999.

30. *Al-Ahram Weekly*, March 10–16, 2005.

31. *Al-Ahram Weekly*, February 11–17, 1999.

32. *Al-Ahram Weekly*, March 10–16, 2005.

33. *Egyptian Labor Protests in 1999*, Land Center for Human Rights, Cairo, April 2000.

34. Howaida Adly Rouman, "Al-Musharaka al-siyyasia li al-umal al-misriyin," in *Haqiqat al-ta'adudiya al-siyasiya fi Misr*, ed. Mustafa Kamel Sayid (Maktabat Madbuli, 1996), 182.

35. Rehab Saad, "The silent 50% percent," *Al-Ahram Weekly*, November 9–15, 2000.

36. Fatemah Farag, "May Day Dilemmas" *Al-Ahram Weekly*, May 5, 1999.

37. Joel Beinin and Hossam el-Hamalawy, "Egyptian Textile Workers."

38. "Ma'zaq al-niqabat al 'ummaliyya wa khiyar al-ta'addudiyya," *al-Musa'ada*, May 1997.

39. Gamal Abdel Nasser Ibrahim, "Représentation Syndicale et Transition Libérale en Egypte: Lecture des élections de 1996," *Egypte/Monde Arabe* 33 (1998): 181–221

40. Karim El-Gawhary, "'Nothing More to Lose': Landowners, Tenants and Economic Liberalization in Egypt," *Middle East Report* 204 (July–September 1997) 41–48.

41. *Report #31*, Land Center for Human Rights, 2005. Cairo, Egypt

42. Al-Sayyid, *Haqiqat al-ta'adudiya al-siyasiya fi Misr*, 39.

43. See Omar El Shafei, "Workers, Trade Unions and the State in Egypt," *Cairo Papers in Social Science*, vol. 18, summer (Cairo: American University in Cairo Press, 1995). Paper series published by AUC.

44. *Al-Ahram Weekly*, December 19–25, 2002.

45. Vickie Langohr, "Too Much Civil Society, Too Little Politics," *Comparative Politics* 36, no. 2 (2004): 181–204.

46. Khaled Ali of the Hisham Mubarak Legal Center notes that the change from appeals courts to courts of first instance had created a backlog of a thousand cases (Fatemah Farag, "Labour backlog," *Al-Ahram Weekly*, no. 689, May 6–12, 2004).

47. Posusney-Pripstein, *Labor and the State in Egypt*, 123.

48. Eberhard Kienle, *A Grand Delusion: Democracy and Economic Reform in Egypt* (London: I. B. Tauris, 2001), 82.

49. This law can be accessed at the Electoral Knowledge Network's website: http://aceproject.org/ero-en/regions/mideast/EG/Law%20no.%2040%20of%201977-%20arabic.pdf/view.

50. For instance, when the regime froze the Labor Party in 2000 after the party's publication criticized the state's banning of Syiran author Haydar Haydar's book, the party's secretary-general said, "The government realized we're capable of mobilizing popular support against its policies. This is an act of serious opposition and they resent us for it" (Maye Kassem, *Egyptian Politics*: The Dynamics of Authoritarian Rule (Lynne Rienner 2004), 59.

51. *Al-Masry al-Youm*, June 23, 2005.

52. "Egypt: Flawed Elections, But . . ." *Democracy Digest* 2, no. 9, September 13, 2005.

53. Faiza Rady, "Privatise the unions," *Al-Ahram Weekly*, no. 747, June 16–22, 2005. Because of the new law, party leaders like Mohamed Abdelaziz Shaban of the NPUP have joined the call for an independent trade union, as existed prior to 1952, "before being shackled to the ETUF."

54. *Al-Ahram Weekly*, November 1, 1995.

55. Joel Beinin, "Political Islam and the New Global Economy: The Political Economy of an Egyptian Social Movement," *New Centennial Review* 5, no. 1 (2005): 111–39.

56. James Toth, "Islamism in Southern Egypt: A Case Study of a Radical Religious Movement," *International Journal of Middle East Studies* 35, no. 4 (November 2003): 547–72.

57. According to the ETUF, 75 percent of its members were working in the state bureaucracy in SOEs, while 25 percent were employed by the private sector. The 25 percent also include independent workers such as taxi drivers who by law have to be union members.

58. Law 12, 1995 Article 36.

59. Law 12, 1995, Articles 23 and 36

60. President of the ETUF, Decree 35, 1996, in *Qarar ra'is al-ittihad al-'Amm li-Niqabat'Ummal Misr raqm 35/1996*, Cairo.

61. Ministry of Employment, Decree 146 1196, Article 6, in Dalil "al-intikhabat al-niqabiyya wa majalis idarat al-sharikat" *Al-'Amal* 30, October 1996.

62. Ibrahim, "Représentation Syndicale et Transition Libérale en Egypte," 183.

63. Eberhard Kienle, *A Grand Delusion*, 35.

64. *Al-Ahali*, January 1, 1997.

65. *Middle East Times*, November 8, 2006; *Al-Ahram Weekly*, November 1–7, 2006.

66. Hossam el-Hamalawy, "Mubarak's NDP Abducts Egyptian Trade Union Federation," *Arabist.net*, November 29, 2006.

67. Joel Beinin, "Underbelly of Egypt's Neoliberal Agenda," *Middle East Report*, May 9, 2007.

68. Joel Beinin and Hossam el-Hamalawy, "Strikes in Egypt Spread from Center of Gravity," *Middle East Report*, May 9, 2007.

69. Bianchi, *Unruly Corporatism*, 171.

70. Richard Jacquemond, "Dix ans de justice constitutionelle en Egypte 1979–1990," in *Politiques législatives: Egypte, Tunisie, Algerie, Maroc, ed.* Bernard Botiveau et al., 79–96 (Cairo: CEDEJ, 1994).

71. *Al-Ahram Weekly*, October 12, 1995.

72. *Al-Ahram Weekly*, October 18, 1995.

73. See Al Sayed Abdel and Dahroug, "The Executive and the National Democratic Party (NDP)," in *The Arab Strategic Report* (Cairo: Al-Ahram Center for Political and Strategic Studies, 1995).

74. *Al-Ahram Weekly*, March 3–9, 2005.

75. Samuel Huntington, *Political Order in Changing Societies* (New Haven: Yale University Press, 1968), 322.

76. *United Nations Human Development Report 2000* United Nations Publications CDROM

77. See Ishac Diwan, "Globalization, EU Partnership and Income Distribution in Egypt," *Working Paper no. 12*, Egyptian Center for Economic Studies, 1997.

78. Hans Lofgren, "Egypt's Program for Stabilization and Structural Adjustment: An Assessment," *Economic and Politics of Structural Adjustment in Egypt* (Cairo Papers in Social Science) 16, no. 3 (Fall 1993): 22.

79. The Economist: Economist Intelligence Unit, *Egypt: Country Profile*, 2006.

80. Ibid.

81. On the Pronasol–Social Fund connection, see Alejankdro J. Grinspun, "Social Funds: Fertile Ground for South-South Cooperation," *Cooperation South Journal* (United Nations Development Programme) 1 (1995); Laura Rawlings

et al., *Letting Communities Take the Lead: A Cross-Country Evaluation of Social Fund Performance* (Washington, DC: World Bank, 2001).

82. *Al-Ahram Weekly*, July 6–12, 2000.
83. *Al-Ahram Weekly*, August 13–19, 1998.
84. "Measuring results for Maximum Effectiveness," report from *The Near East Foundation*, New York, April 10, 2006.
85. Social Fund for Development, *Annual Report 1995*, Cairo, 36, 1996
86. Mubarak told *the Washington Times* that American aid had helped "in developing [Egyptian] infrastructure and it has helped in the privatization of the economy. It has been a great help to the economy. We don't forget that" David W. Jones, "Mubarak to Washington Times: Saudi initiative means full Israeli withdrawal" (*Washington Times*, March 2, 2002). But in a later interview with the Egyptian weekly *Rose El Yusuf*, Mubarak stated that the Bush administration had criticized his government because he doesn't accept direction from Washington, that "because we don't listen (to them) and do not bow to anything that does not match with our interests" (Salah Nasrawi, "Mubarak's son met secretly with Cheney," *Associated Press*, May 15, 2005).
87. Nicola Pratt, "Maintaining the Moral Economy."

Chapter 8

1. Dieter Weiss and Ulrich Wurzel, *The Economics and Politics of Transition to an Open Market Economy: Egypt* (Paris: OECD,1998), 37.
2. Marcelo Giugale and Hamed Mobarak, *Private Sector Development* (Cairo: American University in Cairo Press, 1994), 170.
3. See Ali Soleiman, *Dawr al-Qita' al-Khass fi al-Tanmiyah Ma'a al-Tatbiq 'ala Misr* (Cairo: Maktabat al-Tanmiya, 2000).
4. Neil MacFarquhar, "Melting Icy Egypt-Israel Relations Through a Trade Pact," *New York Times*, December 17, 2004.
5. *Global Development Finance*, CD-ROM, vol. 1, World Bank, 2000.
6. Mohammad El Erian, "Middle Eastern Economies' External Environment: What Lies Ahead?" *Middle East Policy* 4, no. 3 (March 1996): 137–46.
7. World Bank, *Egypt in the global economy: strategic choices for savings, investments, and long-term growth* (Washington, DC: World Bank, 1998), 24.
8. Sherine Abdel-Razek, "Market poised for recovery," *Al-Ahram Weekly*, May 4–10, 2000.
9. Nathan Brown, *The Rule of Law in the Arab World* (Cambridge University Press, 1997), 234.
10. Moheb Zaki, *Egyptian Business Elites: Their Vision and Investment Behavior.* Arab Center for Development and Future Research. Cairo 1999, 134.
11. Nazih Ayubi, "Etatisme Versus Privatization: The Changing Economic Role of the State in Nine Arab Countries," in *Economic Transition in the Middle East*, ed. Heba Handoussa (American University of Cairo Press, 1997), 130.
12. *World Bank, Egypt in the Global Economy*, 18.

13. Howard Handy et al. *Egypt: Beyond Stabilization, Toward a Dynamic Market Economy* (International Monetary Fund Occasional Paper no. 163, Washington, DC, 1998).

14. Timothy Mitchell, *Rule of Experts: Egypt, Techno-Politics, Modernity* (Berkeley: University of California Press, 1999), 275.

15. Mona El-Ghobashy, "Egypt's Summer of Discontent" *Middle East Report*, September 18, 2003.

16. *Financial Times*, September 9, 1999.

17. *Business Week*, June 25, 2001.

18. *Al-Ahram Weekly*, May 18–24, 2006.

19. Sadowski, *Political Vegetables?*

20. Hamied Ansari, *Egypt: The Stalled Society* (Albany: State University of New York Press, 1986), 195.

21. Ayubi, *Overstating the Arab* State, 417.

22. Robert Springborg, "State-Society Relations in Egypt: The Debate over the Owner-Tenant Relations," *Middle East Journal* 45, no. 2 (Spring 1991), 232–49.

23. "Seven Point Foundation of the Agricultural Sector," Speech cited in Yahya Sadowski, *Political Vegetables*, 135.

24. Ngozi Okonjo-Iweala and Youssef Fouleihan, "Structural Adjustment and Egyptian Agriculture: Some Preliminary Indication of the Impact of Economic Reforms," in *Sustainable Agriculture in Egypt*, ed. Mohamed A. Faris and Mahmood Hasan Khan (Boulder, CO: Lynne Rienner, 1993), 133.

25. *Middle East Times*, May 23, 1997. See Ray Bush, "Facing Structural Adjustment: Strategies of Peasants, the State, and the International Financial Institutions," in *Directions of Change in Rural Egypt,* ed. Nicholas S. Hopkins and Kirsten Westergaard (Cairo: American University in Cairo Press, 1998).

26. Salwa Ismail, *Rethinking Islamist Politics: Culture, the State and Islamism* (New York: I. B. Tauris, 2003).

27. Éric Denis, "Demographic Surprises Foreshadow Change in Neoliberal Egypt," *Middle East Report* 246 (Spring 2008), 32–37.

28. Manuel Antonio Garreton, "Political Processes in an Authoritarian Regime: The Dynamics of Institutionalization and Opposition in Chile, 1973–1980," in *Military Rule in Chile: Dictatorship and Opposition*, ed. Samuel Valenzuela and Arturo Valenzuela (Baltimore: Johns Hopkins University Press, 1985).

29. *Akhbar al-Yawm*, February 6, 1992.

30. Mohammed Shuman, "Azmat al-musharak min khilal al-ahzan al-misriyya," in *Haqiqat al Ta'adudiya al-siyasiya fi misr*, ed. Kamel and Al-Manufi (Maktabat Madbuli Mu'taz, 1996).

31. International Crisis Group, *The Challenge of Political Reform: Egypt After the Iraq War Brussels, Belgium: International Crisis Group*, September 30, 2003, 10.

32. Dina al-Khawaga, "Le Parti Nationale Démocrate et les Élections de 1995: La conjonction de nombreuses logiques d'action," in *Contours et Détours du*

Politique en Égypte: Les élections législatives de 1995, ed. Sandrine Gamblin (Cairo: CEDEJ, 1997), 99.

33. Alain Roussillon, "Republican Egypt Interpreted: Revolution and Beyond," in *The Cambridge History of Egypt, Vol. 2, Modern Egypt, from 1517 to the End of the Twentieth Century* (New York: Cambridge University Press, 1998), 391.

34. For more on the "politicized state," see Ben R. Schneider's *Politics Within the State: Elite Bureaucrats and Industrial Policy in Authoritarian Brazil* (Pittsburgh: University of Pittsburgh Press, 1991), 70.

35. Monte Palmer et al., *The Egyptian Bureaucracy* (New York: Syracuse University Press, 1988).

36. Yahya Sadowski, *Political Vegetables*? 89.

37. See Abdelaziz El Shirbini, "Changes and Trends in Public Administration in Egypt," report submitted to the Arab Organization of Devlopment Organization, 1997.

38. Bianchi, *Unruly Corporatism*, 15.

39. *Al-Ahram al-Iqtisadi*, March 22, 1991.

40. Jamil Jreisat, "Faltering Bureaucratic Reforms: The Case of Egypt," *Journal of Developing Societies* 11, no. 2 (1995), 221–32.

41. *Cairo Times*, October 16, 1997.

42. See EPIC 2000, "The Transformation of the Egyptian Labor Market: 1988–1998," EPIC newsletter, Cairo, January 2000, in *Globalization and the Politics of Development in the Middle East*, ed. Clement M. Henry and Robert Springborg (New York: Cambridge University Press, 2001).

43. *Al-Ahram Weekly*, October 7–13, 2004

44. Alain Roussillon, *L'Égypt et l'Algérie au péril de la liberalization* (Cairo: CEDEJ, 1996), 100–110.

45. *Middle East Economic Digest*, July 25, 1997.

46. Mona El-Ghobashy, "Egypt Looks Ahead to Portentous Year," *Middle East Report*, February 2005.

47. Egyptian Constitution, Article 76, chap. 3.

48. Eric Denis, "Cairo as Neoliberal Capital?" in *Cairo Cosmopolitan: Politics, Culture and Urban space in the New Globalized Middle East*, ed. Diane Singerman and Paul Amar (Cairo: American University of Cairo Press, 2006), 47–71. On the privatization of insurance, see "The Toughest Nut to Crack," *Al-Ahram Weekly*, August 25–31, 2005.

49. *Al-Ahram Weekly*, August 3–9, 2006.

50. *Al Ahram Weekly*, March 17–23, 2005.

51. Sherine Nasr, "Proof of the Pudding," *Al-Ahram Weekly*, September 23–29, 2004. Moheiddein declared that there is no such thing as a "strategic commodity or strategic sector . . . [and] the private sector is welcome to step forward and introduce practical solution to save loss making companies."

52. Dieter Weiss and Ulrich Wurzel, *The Economics and Politics of Transition to an Open Market Economy: Egypt* (Development Centre of the OECD, 1998), 124.

53. Dillman, Bradford "Facing the Market in North Africa," *Middle East Journal* 55, no. 2 (Spring 2001): 198–215.

54. Cited in Daniel Brumberg, "Survival Strategies vs. Democratic Bargains: The Politics of Economic Stabilization in Contemporary Egypt," in *The Politics of Economic Reform in the Middle East*, ed. Henri Barkey (New York: St. Martin's Press 1992), 92. Thomas Carothers echoes this argument in his analysis of Mubarak's Egypt, saying "the lack of democratic reforms often blocks efforts to make progress on economic reforms" (Thomas Carothers, "Zakaria's Complaint," *The National Interest*, Summer 2003, 137–43).

55. NDP Document of Basic Principles, principle 17, September 2002. As the party document put it, "the NDP views the market and mechanisms of supply and demand and individual initiative in light of free competition as guarantees of the effective distribution and best use of national resources. The NDP also believes that the state plays a major role in equitably distributing these resources and activating their utilization without obstacles and with oversight by independent, credible and capable institutions" (cited in International Crisis Group Report, 2003.

56. See Al Sayed Abdel et al., "The Executive and the National Democratic Party (NDP)," in *The Arab Strategic Report* (Cairo: Al-Ahram Center for Political and Strategic Studies, 1995).

57. *Al Ahram Weekly*, September 26–October 2, 2002.

58. Mona El-Ghobashy, "Egypt's Paradoxical Elections," *Middle East Report* 238 (Spring 2006), 20–25.

59. *Al-Ahram Weekly*, November 16, 2000.

60. Issandr El Amrani, "Controlled Reform in Egypt: Neither Reformist nor Controlled," *Middle East Report*, December 2005.

61. Ibid.

62. *Al Hayat*, November 19, 2000.

63. In his study of the 1995 elections, Saad Eddin Ibrahim has estimated that at best—in free elections—the Islamist would win 15 percent of the vote, that is, 68 seats out of the 444 seats.

64. *Arab Strategic Report 2000*, Ahram Center for Economic and Political Studies, Cairo.

65. Mona El-Ghobashy, "The Metamorphosis of the Egyptian Muslim Brothers," *International Journal of Middle East Studies* 37 (2005): 373–95.

66. Amr Hamzawy and Nathan J. Brown, "Can Egypt's Troubled Elections Produce a More Democratic Future?" *Carnegie Endowment for International Peace Policy Outlook*, December 2005.

67. Joshua Stacher, "Parties Over: The Demise of Egypt's Opposition Parties," *British Journal of Middle Eastern Studies* 31, no. 2 (November 2004): 215–33.

68. *Al Wafd*, September 1, 2005.

69. International Crisis Group, *The Challenge of Political Reform: Egypt After the Iraq War*, 15.

70. Robert Springborg, "State-Society relations in Egypt: The Debate over Owner-Tenant Relations," *Middle East Journal* 45, no. 2 (Spring 1991): 242.

71. Peter McDonough and coauthors have argued that "depolarization" is crucial to democratization. They note three classes of issues that can divide society: "identity," "ideological," and "interest." See Peter McDonough, Samuel H. Barnes, and Antonio López Pin, *The Cultural Dynamics of Democratization in Spain* (Ithaca: Cornell University Press, 1998).

72. Anne M. Lesch, "The Muslim Brotherhood in Egypt: Reform or Revolution," in *The Religious Challenge to the State*, ed. Matthew C. Moen and Lowell S. Gustafson (Philadelphia: Temple University Press, 1992), 201.

73. Cited in Samer Shehata and Joshua Stacher, "The Brotherhood Goes to Parliament," *Middle East Report* 240 (Fall 2006), 32–27.

74. See the International Crisis Group's recent report on the link between economic-political marginalization and political violence on the Sinai Peninsula. International Crisis Group, "Egypt's Sinai Question," *Middle East/North Africa Report* 61 (January 2007).

75. See Alain Roussillon, "Changer la société par le Jihad; 'sédition confessionalle' et attentats contre le tourisme: rhétorique de la violence qualifiée d'islamique en Egypte," in *Le phénoméne de la violence politique: perspectives comparatistes et paradigme égyptien*, ed. Baudouin Dupret (Cairo: CEDEJ, 1994), 295–319.

76. See also Reem Saad, "State, Landlord, Parliament and Peasant: The Story of the 1992 Tenancy Law in Egypt," in *Agriculture in Egypt from Pharaonic to Modern Times, vol. 96, Proceedings of the British Academy*, ed. Alan Bowman and Eugene Roga (Oxford University Press, 1998).

77. Michael Slackman, "Stifled, Egypt's Young Turn to Islamic Fervor," *The New York Times*, February 17, 2008.

78. Carrie Rosefsky Wickham, *Mobilizing Islam: Religion, Activism and Political Change in Egypt* (New York: Columbia University Press, 2002), 106–10.

79. Ibid., 210.

80. "Lutte d'influence au PND," *Al-Ahram Hebdo*, January 1, 2005.

81. Dina al-Khawaga, "Le Parti Nationale Démocrate et les Élections de 1995: La conjonction de nombreuses logiques d'action," in *Contours et Détours du Politique en Égypte: Les élections législatives de 1995*, ed. Sandrine Gamblin (Cairo: CEDEJ, 1997), 95.

82. *Al-Ahram Weekly*, no. 201, January 4, 1995.

83. David Hirst, "Egypt Stands on Feet of Clay," *Le Monde Diplomatique*, October 1999.

84. Nathan J. Brown, Michele Dunne, and Amr Hamzawy, "Egypt's Controversial Constitutional Amendments," *Carnegie Endowment for International Peace*, March 23, 2007.

85. *Al-Ahram Weekly*, December 1–7, 2005.

86. *International Crisis Group Report*, "Reforming Egypt: In Search of a Strategy," 17.

87. Mohammed Shoman, "Azmat al-musharak min khilal al-ahzab al-misriyya" [Political Parties and Egypt's Crisis of Participation], in *Haqiqat al ta'adudiya al-siyasiya fi misr*, ed. Kamel and al-manufi (Maktabat Madbuli, 1996), 381.

88. Ansari, *Egypt: The Failed Society*, 242.

89. Lisa Anderson, "Prospects for Liberalism in North Africa: Identities and Interests in Preindustrial Welfare States," in *Islam, Democracy, and the State in North Africa, ed.* John P. Entelis (Bloomington: Indiana University Press, 1997), 135.

90. Michael L. Ross, "Does Oil Hinder Democracy?" *World Politics* 53, no. 3 (2001): 325–61.

Chapter 9

1. Joao Guilerhme Merquior, "A Panoramic View of the Rebirth of Liberalism," *World Development* 21, no. 8 (1993): 1265.

2. World Bank, *World Development Report 1997: The State in a Changing World* (Washington, DC: Oxford University Press, 1997), 28.

3. See Edgardo Lander, "The Impact of Neoliberal Adjustment in Venezuela, 1989–1993," *Latin American Perspectives* 23, no. 90.3 (Summer 1996): 50–73.

4. See Katrina Burgess, "Loyalty Dilemmas and Market Reform: Party-Union Alliances Under Stress in Mexico, Spain, and Venezuela," *World Politics* 52, no. 1 (1999): 105–34

5. See Edward L. Gibson, "The Populist Road to Market Reform: Policy and Electoral Coalitions in Mexico and Argentina," *World Politics* 49, no. 3 (1997): 339–70. See also César V. Herrera and Marcelo García, "A 10 Años de la Privatización de YPF—Análisis y Consecuencias en la Argentina y en la Cuenca del Golfo San Jorge," Centro Regional de Estudios Económicos de la Patagonia, January 2003, http://www.creepace.com.ar/secciones/petrolero.htm. Although Argentina's incorporation experience bears similarities to Egypt's, the successive coups and regime changes in Argentina since 1955 preclude a more extensive comparison with Egypt where the regime has known extreme longevity.

6. See Stephen Haggard and Robert R. Kaufman, "The Political Economy of Inflation and Stabilization in Middle-Income Countries," in *The Politics of Economic Adjustment,* ed. Haggard and Kaufman (Princeton, NJ: Princeton University Press, 1992).

7. Scott Mainwaring, "Brazil: Weak Parties, Feckless Democracy," *Building Democratic Institutions: Party systems in Latin America,* ed. Scott Mainwaring and Timothy R. Scully (Stanford, CA: Stanford University Press, 1995).

8. Javier Corrales, *Presidents Without Parties: The Politics of Economic Reform in Argentina and Venezuela in the 1990s* (University Park, PA: Penn State University Press, 2002), 272.

9. Alfred Stepan, "An 'Arab' More Than 'Muslim' Electoral Gap," *Journal of Democracy* 14, no. 3 (July 2003): 30–44

10. Mahfoud Bennoune, *The Making of Contemporary Algeria* (New York: Cambridge University Press, 1988), 122.

11. William Quandt, *Revolution and Political Leadership: Algeria 1954–1968* (Cambridge: MIT Press, 1969), 126.

12. Clement M. Henry, "Algeria's Agonies: Oil Rent Effects in a Bunker State," *Journal of North African Studies* 9, no. 2 (Summer 2004): 68–81.

13. This section draws on the discussion in Clement M. Henry and Robert Spring-borg, *Globalization and the Politics of Development in the Middle East* (New York: Cambridge University Press, 2001), 113–21.

14. Luis Martinez, *The Algerian Civil War, 1990–1998* (New York: Columbia University Press, 2000).

15. Karim Nashashibi et al., *Algeria: Stabilization and Transition to the Market*, IMF occasional paper 165, Washington, DC, 1998. The report notes that "real growth was 4 percent; inflation was declining to single digits, both the budget and current account posted surpluses; foreign reserves were at five months of imports; and external debt indicators had improved markedly" (64).

16. Goerge Joffé, "The Role of Violence Within the Algerian Economy," *Journal of North African Studies* 7, no. 1 (Spring 2002): 29–52.

17. Isabelle Werenfels, "Obstacles to Privatization of State-Owned Industries in Algeria: The Political Economy of a Distributive Conflict," *Journal of North African Studies* 7, no 1 (Spring 2002): 17.

18. "Project Appraisal Document on a Proposed Learning and Innovation Loan in the Amount of US$5 Million Equivalent of the Republic of Algeria for Privatization Assistance," *World Bank Report No. 20257-AL* (Washington, DC: World Bank, 2000).

19. Bradford Dillman "Facing the Market in North Africa." *Middle East Journal* 55, no. 2 (Spring 2001): 198–215.

20. Martinez, *The Algerian Civil War, 1990–1998*, 32.

21. Isabelle Werenfels, "Obstacles to Privatization of State-Owned Industries in Algeria: The Political Economy of a Distributive Conflict," *Journal of North African Studies* 7, no. 1 (Spring 2002): 2.

22. Luis Martinez, "Islamists in the Economy of War," Center of Studies and International Research, Paris, 1999, cited in Blanca Madani, "Algeria: Stronghold of the Pouvoir," *Middle East Intelligence Bulletin* 3, no. 5 (May 2001).

23. See "Diminishing Returns: Algeria's 2002 Legislative Elections," *Middle East Briefing* (Brussels: International Crisis Group, 2002).

24. "Les effets du programme d'ajustement structurel sur les populations vulnérables," Centre National d'Études et d'Analyses pour la Population et le Dévelopement (CENEAP), cited in Luis Martinez, "Why the Violence in Algeria?" *Journal of North African Studies* 9, no. 2 (Summer 2004): 14–27

25. Dillman, "Facing the Market in North Africa," 143.

26. Bassma Kodmani, "The Dangers of Political Exclusion: Egypt's Islamist Problem," *Carnegie Papers*, no. 63, Carnegie Endowment for International Peace, October 2005.

27. Francis Fukuyama, *State-Building: Governance and World Order in the 21st Century* (Ithaca, NY: Cornell University Press, 2004).

28. See Nicholas Van de Wall, "Elections without Democracy: Africa's Range of Regimes," *Journal of Democracy* 13, no. 2 (April 2002): 66–80; and Van de Wall, "The Economic Correlates of State Collapse," in *When States Fail: Causes and Consequences*, ed. Robert Rotberg (Princeton, NJ: Princeton University Press, 2003).

Index